PRAISE FOR
I DON'T

'A liberating alternative perspective on the happily-ever-after take we are sold our whole lives. I often had to rest the book on my chest, close my eyes and whisper "I knew it!"'

Chrissie Swan

'With her signature wit, insight and galvanising ferocity, Clementine Ford lifts the veil on marriage, revealing the history and present of misogyny, violence and oppression that festers behind the fairy tale. *I Don't* is an exhilarating invitation to see marriage for what it is—a building block of patriarchy—and imagine new ways of living, loving and building family.'

Yves Rees

'Wow. An incredible argument smashing the archaic constructs of society. Clementine's articulate brilliance is exactly what I needed to read as a young woman fighting against the ceilings in the public eye and in everyday life. This book made me feel less alone in my anger and will carve space for hope in our future.'

Jaguar Jonze

'An incredible work. Robust, funny, erudite and assertive: Clem Ford at the height of her power. This book will finish what Clem's other books started and change the world forever.'

Alice Robinson

'An enlightening, deeply encouraging work for anyone hoping to remain queen, commander and general of their own life.'

Clare Bowditch

PRAISE FOR
FIGHT LIKE A GIRL

'Brilliant . . . it makes me want to chain myself to a barricade.'

Tracey Spicer, *Sun-Herald*

'Clementine Ford was put on this earth to give courage to the young girl inside all of us. This is an exciting, essential book from Australia's most fearless feminist writer.'

Laurie Penny, author of *Unspeakable Things*

'I'm going to come right out and say it: Clementine Ford's *Fight Like A Girl* should be required reading for all young women in Australia . . . Reading *Fight Like A Girl* reignited my feminist fire, my feelings of frustration . . . Yes, *Fight Like A Girl* will make you angry. It will make you feel uncomfortable. But, ultimately, it will inspire you to create change.'

Marie Claire

'Clementine is furious and scathing when she needs to be, yet compassionate and encouraging every moment she can be. This book is both a confirmation of sisterhood and a call to arms.'

Bri Lee, author of *Eggshell Skull* **and** *Who Gets to Be Smart?*

'There's a wonderful book by Clementine Ford that I advise every woman, and especially young women, to read called *Fight Like A Girl*.'

Kate Beckinsale

'An inspiring, unapologetic, feminist manifesto . . . It's time to change the way we all think about gender. And by doing so, create a brighter future for all humans.'

Shirley Manson from Garbage

I DON'T

The Case Against Marriage

Why, when there is so much evidence of the detrimental, suffocating impact marriage has on women's lives, does the myth of marital bliss still prevail? If the feminist project has been so successful, why do so many women still believe that our value is intrinsically tied to being chosen by a man?

In her most incendiary and controversial book to date, Clementine Ford exposes the lies used to sell marriage to women to keep them in service to men and male power. From the roots of marriage as a form of property transaction to the wedding industrial complex, Clementine Ford explains how capitalist patriarchal structures need women to believe in marriage in order to maintain control over women's agency, ambitions and freedom.

I Don't presents an inarguable case against marriage for modern women. With the incisive attention to detail and razor-sharp wit that characterises her work, Ford dissects the patriarchal history of marriage; the insidious, centuries-long marketing campaign pop culture has conducted in marriage's favour; the illusion of feminist 'choice' in regard to taking men's names; and the physical and social cost that comes with motherhood.

But most importantly, Clementine Ford shows us what a different kind of world could look like for women if we were allowed to be truly free.

Clementine Ford is a writer, broadcaster and swamp witch living in Naarm/Melbourne. She is the best-selling author of the feminist manifestos *Fight Like A Girl* and *Boys Will Be Boys*, which have also been published to great acclaim in the UK and the US, and her memoir *How We Love*, which she adapted into a live stage performance called *Love Sermon*. In 2017, she won the Matt Richell Award for Best New Writer of the Year at the ABIAs. Her favourite colour is pink.

THE
CASE
AGAINST
MARRIAGE

I DON'T

CLEMENTINE
FORD

ALLEN&UNWIN
SYDNEY•MELBOURNE•AUCKLAND•LONDON

First published in 2023

Allen & Unwin
Cammeraygal Country
83 Alexander Street
Crows Nest NSW 2065
Australia
Phone: (61 2) 8425 0100
Email: info@allenandunwin.com
Web: www.allenandunwin.com

*Allen & Unwin acknowledges the Traditional Owners of the Country on which we
live and work. We pay our respects to all Aboriginal and Torres Strait Islander
Elders, past and present.*

 A catalogue record for this
book is available from the
National Library of Australia

ISBN 978 1 76106 966 6

Set in 12/18pt Warnock Pro by Bookhouse, Australia
Printed and bound in Australia by the Opus Group

10 9 8 7 6 5 4 3 2 1

FOR THE ONES WHO ARE WAITING TO BE SAVED

SO THEY MAY FINALLY SAVE THEMSELVES

CONTENTS

'In education, in marriage, in religion, in everything, disappointment is the lot of woman. It shall be the business of my
life to deepen this disappointment in every woman's heart
until she bows down to it no longer.'

—Lucy Stone, 'Disappointment is the lot of women', speech delivered at the
National Women's Rights Convention in Cincinnati on 17 October 1855

'Every one of my female friends is too good for her boyfriend.
I don't know how to explain it, but even if I had a female
friend who was just a pile of rats on a stepladder she'd still
be too good for Brandon.'

—Lane Moore, Twitter

INTRODUCTION

In early 2023, a video of a couple exchanging wedding vows went viral on TikTok. Viral wedding moments have become so ubiquitous that this would be unremarkable were it not for the chasm of difference between the vows themselves.

Standing there in her beautiful white dress, her hair and make-up immaculately done for her big day, the bride expresses gratitude for the ten years she and her groom have spent together. When they met in high school, she didn't let on that she liked him—because she knew he was 'too good for her'. Ten years and two daughters later, she's so grateful to be marrying her 'knight in shining armour' and 'best friend'.

'You are literally making the fairytale that I always dreamed of come true,' she says, tearing up. 'I love you so much, and I promise to choose you every day for the rest of my life and beyond that.'

Awww! I can't wait to hear how this amazing guy—the most 'selfless' person she knows—is going to express his love for her in return.

'You're screwed,' he begins, smirking at her as he unfolds his notes. It quickly becomes clear that while she's brought a delicate soufflé to the proceedings, he's serving up a whole damn roast.

'Only two things are required to keep me happy,' he announces to a tittering crowd. 'Keep my belly full and my balls empty. Though you're amazing at half of them, we really need to get you some cooking lessons.'

Get it? She's good at cock, but not at cook!

Romantic!

Praising his bride for being one of the few women he considers worthy of taking his name, he finishes by allowing her to choose how their night will end: she can either be a Twinkie or a toaster strudel. (For those who don't speak Unbelievable Fuckwit, he's telling her she can choose between emptying those aforementioned balls inside her, or being sprayed with his jizz.)

The celebrant—who is also the groom's mother—chides him and threatens him with a grounding. He's such a naughty little boy!

And of course it's all just so *funny*, isn't it? I'm sure when she imagined her wedding day, the bride (whose vows also included the heartbreaking line, 'I know I'm no model') hoped for nothing more than to have her friends and family picturing her gagging on a dick and being covered in Prince Charming's cum.

Likewise, I'm sure every woman we see being embarrassed, belittled, mocked and disregarded on her Big Princess Day imagined her new husband would smash wedding cake into their faces, despite her explicitly requesting that he not. To have the groom flash a HELP ME sign at the guests from the altar. To be asked to pose for sexualised wedding photographs simulating blow jobs, or to be marrying men so incompetent they couldn't be trusted to organise a single part of the celebration binding them together till death do they part.

And how many women wake up on the other side of their wedding day (the most important day of their life!!!) only to realise that the bliss they were promised hasn't quite eventuated? Now saddled with an overgrown child who can't seem to put his clothes into a laundry basket let alone a washing machine (and given the prevalence of domestic abuse, coercive control and sexual violence that's exerted in homes across the nation and around the world, domestic incompetence can be considered *best-case scenario* for all too many women), which of these lucky, lucky brides would choose to do it all differently?

If we had access to a different kind of story, how many of us would instead choose *ourselves*?

This world has not been kind to women. The men who have built it—which is to say, the world of patriarchy—have deliberately worked to suppress women's power in order to maintain the dominance of their own. We can see this playing out over and over again across the breadth of history, in exactly the same ways. But because patriarchy has become so adept at regenerating itself, the twin stories of *who women are* and *what women need* are always told in ways that conceal how malleable these 'known knowns' actually are and instead present them as immutable facts of life. Throughout these chapters, you'll see that while the reality patriarchy constructs for women has changed over the years, its purpose has always remained the same—to keep women in subservience to men while pretending it's for our own good.

This book is in part an exploration of the depths to which men throughout history have stooped to adjust reality to suit their own needs. It's a comprehensive look at how they have assumed such authority over women that we began to believe the lies they told about us, so that we would keep signing up to support the patriarchal system that works in their favour rather than fight against it.

Marriage and everything it steals from women—our time, our energy, our freedom—has constituted one of the biggest and most successful of these lies. Co-opting women into a life of service used to be achieved by force, with little regard for how women felt about it. Now that we've secured freedom of choice (or the illusion of it, at least), the system has to work more diabolically. The modern woman is told that she *needs* marriage. That without a husband and children, hers will be a life only half lived. She'll be wretched and alone. If she wasn't so gross, you'd feel sorry for her! But she *is* gross, and so you don't. Serves her right for being such a picky bitch.

The spectre of the sad, single woman looms over us all. *Don't miss the boat!* the cultural messages shriek at us. *You'll end up old and lonely with nothing but your cats for company!*

How many of our foremothers would look at the 'choices' women make today and be utterly bewildered? How many of them would have given anything to be left to grow old in peace, tending to their gardens and their cats, sharing their hearths and homes with friends they knew would leave at the day's end, with names, beds and *money* that belonged to them?

But the cultural warning against ending up a cursed old spinster has proven itself dangerously effective. Leaving aside the fact that growing old with cats is actually fucking great, the anxiety felt over single women (the horror!) is determined to demonise them at all costs. So compelling is this narrative that even the most milquetoast of romantic pairings sees women falling over themselves to perform the cultural markers of Chosen Woman. *I said yes!!!!* scream the proposal posts, hands splayed towards a camera that just happens to be there to capture the happy moment.

Her moment.

Where did this fiction come from? Who decided that marriage—the very same institution that has oppressed and dehumanised women through the ages, as they were given against their will to men whose right to rule over them was considered as naturally occurring as the tides—was actually something women *needed*? Something we would be liberated by? Something men, ever the sacrificial defenders of women, had designed with *our* happiness in mind?

Why has it been so important to convince women of the necessity of marriage to our lives? Why, in a world where technological progress has skyrocketed beyond anything we could have imagined in the last century alone, has an archaic institution like marriage retained its influence? It isn't down to human desire; as you'll see throughout the course of this book, marriage rates have always ebbed and flowed just as women have always been single (and punished for it—although not always in the same ways and for the same reasons). Nor is it because marriage makes anyone particularly happy.

The great feminist philosopher, Marilyn Frye, once wrote that men retain the right to author perception and construct reality. Once upon a time, these self-appointed architects of thought (always building worlds, they are!) decided women needed marriage to save us from our wandering wombs; now, they say we need it to keep us from being miserable old cat ladies. Patrolling the perimeters of a reality they created for themselves, men reserve the right to eject or erase women who threaten the integrity of its structure. If a woman challenges male authority or attempts to assert a reality that contradicts the male viewpoint, she will be met swiftly with some form of punishment. As many of us know firsthand, this often translates to physical violence (or at least the threat of it). Just as commonly, though, we are ejected from that reality through the use of crude and basic insults: '*You're just angry men don't want to fuck you!*'

But to do away with marriage would cause widespread chaos!

Really? Chaos for *whom*? Who really needs marriage? Is it the women who receive superficial economic security in exchange for a life spent cleaning, washing, cooking and generally catering to a man's every need? Or is it the men whose lives become easier the moment they begin cohabiting with a woman, who receive tangible economic security and the promise of economic advancement as a result of this partnership, and yet who, despite this increase in privilege, are still given permission (encouraged, even!) to participate in the ludicrous comedic charade that declares marriage to be something that women chase and men resist?

Marriage in its most technical sense—that being the merging of people for the purpose of wealth creation and reproduction—is almost as old as the human race. But this history is full of the silent screams of women compelled to conform to 'tradition' and the reproductive, domestic, sexual and physical labour that has always lurked behind its gleaming smile.

If you're reading this book, it's because some part of you yearns to peel back the facade we've been sold in order to discover the truth. Whether you're married (or engaged to be), a hopeless romantic searching for your 'other half', a gloriously untethered free spirit or simply curious to learn, this book will open your eyes to reality as it is rather than the one patriarchy wishes us to believe in.

This is not a book that seeks to find the good in marriage, or attempts to describe how it can be saved or made better. If you want that book, you can find a thousand different iterations of it in bookshops everywhere. I have no interest in marriage's salvation, and I make no apologies for that. Like the nineteenth-century anarchist Voltairine de Cleyre before me, I seek to abolish completely what is a corrupt and oppressive institution. I reject wholesale any system that gives the government the right to exercise authority over human relationships, and to confer superficial privileges to those who agree to its terms.

I am a marriage abolitionist because I cannot in good conscience support an institution that has enslaved women sexually, reproductively, financially and domestically. To do so would be to betray the very essence of my feminist politics. How could any of us *choose* to add our name to a list of women who had and continue to have no choice—remembering, of course, that forced marriages and child exploitation via marriage still occur all over the world? I don't care how 'unique' a wedding is or how subversive someone makes their vows; marriage is a system whose foundations are built on the erasure of women, and the exploitation of everything that we are and have the potential to be. No amount of quirky decorations or flash mob proposals can change that. And this is why you'll find no great defence or exception made for same-sex marriage in these pages. I understand why queer couples feel compelled to wed, but as a queer person myself I could never willingly celebrate or enter into an institution that fought for so long to exclude me. Love is love—and no one, especially not queer people, should have to prove the extent of that commitment via an official document. That many of us are still forced to in order to have legal recognition of our human rights is something we should be fighting against, not endorsing.

Some necessary disclaimers: An enormous amount of research has been undertaken to ensure the arguments I make in *I Don't* are supported by historical fact and feminist scholarship. Unfortunately (and in a completely rude twist I certainly didn't see coming) it appears you can't summarise six thousand years of patriarchy in ninety thousand words. Misogyny strikes again! With that in mind, I have provided a comprehensive reading list at the back of the book for those who wish to explore the subject further. This is only the start of a much bigger conversation. As a white woman living in Australia, I couldn't possibly speak for cultures outside of my own or assert expertise that I don't have. The context of this book is therefore largely restricted to European history (which, due to the relentless colonisation exercised by the British empire, has expanded across the globe). You may also feel I'm too focused on the experiences of white, middle-class women. This isn't a failure of scope, but rather a deliberate choice. As you'll see throughout the following chapters, white women's allegiance to conservative practices has the destructive impact of upholding economic oppression of marginalised classes, not to mention enforcing white supremacy via legitimising racist anxieties to do with 'replacement theory'. White women have been instrumental in establishing the idea of *success* in marriage as a sign of economic status and moral value, which in turn upholds hierarchical power within the patriarchal system.

I realise some of the arguments you'll read here may feel abrasive or hostile, especially to those of you who feel person-ally targeted by them. If this is the case for you, I humbly ask for your generosity as a reader, and urge you to consider the staunch position I have taken as a response to systemic oppression and not personal actions. I don't blame anyone for being married or even for wanting to be married. Contrary to what some may think, I am quite hopelessly romantic! But marriage propaganda is incredibly persuasive—we're working against thousands of years of well-practised campaigning, after all! And truly equal partnership, built as it must be on love and respect, will exist with or without marriage to confer authority and status. I'm not here to judge, but to make people aware of things that have been deliberately concealed from us. And at the very least, what I can promise is that you'll add some excellent retorts to your collection of comebacks to men who speak out of their butthole about things they don't understand and can't be bothered reading up on.

There is much in this book that will arouse you to a state of fury, especially when you realise the extent to which women have been manipulated into embracing a system that harms us. But I can also promise you a lot of mirth; I am very funny, after all! And although the nineteenth-century scientists would probably warn against such a thing, fearing for the safety of my uterus, I have always found humour to be the best medicine when experiencing rage. I hope you agree.

Although I'm sure this will be dismissed by conservative pundits as my angriest book yet, *I Don't* is a profoundly hopeful love letter to women. It's a rallying cry to reclaim our *right* to be the authors not just of our own perception but of our own stories. It's a message passed back to our foremothers to let them know that we have heard them, and it's a message sent forward to our daughters to urge them to keep going.

This is a book about seeing. It's a book about knowing.

We have been kept from the truth of who we are for too long— and the truth is that this great, glorious, *beautiful* tradition of marriage has been a trap for women from the beginning.

And so the beginning, my dear friends, is where we shall start.

SOMETHING OLD

'She hears her own thick voice deep inside her ears when she says, "I need to know where I am."

The man stands there, tall and narrow, hand still on the doorknob, surprised. He says, almost in sympathy, "Oh, sweetie. You need to know *what* you are."'

—Charlotte Wood, *The Natural Way of Things*

1

IN THE BEGINNING

'I have always thought that there might be
a lot of cash in starting a religion.'

—George Orwell, *Collected Essays, Journalism and Letters of George Orwell*

In the beginning, God created the heavens and the earth. He made light, and separated the light from the darkness. He made water and land and sky, and then made creatures to swim, run and fly through all of it. God made a man—the first man—and called him Adam. God placed Adam in the Garden of Eden, and told him it was his to care for. God loved Adam, for He had made him in His own image.

But the Lord God said, 'It is not good for the man to be alone. I will make a helper suitable for him.'

Adam had named all of the creatures in God's kingdom, but none was good enough to be his companion. And so God caused Adam to fall into a deep sleep, and then took one of his ribs. The Lord God made a woman from the rib, and delivered her to Adam. Adam saw that she was bone of his bones and flesh of his flesh, and recognised that she had come from him. As his wife, she would join to him as one. They would live together in the garden forever, Adam and his helper woman, with only one rule: they must not eat the fruit from the Tree of Knowledge.

But the woman was frivolous and silly. She was too easily led by her own desire, and was drawn to the fruit because of its appealing colour. When a serpent appeared to her and promised the fruit wouldn't kill them but instead open their eyes, she took some and ate it and then gave some to Adam. Their eyes were indeed opened. Adam and the woman now knew they were naked, and the realisation caused them to feel shame. They sewed fig leaves together to cover their bodies, and hid from God when He came to the garden, until He forced them to come out and explain themselves.

Adam blamed his defiance of God's rules on the woman, saying she was the one who had given him fruit from the tree. The woman blamed the serpent, saying it had deceived her. God couldn't contain His fury. He condemned the serpent to an eternity spent crawling on its belly, and created hostility between it and the woman. As punishment for the woman's curiosity and defiance, God cursed her and all women to suffer monthly bleeding and severe pain in childbirth. He commanded that Adam would rule over her, as all men would rule over their wives forevermore. Hearing she would become mother of all the living, Adam at last gave the woman a name: *Eve*. Finally, to rebuke Adam for listening to his wife, God promised his would be a life of toil and sweat, eating food drawn from the dusty ground he would return to upon death.

Then God drove them out of the garden, to the world of men outside. Adam ruled over Eve, wielding his authority to protect her from repeating her sins. She had been made from his bones to be his helper; now she would bring his children into the world and do as he commanded.

This is the word of God. Thanks be to God.

———

In 2004, the Australian federal government passed its Marriage Legislation Amendment Bill. Backed by a collective of hard right, Christian legislators, the bill's purpose was clear: to define marriage by law as only occurring between a man and a woman, thus effectively blocking any attempts to introduce same-sex marriage or recognise those entered into overseas. Australia may have been a secular country, but as far as marriage was concerned the government was resolute—God made Adam and Eve, not Adam and Steve.

Such is the influence of Christianity across the globe that, whatever your personal belief system, you're probably at least vaguely familiar with the story of Adam and Eve. References to the pair have been used for everything from entrenching religious doctrine about humanity's origins to explaining why women are inferior to men and, to really drive home what lies at the cynical heart of cultural narratives, using them as a way to sell stuff to the masses. I don't just mean things like religion or misogyny or homophobia, although the masses sadly love that shit. I mean actual products, like Smirnoff Green Apple Twist (JWT, 2006), CB Insurance (DDB Amsterdam, 2008) or an entire advertising agency named Adam & Eve. A bit weird how God's first human pairing can be used to sell both marital devotion *and* financial security in case of a house fire, but that's capitalism for you.

According to the Christians, Adam and Eve were created by God to be the first husband and wife. This is all the proof we need that marriage is God's plan for us all, as many a Christian minister, legislator or bloke holding court over on GodTok loves to remind us. As it turns out, God's plan also lays out some pretty clear instructions for the wifeys—namely, that we do what we're told. As a Daughter of Eve, I'm expected to surrender all authority to my husband, a Son of Adam. I must allow him to lie with me (i.e. do sex on me) whenever he wishes, because satisfying men's carnal needs is a wife's duty. In exchange, I get to have babies, over and over—as many as my body can handle until it collapses completely, like a three-week-old capsicum languishing at the bottom of the fridge. To be a wife and a mother is the greatest of all gifts, because it allows me to fulfil my purpose on earth and know my place in the order of things—which, conveniently for the blokes running the Church, has always been found in the short walk between the kitchen and the bedroom.

That I might have something to say about any of this is irrelevant, because women 'should be silent and not be allowed to teach or to tell men what to do' (1 Timothy 2:12). Instead of thinking for myself, I must lean into nurturing, recognising 'the husband is the head of the wife as Christ is the head of the church . . .

so also wives should submit to their husbands in everything'
(Ephesians 5:21–33).

I know this, because it says so in the Bible.

You know the Bible. It's that bestseller written by a bunch
of different dudes all professing to be conduits for the word of
God, a magical daddy who lives in the sky doing what daddies
do best, which is to provide and protect. It turns out that Daddy
Dearest is pretty misodgy (not to mention fairly cavalier about
which people He chooses to look after)—but I'm sure that had
nothing to do with the gender make-up of the writers selected
for the task. Yes, it was a total sausage fest. But they were only
reporting *God's exact words* and not, say, making up shit that
would give them more power over women and other creatures
deemed inferior to men, so it's okay.

Here's a random selection of voice notes God sent to earth to
be recorded in the Bible, providing comprehensive instruction
on how all us curious girl cats ought to be handled by our male
keepers:

On where women came from:

'Man did not come from woman, but woman from man;
neither was man created for woman, but woman for man'
(1 Corinthians 11:8–9).

On menstruation:

'Everything on which she lies [and sits] during her menstrual
impurity shall be unclean' (Leviticus 15:20).

On a newly married woman failing to provide proof of virginity (blood) on her wedding night:

> '[She should be] brought to the door of her father's house, and the men of her city shall stone her with stones that she die' (Deuteronomy 22:20–21).

On a woman's failure to scream for help during a sexual assault and man's theft of property:

> 'You shall bring them both out to the gate of that city, and you shall stone them to death with stones, the young woman because she did not cry for help though she was in the city, and the man because he violated his neighbour's wife' (Deuteronomy 22:24).

Cool stuff! I especially like the bits where women were punished for men's crimes. Not much has changed in that regard, but I guess that's because we just refuse to learn. Common sense girlies, try it sometime!

But it's not like men get off scot-free either—not even the ones who respect their neighbours enough to not rape their wives. Sure, women had to submit to husbands and fathers in absolutely everything, but husbands were also reminded to 'love your wives and do not be harsh with them' (Colossians 3:19).

See? *Equal.*

I know that radical, pink-haired, pierced-face, cat lady feminism teaches us to believe in this made-up 'patriarchy', but it's just not real. Whatever gender oppression you perceive to still exist in the modern world is just a figment of your imagination—just one more lie told to you by ugly women who can't find boyfriends and who want everyone else to be as miserable as they are. Like the mythical 'rape culture' they keep banging on about (*ha-ha, as if anyone would rape them!*) or the so-called 'gender wage gap' (which, as any learned fifteen-year-old boy scholar will tell you, is down to the fact women just choose lower-paying jobs and nothing at all to do with the fact that the economic value of an industry drops as its labour force becomes more feminised). It's not that men have colluded with each other and powerful institutional systems over millennia to keep women subjugated to their demands through the coordinated and sanctioned use of force, political, physical and psychological. For that to be true, a lot of men would have to be intentionally bad towards women, which we all know is impossible and frankly offensive to even suggest.

It's that men and women are *different*. God said so. And he's our Heavenly Father!

I do have some questions though.

Maybe it's the radical, pink-haired, pierced-face, cat lady feminist in me speaking, but some of these things just don't add up. Like, if men are so important and sacred, why are so few of them needed to ensure the long-term success of the human species? For that matter, why are they so irrelevant to most animal species found in God's creation playground? Given Daddy designed the whole world from scratch (and made sure we knew to thank him for it), it seems weird that the creatures he made to populate it would be sustained almost entirely by the reproductive cycles of the female species. Weirder still that it's mothers and not fathers who provide the vast majority of food, care and protection for each generation until they come of age, while most male animals tend to sit around doing fuck all.

Why, it's almost as if the whole concept of patriarchal religious figureheads is bullshit from start to finish! Could it be that archaeologist Marija Gimbutas was right, and that the pre-patriarchal world of yore saw more benefit in worshipping goddesses, female deities and the reproductive power that represented a literal portal to the place where all life comes from? How annoying for the boys! Rather than keep dropping to their knees (like simps!) to worship the Holy Mother, maybe these blokes decided it was time for a new story. One where men got to be in charge of the magical fabric of the universe for a change, not to mention its earthly armies. If you didn't like it, guess what? You're dead, sucker! Eventually, to streamline the whole thing a bit and leave no doubt as to who was really in charge, they agreed to convene under the banner of one celestial ruler: a God, made in Man's own image.

Hey, it's a lot more believable than a talking snake.

———

Let me reassure any Christian readers that I'm not ridiculing your faith. I respect that you have a personal relationship with your own definition of God, and that this faith brings you peace and comfort. Nor am I ridiculing the faith of any other denominational worshipper, unless of course their religion involves living in a compound somewhere and waiting for an intergalactic leader named Klenipotik-4 to arrive in a spaceship powered by garlic.

But we have to consider the stranglehold that Judeo-Christian teachings have had and continue to have on western culture. Logic may not be my forte, what with me being a woman and all, but it's hard to take seriously the idea that us gals were created to be subservient to men just because a bunch of dudes said a magical man in the clouds told them so.

Despite being a mishmash of completely unverified reports—most of which seem to have been documented while under the influence of hardcore street drugs—the Bible is still viewed by an altogether frightening number of people as a primary source of historical testimony. While Old Testament Daddy orders the murder of countless people, many of whom are women and children just minding their own business, the New Testament completely shifts gears to tell the story of a child placed immaculately in the womb of another child, who's forced to watch as the baby she never asked for grows up and starts a cult.

On the basis of that alone, you'd think we'd collectively reject the Bible as any kind of instructional manual for living. But the patriarchal society that embraces biblical teachings doesn't just uphold its misogyny as ordained celestial law; it enthusiastically reinforces it. Two thousand years after 'God' chose a *twelve-year-old girl* to give birth to 'His' child, girls even younger than that are being forced to give birth to babies they are similarly too young to bear, by Christian lawmakers intent on keeping women housebound and in subservience to male authority—just as the Bible (which, again, was written by men) decreed they should be.

But here are some things you may not know about Christianity and the supposed 'word of God' it points to as justification for the violence it continues to wield against women and girls all over the world (which includes the use of marriage as a tool of oppression). Buckle up, because we're about to reach into the (very deep) pockets of the Vatican's extensive collection of fancy robes and see how many nuggets of gold we can find there.

Just as Jesus Christ wasn't born on Christmas Day, neither was Christianity as we know it formed during his lifetime or even soon after it. The formal tenets of Christianity and its official doctrines weren't properly established until around 325AD, when a gang of bishops in Turkey got together to form the First Council of Nicaea and basically establish consensus on what the religion's parameters even were. Funnily enough for a religion hell-bent on collecting tithes from its parishioners, 'making money' was high on the list of Church priorities.

Shocker!

Money has always been a primary concern of the Church, despite one of its own commandments warning against the sin of greed. The Bible emphasises the importance of giving a percentage of your income and assets back to God, because it is He who giveth good fortune to you. Seen in this light, God feels a bit less like the source of all divine love and more like a grubby landlord blessing you with the opportunity to pay off His mortgage.

Shortly before the Nicaean Council met for the first time, Christianity was declared the official religion of the Roman Empire—ironic, considering it was Pontius Pilate, the Roman procurator of Judea, who'd ordered Christ's crucifixion. If authors were allowed to quote song lyrics without paying for them, I'd be saying something about Jesus purring like a cat at that news. But I can't, so all I'll say is that three hundred years after they killed him, the Romans were like, damn, that JC has a real swift vibe.

The move granted an extraordinary amount of power to Catholic Church officials, making them basically a one stop shop to wield iron fisted authority over the population while gouging them for 'taxes'. But it wasn't just the congregation who promised to line the coffers of the papal purse. Money that was accrued by the Church could be kept *in* the Church just by making sure no one outside of it could get their hands on it—and that included the wives and children of religious leaders.

Wait, you didn't believe priestly abstinence was sanctioned by almighty God, did you? Nah! When it comes to religious interpretation of the Bible, it's really more of a Choose Your Own Adventure vibe than anything set in (Rosetta) stone.

See, once upon a time, Catholic priests could marry and produce heirs. In fact, for almost one thousand years, clergymen weren't even required to take a vow of celibacy in order to prove their devotion to God (although various attempts were made to prevent or at least curb the dance of the beast with two backs). One of the reasons cited for opposing marriage among the clergy was the fact that if they fathered children, any property or money they owned would be inherited by said offspring rather than passed back into the ownership of the Church.

It wasn't until 1139AD that priests were formally forbidden from fornicatin' or marrying. The movement that would finally secure celibacy as a prerequisite to join the God Squad was led by Gregorian reformers, who were more or less in step with the general public's view that women were dirty, filthy sluzzers with devil vagina magic swirling around their shame pockets. Coming into contact with such sorcery might be all right for the average chap, who only faced the risk of having his knob magicked off and hidden in a tree (more on those fun times later), but priests were not meant to be average chaps. This was *God Squad*. And the Gregorians believed that men who had been called to serve God could be easily lured from him by hip-swinging seductresses, who 'entangled men in the slimy glue of their sexuality'. In perhaps one of the best excretions of paranoid misogyny I've ever read, one such religious leader in the eleventh century denounced women as 'bitches, sows, screech-owls, night-owls, she-wolves [and] bloodsuckers' who tempted men with their 'appetising flesh of the devil', 'lascivious kisses' and their 'wallowing places for fat pigs'.

Wallowing places for fat pigs! I have to hand it to him, the man knew how to paint a picture.

But here we have another example of a story passed around as fact for centuries and then ret-conned to whatever new narrative patriarchy concocts to keep women under its boot. During the Middle Ages, it was widely accepted that women were untrustworthy, sexually depraved harlots with lust at the core of their being and an unquenchable thirst for destroying men's lives. Just a few centuries later, as the notion of 'scientist' shifted from Eccentric Quack to Brilliant Knower Of All Things, women were suddenly declared to be intellectually inferior and naive to the point of being childlike. With sensibilities too fragile to handle the burdensome pressures of an education, it was only right that women be kept from acquiring knowledge—because to know too much of the things only men were capable of understanding could upset the delicate balance of a woman's womb and cause her to become infertile.

From Satan's whores to God's domestic angels, these are the centuries of our patriarchal lives.

Modern Christianity and the 'traditionalists' who advocate for its teachings may have now decided that marriage is a sacred covenant required of all of God's subjects, but this story too has gone through a rampant editing process. In its early days, the Church actually warned against marriage, believing all the sex it promised would distract people from worshipping God and scoring an invite to his Kingdom, the arrival of which was expected to be announced any day. In the Bible, Jesus (who never married #foreveralone) emphasised to his followers the importance of their devotion to God, saying, 'If any man come to me and hate not his father, and mother, and wife, and children, and brethren, and sisters, yea, and his own life also, he cannot be my disciple' (Luke 14:26). Kind of controlling, no? But to form what the actor Jonah Hill might call 'boundaryless, inappropriate friendships' with people outside of God was blasphemous. While women today are actively encouraged by religious teachings to aspire to become that ever important 'helpmate' to a husband, the Bible heralds the superiority of unmarried women, whose service can instead be given to God: 'The unmarried woman careth for the things of the Lord, that she may be holy both in body and in spirit: but she that is married careth for the things of the world, how she may please her husband' (1 Corinthians 7:32–34).

(To circumvent this inconvenient verse, today's Christian 'leaders' urge women to treat their husbands as if they themselves were God, despite this being in clear contravention of one of the oft-cited Ten Commandments: *Thou shalt not worship false idols.*)

From a utilitarian point of view, the only real purpose for marriage in the early days of Christianity was that it could *at best* act as a container for the sin of lust. Even then, one had to be wary of the 'carnal pleasure' derived from marital sex. In the sixth century, Pope Gregory the Great warned that such a thing 'cannot under any circumstances be without blame'. Doubling down on this, Paul (whose name you may know from his experience of being temporarily blinded by light on the road to Damascus) expressed the wish that all men be like himself (single and celibate), but 'if they cannot exercise self-control, they should marry . . . for it is better to marry than to burn with passion' (1 Corinthians 7:8–9).

If sex was considered a distraction from worship that made people's (and more specifically men's) brains crazy, it's little wonder marriage was co-opted by the Church to try to keep those porking loins under control. Nor is it hard to see why men today, raised on a diet of misogyny and patriarchal ideals, would believe that having wives who'll tend to their every need is somehow their spiritual birthright. A newly established Church looking to solidify the devotion and fear of its flock must have figured out at some point that trying to warn men against sex would never work. The next best option was just to give it to them on tap in their home and tell them to bonk if they love Jesus. Let's face it, marriage wasn't going away. And despite all that fanfare, the Kingdom of God didn't seem to be arriving anytime soon. It didn't seem *right* that people could just make choices for their lives without permission from the Church, nor did it seem particularly safe.

Better to take control of it and establish yourself as the spiritual authority on unions than to sit on the sidelines and grumble about the whole thing being overrated. Over the next century, authority over marriage—from who could do it and where ceremonies were allowed to take place—was slowly but methodically removed from communities and assumed by the Church, granting unprecedented oversight to an already monstrously powerful institution.

———

Centuries later, the fiction that marriage has always been the cornerstone of Christianity has become widely accepted fact, exploited not just for the purpose of controlling (and abusing, in many cases) Christian women but also to justify the conservative policies of supposedly secular governments built on the quagmire of Judeo-Christian 'values'.

The harm caused by this garbage can't be underestimated. Countless cults have sprung up in the name of Christianity, most of them run by a hierarchy of patriarchal leaders whose public claims to religious privacy have allowed them to sexually brutalise women and children without consequence for *decades*. Before his capture in 2006, the convicted child rapist Warren Jeffs rose to power as leader of the Fundamentalist Church of Jesus Christ of Latter-Day Saints (FLDS), which preaches 'plural' marriages (for men) as God's will. A self-appointed prophet, Jeffs had inherited the position from his father, Rulon Jeffs, also heralded as a 'prophet'. During his reign over the Church, the elder Jeffs claimed sixty-five 'wives', one of whom was only nineteen when her father 'gave' her to Jeffs, who was then eighty-five. But at the time of Warren Jeffs' arrest, he had eclipsed even his father's capacity for abuse. Among the seventy-eight victims forced into marital and sexual slavery to him, some were girls as young as fourteen. With an estimated ten thousand FLDS members still active in the United States, who can say how many young girls are still being abused in the name of God *just in that cult alone*?

Similarly, the modern Quiverfull movement (which was founded by a woman, proving that while we may not be our own *worst* enemies, we can still be enemies nonetheless) calls for its members to marry and bear as many children as possible—for they are 'like arrows in the hands of a warrior [and] blessed is the man whose quiver is full of them' (Psalm 127). Birth control is verboten for the Quiverfull faithful, with a woman's purpose only to bear and raise children—often for decades. In 2016, a Quiverfull patriarch named Vaughn Ohlman advertised a retreat for parents in the movement to arrange marriages for their *teenage children*. According to Ohlman, a woman of twenty had already started to waste her marriageable years. All she needed was to have developed breasts (which 'promised enjoyment for her husband'), be able to bear children 'without damage' and feel 'emotionally ready' to have sex and 'rejoice physically' in her husband. As with those who've managed to escape the FLDS, women who've left the Quiverfull cult have spoken out against its rampant misogyny dressed up as religious faith.

But aren't these extreme examples, Clamenslime?!

Sure—if they were rare, and if the members of these cults didn't keep getting elected to political office. In 2013, Mitt Romney gave a commencement address to the graduates of Southern

Virginia University in which he urged them all to 'get married [and] have a quiver full of kids if you can'. (By the way, if I could *not* see the word quiver alongside the image of a man spraying his jizz around ever again, that would be great.) But Romney isn't just some God botherer—he's a former US presidential hopeful and a current senator in Utah. His views on marriage and reproduction directly impact the constituents he's elected to serve. And although he's spoken out against other state legislatures effectively banning abortion, he also had this to say after the Supreme Court's 2022 overturning of *Roe v. Wade*: 'The sanctity of human life is a foundational principle, and the lives of our children—both born and unborn—deserve our protection. I support the Court's decision, which means that laws regarding abortion will now rightfully be returned to the people and their elected representatives.'

As of 2023, just under 88 per cent of members of the US Congress were Christian. Australia may be less in love with God than our neighbours across the Pacific, but that doesn't mean our government isn't influenced by the beliefs (and money) of His loyal followers from both in and outside its ranks. This manifests in countless gross ways (does it get more disgusting than the Australian Christian Lobby fighting to destroy an anti-bullying program that would help support schools to be safe for trans and gender diverse kids?!), but the one this book is concerned with is this: *why* is it so important that governments need citizens to embrace marriage, to the point where a raft of (superficial) financial, social and political benefits are provided to those who comply? Could it be that the conservative policies that protect the powers of the elite are easier to institute when delivered inside that pesky (white) Trojan horse known as 'family values'?

People in positions of power rarely care if their underlings are happy. What they need is for them to be compliant. One of the easiest ways to secure this is to make the people they rule over feel aligned to a small unit (in this case, the family) who benefits from the benevolent authority of their leader, whether they act as head of the country, head of Church or just head of the household. Compliant followers are far less likely to look beyond their own conditions, which makes them less likely to join up with anyone (the proletariat, the atheists, the feminists) who threaten the status quo. So again I ask, *why* is it so important that marriage still be spoken of as some kind of cosmic present bestowed by Daddy when we know it not only existed long before He did, but for centuries afterwards still rarely, if ever, considered women's choice in the matter?

The truth is, marriage doesn't exist to provide women with spiritual fulfilment or happiness. It exists to prop up patriarchy, and to keep women's hands busy tying the knots that hold our ropes in place. It may well be the bedrock of western civilisation, but here's what you won't hear at the local Sunday service: as far as marriage is concerned, men sleep on the beds, and women on the rocks.

———

Religious texts and doctrinal codes are not accurate depictions of how and why we came to be. The Bible isn't a cliff face sculpted over millions of years by the rise and fall of oceans; it can't be read through a scientific lens, and therefore it should never be deferred to as an authority on human existence. Patriarchal religions have endured largely because they reassure men of their own divine power, and keep women in check by convincing us this is what the Creator wants. But humans didn't descend from a man made out of celestial playdough and the lesser woman who was created to serve him. The biblical depiction of Woman as having been plucked out of Man's rib and therefore obliged forever more to live in deference to his authority isn't just a problematic footnote in an otherwise thumpingly good read—it's at the core of Judeo-Christian beliefs, which are consistently invoked by modern-day lawmakers as being integral to the 'foundation of western civilisation'. It *matters* that these cultural touchstones were conceived of by men to enforce their own supremacy. And it's frankly terrifying that they're still being used to justify the oppression of women worldwide, in both overt and covert ways.

Here's another story for you.

Before Eve, there was Lilith. You won't find much mention of her in the Christian world (the Bible mentions her by name exactly once), but there are references to her in art, engravings and folktales over the last four thousand years at least. Mostly, she's been depicted as a demon—specifically, the twisted feminine monster responsible for stealing women's babies, either in the womb, at the moment of their first breath or unexpectedly while they sleep. But every good villain needs an origin story, and three thousand years after her first recorded appearance, *The Alphabet of Ben Sira* (one of the midrashic texts of the Middle

Ages offering rabbinic interpretations of the Hebrew Bible) recast Lilith as a member of the First Wives Club.

God made Adam and Lilith from the same material and gave them both the Garden of Eden to live, laugh and love in. Being made of the same material, Lilith sees herself as equal to Adam. But when Adam tries to force Lilith to lie beneath him, she refuses, inciting God's wrath. He banishes her to a cave in the desert, where the Angel Samuel impregnates her repeatedly. Using His angels as emissaries, God commands Lilith to return to the Garden of Eden, warning that one hundred of her babies will be murdered each day until she complies. Again, she refuses. Her babies are slaughtered as promised, and God creates Eve to be a 'helper' to Adam in Lilith's place. Forgotten in the barren desert, Lilith grows wings and becomes the demon thief of babies' souls. Pregnant women are taught to fear this hate-filled creature who threatens their ability to create and keep life. Mothers in grief are taught to blame her, their babies stolen in the night by the monstrous aberration of femininity she has become. She is a femme fatale, trapping men with her beauty and then consuming them. She is a devil, a monster, a *screech owl*.

This is all a fiction, too, of course. But real or not, the story of Lilith is just one of many cautionary tales that work to dissuade women from seeking liberation, just as the story of Eve works to dissuade women from seeking knowledge.

See what happens when you girlies reject the role God has created you to fulfil, disobeying your father/husband/brother/ your own biological instincts? You become a dried-up old husk languishing in the barren cave of your womb; an angry, bitter, twisted witch, jealous of the pretty girls and all their fertile soil. People will warn their children to avoid you, the winged demon who threw it all away for her 'freedom'. And look at her now! Lonely and sad, with no one to visit her in the Old Demons Home.

How could women ever hope for something more, with the stories of women like Eve and Lilith warning us against transgressive behaviour? When men are the only ones allowed to write our collective stories—literally HIStory—then it's little wonder we have to deal with so many shitty endings for women who step out of line.

Don't stray too far from the path, girls, or you'll get lost in the woods. Don't forget your purpose, girls, or you'll lose your one chance at happiness. Don't hunger for knowledge, experience or adventure, because you'll destroy the world as we know it.

Christ on a fucking bike.

2

CAT LADY

'If man could be crossed with the cat it would
improve man, but it would deteriorate the cat.'

—Mark Twain, *Mark Twain's Notebook*

If one of the most pitiful things people can imagine is a woman who misses out on the marital adventure *despite* her best efforts, then surely one of our most frightening cultural bogey monsters is that of the woman who does so *because* of them. We can (and should!) make jokes about the paper-thin fragility that's been passed down between men for generations, but this inherited hatred is constructed more deliberately than you might have thought. Understanding its history will enable you to annihilate the next ding-dong who tells you that women need to partner up in order to be happy *and everyone knows it*.

THE SHOCK COLLAR

Spinsters, misandrists, shrews, demon spawn from hell encased in human skin suits—no matter what euphemism our unrelentingly misogynistic society has coined to describe women who choose to live alone, the underlying message from the outside world is always the same: *We don't fucking trust you, WITCH.*

Nothing unsettles people more than the terrifying spectre of a woman who exists on her own terms. Women are supposed to be owned! We can't just be left to our own devices, wandering about the place unsupervised with nothing to keep our aimless wombs from driving us slowly mad. We need to be captured and monitored, lest we accidentally unleash the volatile nuclear energy source contained within our Pandora's box. One false step (especially with a big stride) and we could destroy the entire world!

Or so the story goes.

The writer and philosopher Kate Manne likens the use of misogyny to shock collars put on dogs to train them to stay behind invisible fences. While misogyny can and does inflict terrible violence, Manne argues that the *threat* of it is often enough to 'discourage girls and women from venturing out of bounds'. In this respect, the virulent backlash women are subjected to when we reject marriage and other heteropatriarchal demands functions as a crude training system to teach us what we are and aren't entitled to want. Happily single women are a threat to patriarchal order, because we contradict everything society has ever asserted about women's autonomy and value—to wit, that we cannot be trusted with the former and that we only attain the latter in relation to someone else. What are men supposed to do with all us misguided women, living in defiance of the social order and with such little regard for *our own happiness*? Us daffy little flibbertigibbets who don't realise that no amount of money, autonomous living and/or blissfully quiet Saturday mornings could ever make up for the fact we'll die old, sad and *alone*? How are we to be summarised in one neatly packaged trope, a derisive, dismissive stereotype that can be used to strike fear into the hearts of all women everywhere who might be tempted to follow in the (comfortably shod) footsteps of us unfuckable shrews?

This is where Manne's 'shock collar' comes into play, training us to remain within our invisible fences. While we can point to the complex system of economic, social and political coercion used to conscript women into the domestic service required to maintain patriarchy, nothing is quite as immediately effective as the use of insults and mockery. Misogyny has ejaculated all manner of words and phrases over the centuries to turn women who reject its rules into pitiful creatures living hideously unfulfilling lives in sad little garbage piles by a swamp.

In this construction of reality, we are *careerists*, driven by ambition and the pathetic desire for success and financial security at the expense of our own natural instincts. Those of us who don't care to become mothers are *deliberately barren*, refusing to use the body God and nature gave us for the only thing it was built for, and consequently missing out on the greatest happiness a woman could ever be blessed with—a destroyed pelvic floor, a baby to care for and clothes that will never again be free of peanut butter stains. Those among us who did become mothers but made the criminal choice to leave unsupportive (or just unfulfilling) partners and go it alone can enjoy being called *gold diggers* and *baby trappers*—used-up, run-through hags who've been thrown away by men who no longer want us yet now have to contend with having their hard-earned money stolen from them to support children they're not allowed to see. *Who would ever want you now?* the threat goes, as if the worst possible fate to befall a person who can't even spend five minutes on the toilet without interruption would be to never again be blessed by another person demanding she look after them. Then there are the *feminazis*, the deranged, angry, UGLY (how dare they!) battleaxes whose desire to see an end to the rape and abuse of women is somehow akin to an insane psychopath invading Poland and murdering six million Jewish people. Scold, shrew, harridan, nag, bitch, whore, slut, cunt . . . if you're looking to discredit a woman, there's a range of poisons to choose from.

But there is no more enthusiastically applied stereotype for women who reject the demands of domestic service and male authority than one that's been rattling around for almost a thousand years. She is old, she is sad, she is friendless. Once upon a time, she might have supped on gruel and stared at the walls, gnarled fingers gripping a bowl made of dried mud. Now she eats dinners for one in front of the television, watching game shows and shrieking the answers at the screen, her only source of satisfaction found in her uselessly clever brain and all of its pointless education. She is dried up, she is grotesque, she is unworthy of that most precious of resources: *male attention*. In one of the many paradoxes of misogynist logic, she is both bereft of sexual experiences and yet also boasts a vagina the size of a shipping container, thanks to the absolute walloping she gave it in her youth. It is in this enormous cavern of misery that she stores all of her regrets, each of them keening for the baby she failed to create to give her life meaning. She is the most nightmarish vision the world can imagine, a rotting witch clattering about in a dank house with the dozens of feral animals she keeps to stave off her wretched loneliness.

She is . . . Cat Lady.

Boo!

—

If you're a woman somewhere between the ages of birth and death, you'll have most likely been warned about Cat Lady. Hers is the fate that awaits any woman who wanders too close to the shores of independent thought, especially if she's doubly cursed by the kind of foolhardiness that sees her voicing such thoughts *out loud*. But although she's haunted society for centuries, her critics (most of whom are men, let's be real) still seem to believe she's a new invention—something only they could conjure up with their clever, clever wit and more sophisticated grasp of comedy. Watching adult men try to invoke her spirit as a kind of curse against disobedient women is always amusing, like watching children line up in front of a mirror to whisper *Bloody Mary* at their own reflections—except when these men utter the name of the she-beast five times, she appears behind them and screams PUT THE FUCKING TOILET SEAT DOWN.

Cat Lady has been a particularly popular subject among conservative commentators of late, many of whom are also *very* distressed at the thought of women having Too Much Access To Education. In May 2022, shortly after a US Supreme Court majority opinion was leaked making it clear the archaic toads sitting on the bench were finally coming for reproductive healthcare rights, the far right Republican congressman Matt Gaetz tweeted the following: 'How many of the women rallying against overturning Roe are over-educated, under-loved millennials who sadly return from protests to a lonely microwave dinner with their cats, and no Bumble matches?'

Less than a year earlier, in July 2021, the Republican Party's Senate candidate J.D. Vance (author of the memoir *Hillbilly Elegy*) appeared on Fox News pundit Tucker Carlson's show to rail against child-free people who had the audacity to behave as if they had any right to political influence. Vance (whose bid for the Senate was successful) was in full-on campaign mode as he performed one of the central tenets of the Republican Party—virulent misogyny— to the millions of Fox viewers similarly dismayed by the prospect of women thinking for themselves: 'We are effectively run in this country—via the Democrats, via our corporate oligarchs—by a bunch of childless cat ladies who are miserable at their own lives and the choices that they've made, and so they want to make the rest of the country miserable too.'

Vance was appearing on Fox to extrapolate on comments he'd made while speaking to members of a conservative think tank. By Vance's reckoning, child-free Americans of voting age couldn't possibly have the kind of emotional and political experience necessary to decide what good democracy looks like. Instead, their votes should be taken from them and given to children, whose votes in turn would be given to their parents to use judiciously.

'It's an interesting idea,' *Fox & Friends* host Will Cain said later, proving once again the dearth of intelligence that exists at the network. 'Parents have a stake in the game, they have children, so give parents a bigger say.'

These are the same people who refuse to accept the probability of climate collapse but, yes, let's pretend they care about children. As to the assumption that non-parents are ill-equipped to vote in the best interests of the next generation, this reverence for personal experience is curiously absent when it comes to conservative men like Vance, Carlson and Cain assuming reproductive authority over women's bodies. But I guess that's just one of those paradoxical quandaries I don't get because of my frivolous girl brain.

It isn't just media pundits and right-wing politicos who seem to have a problem with women exercising choice over who, when, how and even if they decide to partner and/or have children. In August 2022, an article titled 'The rise of lonely, single men', penned by psychologist Greg Matos, went viral on social media, mostly accompanied by amused commentary. It came as no surprise to women that modern heterosexual men were finding their opportunities for romantic attachment diminishing. Although the bar for women's expectations of men still tends to be about as low as the molten centre of the earth's core, there has been some slow movement up in recent years. The general consensus for this revelatory new information was *no shit.*

But rather than use this as an opportunity to reassess what they've been taught is their birthright and entitlement when it comes to love, much of the response offered by men was of the embittered variety. *Enjoy your bloody cats, you bloody selfish girls! WE DON'T WANT YOU ANYWAY!* Matos—who had identified poor communication skills and lack of emotional maturity as one of the main reasons for men's lack of romantic success—received death threats and hate mail.

'Why?' he asked in a video posted to TikTok. 'When all I am doing is asking you to be the best version of yourself. That's all. All I am inviting you to do is just be the best version of yourself.'

It's a reasonable question, but my own anecdotal experience with men online indicates it will never be satisfactorily answered. Nor does it seem probable men en masse will take Matos up on his invitation, and look inwards to consider what they might be doing (or not doing) to stoke women's aversion to settling for the bare minimum.

No matter how many women turn our backs on domestic servitude, men always act surprised at the idea we would want to. They really do find it easier to believe that women (whom they usually refer to as 'females') are born hardwired to keep houses clean and balls empty, and that a life spent doing literally anything else will send us into a state of chronic depression that can only be cured by a man telling us to smile. Females, these men intone, are natural caregivers. It's *biological*. (Curiously, men who argue for women's biological compulsion to nurture have never much liked it when I've thanked them for agreeing we should automatically receive full custody of children on the basis of our superior ability to care. In fact, they get very cross! It's an enjoyable way to spend an afternoon, and I highly recommend it.)

No man who makes this argument is ever able to bolster it with anything more than the insistence that 'it's just obvious'. The same intellectual rigour is used to support their claims that women *need* a relationship in order to be happy. Everyone knows it, and that's that. The lack of real evidence to support this (in fact, the longitudinal data indicates the exact opposite) is irrelevant. It feels true to them (which is convenient, given it satisfies their needs), so they insist that it must *be* true. But you'll note that the more confident a man is about what women want, the less likely it is that he's actually spoken to any to find out. He doesn't read books by and about women, nor does he watch movies devoted to women's stories, listen to music made by women, follow the work of intellectuals who are women or count women among his close friends. It isn't necessary for him to engage with women as a set of complex humans with unique and legitimate perspectives separate from his own; his own instinct is all the proof he'll ever need, and no amount of 'broken' women telling him he's wrong will ever change his mind.

This idea of brokenness is at the heart of the Cat Lady insult. When a woman's behaviour deviates from what *men* want and need to be happy—care, unending labour, sex on tap, provided by someone who never complains, nags or asks for anything in return—it isn't because she has agency and humanity of her own. It's because there's something wrong with her. Her own natural instincts have been perverted in some way, poisoning the well of love she's supposed to *want* to give a man lifelong access to and channelling it instead into an animal known for its self-sufficiency, ability to self-clean and ambivalence towards attention. *Who hurt you, bitch?!*

I mean . . . they're just *so close* to getting it, aren't they?

—

While feminist progress has made it more possible than ever for a single woman to survive and even thrive on her own terms, the existence of such women is nothing new. Time and again, whenever women's liberation from oppression has come within reach, we see the culture reinforcing its well-worn moral framework that positions unleashed women as absurd, pitiful and ridiculous.

For a society that relies not just on women's performance of domestic servitude but also our aspirations to it, happily single women represent a threat to the natural order of things—the 'natural order', of course, being a carefully cultivated social design spanning millennia that positions women as both the supporting characters in men's lives, the well-trodden stages on which they present their narratives and the wardrobe assistants who clean up the post-show mess. It's our job to help them shine, and then to ensure the costumes are washed, freshly pressed and hanging in the dressing room for the next day's performance.

Who said we can't have it all!

Adherence to this system isn't just a matter of tradition. It's an essential part of the patriarchal project, driven by one specific goal: to seamlessly maintain the fiction that positions men as the architects of all of human history and women as the willing subjects just grateful to be included. Without women lining up to act as the stage managers for men's lives, how could those same men possibly assert themselves as the creative minds behind the world's longest-running cultural almanac: *Boys Rule and Girls Drool.*

In this modern fantasy of male superiority and world-building, women are little more than single-cell organisms floating around looking for something to help us to evolve into a more complex state of existence. My way-back foremothers had scant choice in their marital unions, being traded around like stocks and bonds among men either looking to build their property portfolios and/ or wanting to end longstanding diplomatic disputes between clans and nations, while my more recent ancestresses (at least on my Celtic father's side) were constrained by the fact they had no legal identity and therefore needed to attach themselves to a husband to have any social mobility at all. Companionate marriages built on the flimsy notion of 'love' were still centuries away from becoming fashionable, and marriage for most people was often the choice between being really poor or being slightly less poor. In a world designed to service men's needs by denying women their human rights, the use of shame as a motivator to sign on to compulsory heterosexuality and domestic drudgery would have been laughable. Why would people treated as the legal property of men be consulted about marriage at all, let alone given a choice in the matter?

But every time women's liberation movements have delivered an increase in agency, however fractional, our success has encountered resistance and fury from the forces which rely on our subjugation. When the ties women seek to sever are those that bind us to men's service, the backlash is especially vicious. As the notion of marital *choice* has become more attainable for women over time (even if still illusory in many ways), the punishment for exercising it to opt out of the system has reared its ugly head.

So how does a culture that benefits from women's forced subservience respond when those same women look to acquire power, even if just over their own lives?

It establishes those women as aberrations of 'correct' femininity— a mutant organism whose programming has gone awry somehow, filling her mind with ugly thoughts and quite often reflecting them via an even uglier physical appearance. If one of the few currencies a woman is allowed is her beauty and desirability to the male gaze, then these will be the first things denied to her should she threaten to upset the apple cart. She will be stripped, too, of her more interior 'feminine' traits: her gentility, her capacity for nurture and the likelihood of her becoming a mother—thus rendering her obsolete entirely. None of this is based in reality, of course, but as a general rule men have never allowed facts to get in the way of the goalposts they're constantly shifting.

Disruptive women have always been punished in one way or another, whether that's through mass social ridicule, exile or just a good old-fashioned murder. Given that the latter isn't as easy to get away with these days (although there are still far too many men who seem willing to keep trying their luck on that one), shame and mockery prevail.

But why has the trope of the pitiful Cat Lady become so ubiquitous?

Well, like all edgelord comedy, it's far less original than you might think. Derek from the bar might think he's torching you with his wit when he tells you to enjoy dying alone with your cats, but disagreeable women—aka Cool Bitches—have been dealing with Dereks for almost a thousand years. Because what can't you do with a cat that you can do with almost every other domesticated animal, a category into which men have always wanted to place women?

Bend it to your will, and force it to respect your God-given authority.

DANCING WITH THE DEVIL

Really, it was the establishment of Christianity across the European world that signalled the death knell for cats and the hitherto unparalleled popularity they'd enjoyed as mystical creatures. The ancient world revered them, going so far as to associate them with multiple deities.

Consider Bastet, who was the original Cat Lady and the Egyptian goddess of hearth and home. Bastet had the body of a woman and the head of a feline, and—as the protector of women's secrets—was probably considered especially threatening by a religion obsessed with male power. The Zhou dynasty was said to have held an annual sacrifice in the honour of cats. And while most people have heard of Valhalla, the majestic hall presided over by the Norse god Odin which was the resting place for the souls of fallen warriors, a lesser known fact is that only half of all soldiers ended up there. The other half were called to Fólkvangr, a meadow ruled over by Freyja, the Norse goddess of fertility, gold and death. Ancient religions were far more likely to worship goddesses as well as gods, which was a bit of a problem for a religious doctrine devoted to patriarchal rule and a single Holy Father. It probably didn't help that Freyja's preferred mode of transport was a chariot pulled by two glorious cats.

Wanting to put an end to the mysticism and bacchanalia that had run rampant across Europe since a bunch of druids got drunk one day and decided to build a henge out of stone, the Catholic Church decided it was time for a crackdown. Anything remotely associated with pagan rituals or the worship of multiple deities was demonised—literally—as representative of Satan. With cats now considered to be one of his preferred forms (not to mention strongly associated with women who refuse to do what they're told), our feline friends were rebranded as 'familiars'—creatures sent from Beelzebub to act as messengers for the she-devils who served him. In 1180, the writer Walter Map immortalised this cultural fear, describing how 'the Devil descends as a black cat before his devotees. The worshippers put out the light and draw near to the place where they saw their master. They feel after him and when they have found him they kiss him under the tail.'

Raunchy stuff!

For obvious reasons, women were far more likely to engage in pagan rituals involving nature and the moon (not to mention being more proficient as midwives, healers and medicinal suppliers), and were also able to create life in a way priests and their made-up man in the sky were incapable of. The idea that women might be respected as religious leaders contradicted the authority of a singular Father creator, so the men trying to make Him happen decided the best way to put a stop to this was to turn women *and* their cats into objects of fear, and then use the resulting paranoia as an excuse to go on a killing spree. On the advice of one of his chief inquisitors, the thirteenth-century pope Gregory IX even ordered the mass extermination of cats, which led to the eradication of roughly two hundred thousand of them. (According to some tellings, this is what led to the bubonic plague; with no cats left to kill the rats blamed for it, the disease was able to spread like wildfire. However, this is likely a myth. It was fleas that carried the plague, and whether they travelled about on rats or cats would have been largely irrelevant.) So enthusiastic was the public desire to stamp out witches and their familiars that if you were to ask a child in the thirteenth century what they wanted to be when they grew up, you'd not be surprised to hear them chirp, 'A witch-hunter!'

Hunting witches was a messy business, and undoubtedly led to many a debrief at the local tavern. There's some degree of irony in the fact that—in probable homage to their forefathers—modern men's dissection of horrible women and our ugly feminism might take place over a beer, and it's to this topic that we must divert for a moment. The drink has long been identified as a Special Interest Topic for men, and they're certainly very eager to share their love for the fancier versions of it across all of their online dating profiles. But despite its popularity among men (79 per cent of craft beer drinkers are boys), the brewing of beer used to be a woman's game. That is, until they were demonised and vilified by the Church for—you guessed it!—being witches.

The first-known records of female brewers—or 'brewsters', as they used to be called—can be traced back to Mesopotamia, roughly four thousand years ago. The Ancient Sumerians worshipped the goddess Ninkasi, whose name translates to 'mistress of beer', and celebrated her with a hymn containing what is now the world's oldest-known beer recipe, which included the soaking of malt in a jar and the spreading of cooked mash on large reed mats. Ceremonial, for sure, but also a clever way to make sure the recipe would never be forgotten.

The Ancient Egyptians surpassed the Sumerians as master brewers, with smoother, silkier concoctions that could be drunk from a cup or a glass instead of the bowls 'n' straws combo favoured by the Sumerians. Beer became an integral part of Egyptian festivals, including those celebrating the goddesses Hathor, Sekhmet and Bastet (our OG Cat Lady). Just like in Mesopotamia, it was the women who were responsible for brewing it. The beer itself was considered a valuable source of nutrition, being consumed by men, women and children and used as payment for labour and goods. So essential was it to the Egyptians that they needed it even in death. Forget flowers—for the wealthy, jars of beer were one of the most common grave offerings. Two thousand years later, Incan society in South America considered beer so important to the functioning of society that the brewing of it was *only* entrusted to women.

For eons, beer was considered a staple part of the average person's diet all over the world and an important part of ceremonial protocol. Not only was it a cheap and convenient way to use grains, the pleasant feelings of intoxication no doubt went a long way to making up for the lack of proper septic systems in a time when people still only bathed once a year.

But although men took to the consumption of beer then with as much enthusiasm as they do now, brewing was dismissed as a domestic job. I suspect that all the milling of flour, soaking, filtering and fermenting also made it quite fiddly and time-consuming, which are two things men rarely seem to involve themselves in at home unless it means talking loudly about the best way to barbecue meat. It was also a task performed mostly in the kitchen—and as every Clever Online Boy will tell you, this is where women belong. In a chapter about the demonisation of single women, it's nice to be reminded that one of the selling points men love to recite from the marriage brochure is the expectation we work our hardest to keep their tum-tums nice and full.

But women are nothing if not packed with ingenuity and can-do pluck. Men might need the fishing net to feed their family for a lifetime, but women will figure out how to make one using nothing but the scales and bones of the fish itself. With limited options for financial independence (or as close to it as a woman could get at the time), entrepreneurial gals made use of what means were available to them. A knack for brewing beer being one of these, some women in possession of this ability were clever enough to monetise the operation. Exceptions to deeply misogynistic attitudes about money were often made for women to sell beer either as independent traders or as tavern owners. Brewsters everywhere were able to eke out a living, sometimes marrying and sometimes not, but always able to make use of the skills they had. And so it would have remained had it not been for two major moments in whiny man-baby history: the publication of the *Malleus Maleficarum* in 1486, and the Reformation.

THE SEASON OF THE WITCH

For a community gripped by both religious paranoia and abject misogyny, the *Malleus Maleficarum* (also known as *The Hammer of Witches*) was considered the definitive guide to witch-hunting, providing (supposedly) much more rigorous instructions than the previous two hundred years of trial and error had been able to achieve. Just as they had done in the Dark Ages, Medieval Europeans held firmly to the view that witches were almost always women, to the degree that most authors had stopped bothering to explain why. Those who did were happy to elucidate the scientific link, this being that witches and women were both naturally deceitful and vengeful, and that women's unrestrained sexual voracity in particular made them ideal tools for Satan's misdeeds. The *Malleus Maleficarum* itself describes women as 'more credulous . . . more impressionable . . . more carnal than a man . . . [with] slippery tongues and weak memories'. This duplicity was due to a defect in our creation that could be traced right back to Eve, 'since she was formed from a bent rib . . . which is bent in the contrary direction to a man'.

Science!

Just over a century later, King James I (you've probably found one of his Bibles in a motel drawer at some point) would write in his own 'women are scary' book, *Daemonologie*, that women were in fact *twenty times* more likely than men to be witches. The reason for this was threefold: first, that women were more curious than men; second, that our thirst for revenge outstripped theirs; and third, that we had a 'greedy appetite caused through great poverty'.

To be honest, all of that sounds quite accurate to me. But somehow, I don't think King Jim considered it a compliment to call us both curious and diabolical, or thought it necessary to reflect on why 'great poverty' might encourage our ambitions. What he did do was use it to justify the murder of thousands of Scottish women who had been accused of witchcraft, which makes the casual endorsement of his Bible in accommodation services across the globe fairly questionable.

Despite its obviously nonsensical theories and outright misogyny, the *Malleus Maleficarum* was considered an essential weapon in the battle against Satan and his horde of evil brides. Proving once again that patriarchy will always change the rules to suit itself, the devil had begun life as a sort of useful imp, subordinate to the will of his more diabolical (male) masters. But the prospect of vilifying women led to a revamp in the centuries that followed his creation. As Silvia Federici writes in *Caliban and the Witch: Women, the body and primitive accumulation*, 'The witch-hunt reversed the power relation between the devil and the witch. It was the woman now who was the servant, the slave, the *succubus* in body and soul, while the Devil functioned as her owner and master, pimp and husband at once.' This reversal, Federici argues, was not only a clear reinforcement of male supremacy (for even in violation of morality and God, women had to be presented as being subservient to a male entity) but also a 'pre-figuration of women's matrimonial destiny', with the so-called witches having given themselves to Satan mind, body and soul.

Women aligned with Satan weren't just at risk of sinning against God but also of destroying men. Obviously, such women need to be annihilated. And luckily for the Church, the perfect opportunity to rid themselves of the threat of women presented itself in the form (ironically) of a power grab from a man and his earthly followers. Until the fifteenth century, the Catholic Church had enjoyed a comfortable monopoly on religious power, imprisoning or killing anyone who challenged the notion of the Big Guy Upstairs. But the Reformation changed that, with the newly established arm of the Protestant Church vying to steal some of the flock.

The papal system had been challenged by reforms before, but none had been so effective as those proposed by Martin Luther. Aided by Johannes Gutenberg's new industrialised printing press, Luther and his mates were able to disseminate their calls to the Protestant Church across Europe more rapidly. Desperate to maintain its domination of the soul market (and, more importantly, the wealth it brought) the Catholics and Protestants battled to prove whose leadership was best. This involved demonstrating who could hunt and kill the most witches.

Surprise!

In a very on-brand move for men through the ages, women were yet again used as a kind of Thunderdome in which to stage power grabs and dick-swinging competitions. As you might expect carnage ensued. The violence inflicted by the state against entire generations of women (and some men) was devastating. Over the next century and a half, from about 1550 to 1700, more than forty thousand people (the vast majority of them women over the age of forty, whose 'useful' reproductive years were most likely past them but whose reproductive *knowledge* was considered a threat) were murdered as witches across Europe. The lion's share of these executions occurred in Germany and Scotland, both of which happened to be ground zero for the fiercest competition between the Catholics and the Protestants. Women were tortured brutally in order to force confessions, with sleep deprivation and sexual sadism both enthusiastically employed. Thanks to a 1468 declaration by the Pope that identified witchcraft as *crimen exceptum*, or 'crimes apart', the usual legal protocols that protected citizens from unreasonable interrogation tactics were thrown out the window. With no limits to the depravity available to them, officials applied what Federici calls 'some of the most sadistic tortures ever invented'. Preferred methods varied depending on the person or people extracting these 'confessions', but often involved rape and other forms of sexual violence; some women had their bones crushed or their limbs torn from them, or were forced to sit on iron chairs that would be heated to boiling point. To make sure the message was delivered loud and clear—to ensure, as Kate Manne might have it, that every last woman watching felt the sharp, invisible sting of a warning pierce her neck—members of the community, including the children of those women accused and sentenced, were expected to attend any and all executions. Sometimes, as a sort of side act to the main event and an assurance against inherited wrongdoing, the daughters of these women 'would be whipped in front of the stake on which they could see their mother burning alive'.

Men threatened by feminism ask women like me why we hate them. The more I read of history, the less concerned I am with trying not to. The capacity men have shown for destroying the very people who gave them life is unparalleled. How dare *any* modern man compare the long-overdue and still-not-far-enough uprising of women against the rapists, abusers and misogynists who have terrorised us for millennia as a *witch-hunt*.

Fuck them all to hell.

SLIPPERY WOMEN

The trials and resulting executions of 'witches' only began to abate in the mid-seventeenth century, with a series of treaties to broker relative peace between the arms of the Christian Church. By 1700, the formal persecution of witches had been essentially abandoned. They'd got it wrong, see. Only daft superstition would cause people to believe in that rubbish! *Har dee har har.*

But the legacy of the witch-hunts runs deep. In fact, it directly informs the oppression women experience across multiple layers of modern society. It introduced a policing of women's sexuality that has persisted to this day, with sexually active women considered impure and ungodly. It marked as dangerous the 'rebellious' woman—she who spoke out against feudal hierarchies, religious oppression and domestic abuse. Proving the effectiveness of Manne's metaphorical shock collar, the threat of accusation worked to distance women from one another—because even *connection* between women was enough to create suspicion that they might be colluding with the devil. Women who were accused (and horrifically tortured) were sometimes compelled to accuse other women in the hope that their own life might be spared. This fear of each other continues today. We can see it in the behaviour of Pick-Me girls and their appeal to male authority and approval. *I'm not like other girls, I just get on better with men, women are too bitchy/mean/vindictive, you never have to fear that I'm on their side, I'm not I'm not I'm not.* We can see it too in men's inherited suspicion that women might be colluding against them—because when two or more women spend time together without men to oversee the proceedings it isn't a gathering, it's a coven.

But one of the worst outcomes of the witch-hunts was in how they wrestled the control of reproduction away from women and delivered it into the hands of the patriarchal state. It was the midwives and the wise women, with deep knowledge of birth, medicine and nature, who were most often targeted. Childbirth in particular had always been seen as an 'inviolable mystery', but the Church decided they didn't like being excluded from the process. Who knew what those midwives were doing behind closed doors? Who was to say they weren't responsible for the tragic loss of infant life, rampant as it was in the otherwise notoriously sterilised environment of state-of-the-art medieval hospitals? That they hadn't used their dark arts to murder babies and offer them up to Satan? So dangerous were midwives that the *Malleus* dedicated an entire chapter to how they were the 'worst of all women'. Worse even than scrapbookers! By the end of the sixteenth century, as the witch-hunts were gathering steam, few women in France and England were allowed to practise midwifery. By the beginning of the seventeenth century, the control of obstetrics had shifted almost entirely to men in the medical profession. And because women were denied access to education and professional training (*why don't you just try harder to succeed?*), the belief that men were more capable of overseeing reproduction and *women's own fucking bodies* became undisputed.

This didn't end with the witch-hunts. In the absence of Satanic-based accusations, the legal system simply shifted the witchy-woo arguments they'd used as proof of women's 'slipperiness' and regurgitated them to discredit their allegations of rape and domestic abuse—an outrageous codifying of misogyny that also continues today, in both the legal system and broader society. According to Federici, the word 'gossip' in the Middle Ages meant only 'friend'. But because friendship between women (who were untrustworthy, vindictive and weasel-tongued) was a source of suspicion, 'gossip' took on the meaning that we understand it to have now—that it's something meddlesome women do with the intention of causing harm to innocent people. The *Malleus* had warned of the capacity of witches to destroy men, drawing them in with the allure of beauty and the scent of sex and then castrating them for laughs (or, as one witch was accused of doing, hiding dozens of their penises in a tree). This suspicion of women's motives didn't disappear alongside the diminishing spectre of witches, but has only grown more robust in the intervening centuries.

Consider the foundation of the western legal tradition, and the men still lauded for having designed it. This is where we can find the celebrated British legal scholar Sir Matthew Hale, who was appointed chair of the Hale Commission (a seventeenth-century entity designed to investigate law reform), and whose posthumously published work *Historia Placitorum Coronæ* (1736) directly influenced the establishment of English common law that is practised today.

Hale's legacy was indeed great, if by 'great' you mean 'greatly fucked'. It was Hale who contributed the British legal doctrine that stated a man couldn't rape his wife, because he was already entitled to sex by virtue of 'their mutual matrimonial consent and contract'. Far from being opposed as horrifyingly dehumanising, Hale's views on marital rape formed the basis of common law until the late twentieth century, granting three centuries worth of men more claim over their wives' bodies than the women themselves. And it wasn't just husbands who were entitled to sex. Hale's broader view on rape held that it was 'an accusation easily to be made and hard to be proved, and harder to be defended by the party accused, tho never so innocent'. In his view, when dealing with the 'detestable crime' of rape, the jury (which, in Hale's era, was always limited to men) must consider the reliability of the woman. Was her reputation good or bad? Did she fight back or try to escape? How soon after the alleged attack did she make a complaint? So valued was this insight into women's naturally vengeful nature that, in 1973, US appellate judge Justice Bazelon described Hale's cautioning against the risk of false accusations as one of the most commonly quoted passages in US jurisprudence. American juries retiring to deliberate in rape trials were reminded of it well into the 1980s. Though they may no longer be formally instructed to question a woman's motives, members of a jury (not to mention members of the public) cannot so easily shake off these cultural beliefs. When you encounter victim blaming, understand that it isn't caused by ignorance but by deliberate patriarchal design.

Should we be surprised by Hale's disdain for women's agency or motivations for defending it? No, given he believed women were inherently duplicitous and had no qualms about killing them as punishment for it. In 1662, he presided over the trial of Rose Cullender and Amy Denny, who had been jointly accused of using witchcraft to harm the children of men said to have upset them. Hale instructed the jury to remember that witches were *real*; not only had the Bible confirmed this, but 'the wisdom of all nations had provided laws against such persons, which is an argument of their confidence in such a crime'. Rose and Amy were both found guilty, and Hale ordered their executions. Thirty years later, the trial and his particular instruction would provide great inspiration for the persecution of witches in Salem, Massachusetts.

As unbelievable as it should be—as absolutely *baffling* and *outrageous*—this piece of shit seventeenth-century rape apologist is still being given power to determine women's lives today, facilitated by the misogyny of (at least some of) his successors in the legal system. In 2022, some three hundred and fifty years after Hale's death, US Supreme Court justice Samuel Alito referenced Hale (whom he referred to as an 'eminent common-law authority') and his views on abortion (he called it a 'great crime . . . and misprison') in the majority opinion that successfully put an end to *Roe v. Wade* and thus abolished access to reproductive health care for millions of American women and people with uteruses. Well might social fantasists argue against the need for feminism because 'everything is equal now', but that can never be true while women have less authority over our own bodies than a man who's been dead for more than three centuries.

But what does all this have to do with today's spectre of the Cat Lady—or beer, for that matter?

Well, as the Reformation began to gather steam and witch-hunting began in earnest, so too did society cling harder to beliefs about strict gender norms. As Federici lays out, the witch trials worked to entrench the idea of marriage as a necessary means for containing women, and subsequently to separate us from the solidarity we had once enjoyed with each other. A divided force is a conquered force, after all. Meanwhile, men had started to see the financial benefits in brewing beer themselves, and didn't quite fancy the idea of competing with women for their share of the market, especially not since those women had shifted their operations from the home and into the actual *marketplace*. Brewing beer was a time-consuming activity, and it was feared that women who did it would be less inclined to marry and produce children (which was perhaps why they were now referred to as 'alewives').

It would have been pointless to try to force compliance using the basic mockery of single women that would prove so effective in later historical periods, because marriage hadn't yet been reinvented as a signifier that one is loved; it was still primarily a means of forming economic or genealogical alliances. Instead, men used what was available to them—this being the rampant paranoia surrounding witches and aberrant women—to drive their competitors out of the industry. Aided by the occasional bout of hallucinations that occurred when the grains used to brew beer were infected with ergot (a fungus that grows on grains, and from which the first batch of LSD was synthesised in 1938), these men began to circulate the idea that the alewives were witches—dangerous women brewing potions instead of beer, and using them to cast spells on unsuspecting folk just looking to quench a hard-earned thirst. The accusations stuck, and hundreds of years later we still have to listen to dudes discuss their preferred level of hops with no mention at all of Hildegard von Bingen, the twelfth-century Benedictine nun and medicine woman who was the first known person to write accurately about the medicinal properties of the flower when added to a hearty brew.

This is where some historians have suggested the iconography we associate with witches originated, and it's a good example of how ridiculously susceptible humans are to propaganda. Alewives wore tall, pointed black hats as they walked through the market so that they could be seen above the heads of the crowd. Their beer was carried in cauldrons to serve to patrons. To signal their shops were open, they'd hang brooms above the doorway—brooms that were also useful for sweeping up the grains used to make the beer. Grains have always been a major holiday destination for mice and rats. And what did the world's oldest agriculturists, from the Egyptians to the Greeks to the Chinese and the Norse Vikings, know you must always have around if you want to keep the vermin away, to the point even of revering them as spiritual deities?

Cats.

Blessed be.

3

SPINSTER CITY

'I put in my list all the busy, useful independent
spinsters I know, for liberty is a better
husband than love to many of us.'

—Louisa May Alcott, *Her Life, Letters, and Journals*

As we now know, all single women who live alone risk one day becoming all-you-can-eat buffets for their hungry felines. With neither husbands nor children to act as interpreters for the human experience we've lost all ability to understand, we are destined to drift through our twilight years like forgotten ghosts. Ignored by the outside world, the day will eventually come where we'll fail to wake up, the couches we treated as lovers providing an eternal embrace for us at last. There we'll remain for days—months, even—while the shells we once called bodies are slowly picked of all their meat by the creatures our annoying feminism cursed us to grow old with.

Of course, a woman doesn't need to be *old* to risk consumption-by-pet. All she needs to be is single past the age of thirty, which is practically the same thing. The most famous modern heroine to voice such a worry out loud was Bridget Jones, who confessed to her diary that she feared the most significant relationship of her life would be with a bottle of wine, and that unless something changed, she'd 'finally die, fat and alone, and be found three weeks later half-eaten by Alsatians'. (You'll note that not even Bridget saw cats in her future, but a trope is a trope.)

For Bridget, being relegated to the state of 'spinster' at the tender age of thirty-two wasn't just a cultural paranoia spawned by hundreds of years of bad press; it was a legal certainty for unmarried women coming of age in late-twentieth-century Britain. Prior to the UK's *Civil Partnerships Act 2004* unmarried women were forced to tick a box marked 'spinster' when listing their previous relationship status on marriage certificates. Men could record themselves as 'bachelors', a term that carries significantly less social stigma (if you care about that sort of thing) and certainly none of the associations with pet-devouring. The legalisation of same-sex civil ceremonies resulted in options for both being changed to the more accurate use of 'single', but the terms still remain fixed in people's minds. As recently as 2019, 'spinster' was still being used to describe unmarried women in legal documents in Hong Kong.

Relatable though Bridget's desperation to find love might have been to women raised to believe in the promise of a happy-ever-after with a you-complete-me, the evolution of 'spinster' as a pejorative term is just another example of how determined patriarchy has been to keep women in our box. What can I say—misogyny has always teamed up with cultural anxieties to produce some truly bargain bin comedy.

How did 'spinster' become the 'cat lady' of its time? It didn't begin that way. For hundreds of years, it was just a job title for people who spun wool. The first recorded use of it can be traced to the 1300s, when a poet named William Langland wrote, 'And my wyf . . . Spak to the spinsters for to spinne hit softe.' (Sidenote: reading Middle English is an excellent reminder that language changes constantly, so stop shaming people for being 'bad' at spelling!)

This being a few hundred years before the establishment of the economic middle class and the sparkly new opportunities to outsource labour this created, almost all women were required to work in some capacity. Modern-day conservatives like to pretend that feminism invented jobs in order to lure unsuspecting women out of the home, but the reality is that we've always been on the front line of world-building, particularly in the manufacturing and textile industries. The idea that humanity got to where it is now through the contributions of men alone is ludicrous. If it weren't for women, men would be building all their precious roads while still draped in loincloths and dried leaves pasted together with mud, and the tiny skirts favoured by Bridget Jones would quite literally be nowhere to be seen.

Being married didn't deliver women from the indignity of work. On the contrary, it often improved the employment options available to women at the time. Married women working with textiles in the fourteenth century were usually able to access better, more expensive materials because of the economic advantage gained by combining resources with their boo, thus increasing their returns overall. Yay, capitalism! Single women with limited economic means were more likely to spin wool for a living, because the initial outlay of costs was much lower.

Well-meaning modern feminists have sometimes misinterpreted this history, presumably to deflect the frustrating nonsense men bombard us with daily. A few years ago, a woman named Gemma Milne tweeted the following: 'Just learnt that "spinster" was originally the word for a woman so good at weaving that she was financially independent. HOW INTERESTING.' Listen, I get the temptation to recast spinsters as the original Boss Babes, but it's just not true. Women who worked on the wheel weren't off galivanting about the countryside or dressing themselves in the latest Parisian fashions. Like all people oppressed by poverty and class warfare, they scraped by because they had to. It would have been shitty, repetitive work that eventually decimated their eyesight, gnarled their fingers and strained their backs. Under those conditions, I'm sure many of them would have preferred the economic security of marriage—and the not insignificant financial privilege (at huge invisible cost) that marriage promises to women goes to the heart of why it's so manipulative and fucked. Still, from a moral point of view, whether a spinster had a himster was irrelevant. If she were maligned for anything back then, it was more likely to be because she was poor than because she was unmarried. (To be fair, there may still have been a legitimate risk of her dead corpse being eaten by cats. Medieval England was a grim place, and the proper disposal of bodies was kind of hit and miss.)

For a few centuries, spinsters quietly went about their business. It wasn't until the mid-seventeenth century that the term 'spinster' assumed any kind of legal authority in England, being used to refer to unmarried women in general, regardless of the nature of their employment (or class bracket). But it was during the eighteenth century that the idea of turning spinsters into a kind of hurricane warning system for disobedient women really began to capture the public imagination. Having survived three hundred years of relatively mundane meaning, the word quickly entered the zeitgeist as a misogynistic shorthand for a new breed of woman: one who already had or was in position to create financial capital without needing to marry, and whose growing financial independence posed a threat to the institutional power traditionally hoarded by men.

The possibilities presented at the time for ordinary dames with a mind for money were greater than at any point in Anglo history. Western Europe was undergoing rapid change, colonialist Britain was seeking to expand its brutal empire, and the resulting emergence of the economic middle class was well underway. Women may have always worked, but they had rarely been in a position to amass any kind of institutional economic power on their own. Thus, whether or not they had married was largely irrelevant, carrying with it only personal implications for a small group of people—a family looking to combine land or resources, say, or to give legitimacy to children born outside of wedlock.

But these women . . . well, they worried the men. They seemed to have come out of nowhere, and who knew what demands they might make? According to Judith Spicksley, in her paper 'Women alone', 'As never married women moved to fill a greater physical space in the English landscape than at any time previously in living memory, institutional structures had little choice but to recognise their presence: their access to capital ensured they were more likely, as wealth holders, to appear in the records of civil and ecclesiastical organisations.'

Recognising women's presence in public life? Preposterous! Next they'll be wanting the vote!

You see the conundrum.

Then there was the issue of baby-making. With more and more women opting out of marriage and the reproductive service this entailed, the aspirations of an increasingly powerful British Empire were under threat. Remember, it's never been for our own fulfilment that women are expected to produce babies; it's so the state has an endless supply of bodies to be productive for itself. The commentariat decried the existence of unmarried, loathsome old hags (and at *twenty-five*, no less!) for exactly the same reasons women today are warned against too much independence: because fewer women were getting married, and that meant fewer babies were being born. In her research into the prevalence of single women in early modern England, historian Amy Froide found that just over half of all adult women at the time were either unmarried or widowed, which effectively halved the reproductive labour women were performing in service of an expanding empire. Britain was extremely anxious to grow both its military and its manufacturing industries. How could the empire continue to flourish when more and more of the state's glorified incubators were refusing to fulfil their obligations to King and Cuntry?

It was a problem Britain had never faced before. It used to be that women could just be traded or sold into marriage, as they were considered the property of fathers, brothers and any other man vaguely connected to their bloodline. But although not much had changed in regard to women's property (or bodily) rights, marriage itself had undergone some cultural changes, at least for the upper classes. The economic benefits of marriage were still considered unavoidable for many women without means, but those establishing a degree of independence for themselves had far more leeway. Choice may be a concept relative to one's available options, but there's no doubt the capacity of the first increases alongside the second. Women with economic security have always had more choices than women without, and this was no less true for the independently minted women who were in a position to weigh up what marriage could possibly give them versus what it would definitely take.

And boy, could it take a LOT.

The *Married Women's Property Act 1882* was still almost two hundred years away from being signed into law, and coverture—which had been practised for centuries but was formally outlined as part of British law in the mid-eighteenth century—held that everything a woman owned, including her identity, automatically belonged to her husband. Until the *Matrimonial Causes Act* was passed in 1857, divorce was basically impossible.

To secure one required a private Act of Parliament, which was incredibly expensive. To avoid this, men who had grown tired of their wives could either force them out of the family home or shack up somewhere else with their new girlfriend, leaving a woman with nothing.

But more frightening than abandonment was the prospect of institutionalisation. Beginning in the eighteenth century, and really hitting its stride in the nineteenth, an increasing number of men keen to move on with someone new began to collude with the medical establishment to have their wives committed to mental asylums. Consider the case of Hannah Mackenzie, whose husband Peter conspired to have her sent to Peter Day's Paddington Madhouse in 1766. Peter had been having an affair with Hannah's niece and, wanting to install her as the lady of the house, arranged for a doctor well known for assisting in such circumstances to visit with Hannah and confirm that she was insane. Clever Hannah knew what her husband was doing and managed to run away, but she was soon caught, placed in a straitjacket and sent to the madhouse. She only managed to escape after attracting the attention of a boy working next door; through him, she was able to secure the help of John Sherratt, whose legal training assisted in his lifelong campaign against private asylums. Countless other women weren't so lucky; by the nineteenth century, more women than men languished in asylums, and could be committed by fathers and husbands alike for such signs of mental collapse as 'reading too much' and 'asking for a divorce'.

Those crazy bitches!

Not all husbands were in a position to pay doctors to sign committal forms, but don't worry—men of humble means could free themselves of inconvenient marriages *and* make a little bit of money on the side by engaging in the technically illegal but often overlooked practice of wife-selling. Had Peter Mackenzie been poor, he might have paraded Hannah around with a halter and auctioned her off to the highest bidder.

And so while marriage (and all of the physical obligations that came with it) might have been a practical economic decision for a woman with few options, it was still precarious. Husbands could be punitive with the law's blessing, leaving women abused, depressed, destitute or abandoned as lab rats in mental asylums. Why would any woman want to risk it, especially if she had managed to establish financial independence on her own terms?

Having stumbled upon the secret to a happy life, some of these trailblazers were eager to shed light on society's subjugation of women and the materially shit conditions they were expected to live under. Through art, books and poetry, these renegades offered different ways of understanding womanhood and our capacity to imagine a world beyond our own spheres. Consider the ground-breaking work of Emilia Bassano. She was the first woman to publish a book of poems in England, and her work advocated for the rights of women to exist independently and be allowed a voice equal to that of men. There's suggestion she may have written or at least strongly influenced the work of Shakespeare's, with whom she may have had a longstanding affair. (Morgan Lloyd Malcolm's magnificent play *Emilia* imagines the life of Bassano, and if you ever have the opportunity to see it then run, don't walk!)

Then there was the pioneering feminist philosopher Mary Wollstonecraft. She may be best known for her manifesto, *A Vindication of the Rights of Woman*, but Wollstonecraft wrote a number of other treatises and novels in her short lifetime, including the 1787 'conduct book', *Thoughts on the Education of Daughters*.

Wollstonecraft had seen her abusive, alcoholic father beat her mother, squander the family's money and ultimately steal the inheritance intended for her. She understood how integral independence (and money) was to women's wellbeing, and her work championed the importance of education for women and solidarity among them. She also knew that marriage could be a prison. Wanting to avoid it for herself, she made plans with her best friend to live together and offer the egalitarian exchange of financial and emotional support, but the plans were scuppered when her friend married, moved to Portugal and then died shortly after. Wollstonecraft was devastated. But she continued to live a wild life, taking multiple lovers outside of marriage and even having a child by one of them.

Although she did eventually marry, it was to a fellow radical whose own transgressive views mirrored hers so closely that he inadvertently destroyed her reputation by publishing a posthumous tribute to her life that described in detail what a cool bitch she was. She died from postpartum sepsis shortly after the birth of her second child (who would grow up to become Mary Shelley, the author of *Frankenstein*). There's a terrible irony in the fact that someone so far ahead of her time, who resisted the entrapment of marriage and all the risks it posed to women, was ultimately felled by the very thing that has robbed so many women of their lives, even as it continues to demand that they do it: childbirth.

Wollstonecraft's final gift to feminist thought came via the novel *Maria: or, The Wrongs of Woman*. Published after her death and now considered a triumphant articulation of radical feminist ideas, *Maria* tells the story of a woman whose husband has had her committed to a mental asylum. The novel served more broadly as an excoriation of the suffocating limitations society placed on women. Needless to say, her publisher hated the early drafts, arguing that no one would be interested in the topic of women's oppression at the hands of brutish husbands. Chicks want to read about *nice* things. Like romance and men taking care of them! Not that nasty Ken Loach shit.

Wollstonecraft was just one of many feminists at the time using stealthy means to awaken women to the realities of their lives, and this was yet another source of concern for the Powers That Have Always Been. These early feminist offerings were welcomed by the status quo with about as much enthusiasm as they're met with today, which is to say they were feared and loathed in equal measure, with men regularly crying themselves to sleep over how mean women were being.

Think of the fabulously named Olympe de Gouges, who pissed off her contemporaries so much they put her to death. As well as being a furiously outspoken opponent of the French colonial slave trade, her political pamphlets (of which she wrote sixty-eight in her lifetime) included the incendiary manifesto *Declaration of the Rights of Woman and of the Female Citizen*. She was also against marriage (a true icon), describing it as 'love and trust's grave'. Because of this, she worked alongside her feminist peers to give French women the right to divorce, proposing a new *contrat social* to Queen Marie Antoinette. The prolific and brilliant Olympe railed against the injustice of women being excluded from personhood in the recently ratified French constitution, writing: 'A woman has the right to be guillotined; she should also have the right to debate.' Unfortunately for Olympe, the men in charge didn't agree. After criticising Robespierre one too many times, she was sent to the guillotine, a move Jennifer Robinson and Keina Yoshida called 'a warning to all politically active women' in their excellent exposé of the built-in misogyny of the legal system, *How Many More Women?* Infuriatingly, the divorce laws Olympe helped to deliver didn't last—they were overturned in 1804 by the Napoleonic Code. Many more outspoken women would be executed in the years that followed.

But there's a footnote to this story that Olympe would no doubt love, a testament perhaps to the fact that the fiercest among us might just live on in our descendants. Olympe's final words as she approached the guillotine called for ongoing resistance. 'Children of the fatherland,' she declared, 'you will avenge my death!' Centuries later, a child born on the other side of the world would do something of the sort—although they'd be less a product of the fatherland than of Olympe's own lineage; the remarkable Helen Mary 'Molly' Groom (who became Bencke after her marriage). A descendant of Olympe, Helen was one of the first women to enrol at the University of Queensland, graduating with a science degree. Although she spent much of her early life being a homemaker and raising children, in her later years she directed her attention to establishing a branch of the Marriage Guidance Council in Rockhampton and becoming a fully qualified counsellor. Her excellence in this field led to Chief Justice Sir Garfield Barwick seeking her input in the framing of a new piece of legislation being drafted: the *Family Law Act 1975*. Centuries after her fierce ancestor Olympe had helped secure the right to divorce for French women (however briefly), Helen Bencke would do the same for her Australian sisters—and this time, the new legislation would stick.

Perhaps witchcraft is real after all. Thank the goddess for that.

But all of that is yet to come. And back in early modern England, where more and more women were rejecting men's authority entirely, or at least attempting to negotiate a better deal for themselves, the men in question reacted as you'd expect: with a coordinated campaign of ridicule, abuse, disparaging names and crudely drawn cartoons (which were really just more laboriously created versions of the same boring memes they make today) that only grew more agitated by the *outrageous* behaviour of suffragettes demanding the right to vote. Unmarried women weren't just inconvenient to the system and personally annoying to men; they were also deranged and grotesque. They were bucktoothed, myopic, too skinny or too fat, ugly, old and considered absolutely pitiable by *normal* women, all of whom simply *adored* men and craved the love and protection they could offer. And this was why those spinsterish old maids hated the young, fresh, rosy-cheeked maidens most of all: because they had secured the (ever so important) admiration and desire of men, and would now be blessed with the gift men had always denied to the reptilian monsters who grew more and more repulsive with every year of its absence.

Sex.

How very, very familiar.

———

While writing this chapter, I followed a lot of posts on social media concerned with women either happy to stay single, happy never to have children or who just have *standards*. The RAGE that spewed forth in the comment threads was truly a sight to behold. Nowhere will you find men more concerned about the cavalier disregard women have for their future happiness than in conversations about women's independence. *When will you women realise that being too picky will only hurt you in the end? Don't you know there's no amount of financial security or career satisfaction that could ever rival the joy you'll feel by having a gaggle of children to bring purpose to your otherwise pointless lives? Designer handbags* (the apparent obsession of frivolous, unmarried women everywhere) *won't be there to hold all of you decomposing crones at night! Nor can they visit you in the care home you're destined to end up in* (at the decrepit old age of sixty, according to one young chap), *the stretched-out emptiness of your days a cruel imitation of the beaten-out vagina you took on tour when you were young and the cavernous vault at the end of it that you call a womb.*

So concerned are they for women's wellbeing that they need to state over and over how *stupid* we all are; how we've been brainwashed by feminism to reject our most basic biological functions, all so we can feel *special* (imagine that!); and that, ultimately, our refusal to embrace the roles of wife and mother (when we're still young enough to be attractive to men, and therefore relevant) will be our greatest regret. It's hard to imagine regretting something more than that time I got drunk and decided to give myself a fringe with the nail clippers, but what would I know? I am but a woman, and as such I need to have men explain the circumstances of my life to me.

This refusal to allow women the right to report on our own lives, and to outline exactly what it is we want those lives to be, is rooted in more than men's basic indifference. It's a philosophical quandary: the paradox that exists between men's essential need for women and the belief that has been embedded in them that we don't exist at all.

As a Very Online Feminist, I can't say I'm surprised to see that dudes today haven't improved on the style of attack perfected by their ancestors. Nor have they stopped pointing to the distant past as an example of some kind of golden era of romance, a time when women knew how to behave and were happier because of it. I've no doubt the agitated men of eighteenth-century England whinged about the arrogance of their female contemporaries with as much force and historical revisionism as the male podcasters of today pine for the (heavily medicated) women of the 1950s. Both sets of men seem gobsmacked to discover that the women whose service they were told would be theirs by divine right might not share their enthusiasm for the prospect.

Certainly, they seem to share the same compulsion to use sex (or the lack thereof) as a shaming mechanism. Feminists today are accused of being either massive sluts or completely deprived of touch, with our only avenue for pleasure coming via our ample collections of dildos, vibrators and rubber dongs. (The fact that toys designed to vibrate on multiple different speeds offer a much higher guarantee of sexual pleasure than being ploughed for seven minutes by a man who's watched too much porn and may or may not commit to regularly washing his own butt is apparently lost on them.) Similarly, the single women of the eighteenth century (interchangeable with feminists, really) were warned that dying without having fulfilled their carnal duty on earth would result in them 'leading apes in hell'. In Tudor English, 'to lead' was a euphemism for sex, and this was what spinsters of the time were being *hilariously* threatened with—an eternity of being fucked by apes, as punishment for refusing to fuck men. The trope (which almost certainly drew on racist stereotypes about men of colour, once again demonstrating how white women in particular were conditioned to aspire to marriage with white men as a form of 'respectability') was so common that it spawned a raft of cartoons, appeared in poems, proverbs and letters, and was referenced in two of Shakespeare's plays.

Plus ça change etc.

Women's aversion to the marriage state has nothing to do with the men we find on offer at its gates—it's because we're too ugly/ crazy/old/fat/disordered or just plain gross to have been considered suitable for it in the first place, and so any complaints we make now have to be understood in that context.

Again, this behaviour has remained extremely consistent! 'A Satyr upon Old Maids' (published anonymously in 1713) described never-married women in such glowing terms as 'a pestilence' and 'nasty, rank, rammy, filthy sluts'. We can continue to marvel at the extraordinary ability of women to be both buttoned-up prudes *and* filthy fucktrucks, the two things treated as interchangeable by men whose true grievance lies not in how we use our bodies but how we use our brains.

Nor do the excuses change. Despite an almost four-hundred-year gap, men frothing on social media today tout the same arguments their forefathers were chiding women with in pamphlets and crudely drawn comics: that the population is declining and the human race will die out unless women surrender all this nonsense and embrace the natural biological purpose we were designed for (which was conveniently discovered when eighteenth-century scientists set out to prove women's intellectual inferiority).

I realise social media and the content shared across those multiple platforms isn't a definitive representation of public thought, but we should still be concerned by the magnitude of garbage that exists online purely to do the heavy lifting of historical revisionism.

In this fantasy land, men are responsible for creating everything of value and constantly propelling society forwards. We're reminded ad infinitum that they 'do all the dangerous jobs'. Men are responsible for building all the infrastructure we need in order to have functional lives. We can thank them for our roads, our skyscrapers, our technology, our food transport systems, our farming, our innovation and basically anything else you can think of that is worthy of credit. That so many of the people making these arguments are teenage boys responsible for building exactly nothing other than mountains of washing is apparently irrelevant, as is the fact that this collegiate approach to claiming credit for men's perceived collective achievements in the world doesn't seem to extend to the violence they are overwhelmingly responsible for meting out. Men build the world, so the least women can do to show their appreciation is clean it for them, and pop out a few kiddies to keep their bloodline strong.

One might think that if the state needs babies (some of whom will be the very same men who claim to have built everything) just as much as it needs roads, then the people charged with doing this work might be recompensed for it. But this is the annoying double bind that patriarchy finds itself in. If we admit society *needs* women to do this work, then recognising its inherent value might mean putting an economic price on it. And this in turn provides women with both an income *and* enterprise bargaining power. Financially independent women are harder to control, which causes a bit of a headache for men who've historically been able to exchange basic economic security for an endless supply of domestic, sexual and reproductive labour. If patriarchal society can't function without women bearing the brunt of this work, then convincing us of its necessity to our lives is an industry in and of itself.

Given the mind-numbing options for domestic excitement on offer to women, is it any wonder so many of us have chosen to opt out? To withdraw our devotion and service to men and reclaim it for ourselves, fulfilling our own ambitions and pursuing our own dreams?

Let's face it, if the system was honest about what it expected from women—domestic servitude, reproductive labour, removal to the fringes of society and away from the power that lies at its core—then women would chew their own legs off to avoid being caught in the trap. It's much easier to use tactics of intimidation to prevent as many women as possible from listening too closely to those of us who've figured it out.

By relentlessly and viciously mocking single women (most of whom are just minding our own business, to be honest), a clear message is sent to *all* women: don't even fucking try to resist your obligation to service male authority, or we will use every tool at our disposal to turn you into a figure of ridicule. And the most egregious part?

It works.

And so single women who reject society's demands become witches, spinsters, old maids and cat ladies. We are turned into a source of derision and spite, each sneery accusation designed to send a little zap through the invisible collars that were strapped around our necks the moment a (probably) male obstetrician looked down and declared us to be a girl. All of this propaganda is designed to keep us in line and afraid of giving in to curiosity. Don't buy what the old witches are selling! They don't want to help you, they want to hurt you! They hate you! They're jealous of you! Only true love's kiss can save you from their fate!

What was the weapon the evil old fairy uses to prick Sleeping Beauty's finger and send her into a deep slumber?

Oh yes. A spinning wheel.

4

A WOMB OF ONE'S OWN

'Do you really believe ... that everything historians tell us
about men—or about women—is actually true? You ought
to consider the fact that these histories have been written
by men, who never tell the truth except by accident.'

—Moderata Fonte, *The Worth of Women*, 1600

A few years ago, I made the mistake of trying to have a sincere
conversation with a family member who'd fallen deep into the
meat grinder of the Murdoch right-wing propaganda machine.
This person confessed to having earlier felt some anxieties about
my son, because of his long hair and the fact he had on occasion
been photographed doing such terrifying things as pushing a doll
in a stroller and wearing a tulle skirt.

'But looking at him now,' the man said, 'I can see that he's
a *boy*!'

At the time, my son was only four years old. He had begun to
assert his gender clearly; he corrected people when they referred

to him as 'she' but seemed unfazed by the need to do so. I wasn't surprised that this particular man considered the details of a child's gender expression to be of vital importance, but I did suggest that a small boy playing with a baby doll was probably more at risk of learning how to be a dad than of destroying the fabric of society as we know it—although to some men, perhaps that's the same thing.

'Listen,' I said, wanting to be at least one contrary voice among the otherwise hate-filled chorus of lunatics he confuses for being hard-hitting journalists working on the front line of courage. 'I don't know what makes any of us who we are. I don't know how I know that I'm a woman, I just do.'

'Ah, but can you even say what a woman *is*?' he asked smugly.

I answered that a woman is an anomaly in the animal kingdom in that she's conditioned to love her most dangerous predator.

He didn't seem to like that, which pleased me.

As the culture war against trans people and their right to be afforded both dignity and humanity has grown uglier, the rhetorical challenge of what it means to be a woman has emerged as a kind of checkmate move for conservatives. In 2022, during the US Senate Judiciary Committee's confirmation hearings for nominee Judge Ketanji Brown Jackson's seat on the Supreme Court, Republican senator Marsha Blackburn delivered in one neat sound bite a question that would be repeated giddily by conservatives for months to come: *Can you provide a definition for the word 'woman'?*

Blackburn's question was a cynical attempt to highlight the threat posed by so-called 'radical cultural shifts'. She framed

Jackson's inability to 'give a straight answer about something as fundamental as what a woman is' as proof of the dangers of 'progressive education'—which is shorthand for terrifying things like critical race theory, respect for gender fluidity and, if you take Blackburn's voting record into account, the banning of firearms in schools. Considering that, shortly after Jackson's confirmation, the Supreme Court voted to overturn *Roe v. Wade*, perhaps the most accurate answer to Blackburn's question would have been 'someone to whom the government will give fewer bodily rights than a corpse'. Despite the obviously bad faith nature of the question, conservatives and TERFs (trans exclusionary radical feminists) alike have been parroting it wherever they can, seemingly unaware that it makes them look like complete idiots.

Consider the human-sized lizard known as Piers Morgan. Ahead of the coronation of Charles Mountbatten-Windsor (the unelected leader of the colonising British monarchy), Australia's prime minister, Anthony Albanese, appeared on *Piers Morgan Uncensored*, where the question was—inexplicably—put to him.

'What is a woman, Prime Minister?' Morgan asked.

'An adult female,' Albanese replied, clarifying further that he believes it's up to individuals to determine how they identify.

But did Albanese think it was 'fair' that people born with the 'physical advantage' of being 'biologically male' should be allowed to compete against those born with female sex characteristics? Morgan persisted.

Albanese suggested it was the responsibility of sporting organisations to determine for themselves who should be allowed to compete, saying he never observed the inclusion of trans people to be a problem while his son was playing junior sports.

'That's because it wasn't happening then,' Morgan protested. 'You didn't get biological males competing against biological women. And that's the problem. To me, I can support transgender rights to fairness and equality right to the point where they infringe on women's rights. I mean, they've got to also have fairness and equality.'

Fairness and equality.

It's an interesting choice of words for Morgan, especially given he doesn't accept the existence of the gender pay gap, has conducted a years-long campaign of hostility against and weird fixation with Meghan Markle, which may or may not be because she rejected his lunch invitation, and he once hosted an on-air television 'debate' asking whether feminism and the #MeToo movement had gone 'too far'. As I write this, he's turned his attention to protesting the new *Barbie* movie—because its tongue-in-cheek depiction of Ken as little more than an accessory to Barbie is apparently an attack on men. *First they came for the boy dolls, and I did not speak up.*

Alongside his obsession with overseeing the physical parameters of a woman, Morgan also loves to chastise young women when they show more of their bodies than he considers respectable. After the model and feminist podcaster Emily Ratajkowski shared some photographs of herself posing in lingerie for a magazine's annual advent calendar, he tweeted, 'Somewhere, Emmeline Pankhurst just vomited.' When Lady Gaga spoke about having PTSD as a result of being raped, he not only publicly mocked this as 'vain-glorious nonsense' (according to Morgan, only people in the military can experience PTSD), he also expressed doubt that she'd been assaulted at all—because a *real* victim would have reported the crime to the police.

Questioning the authenticity of rape survivors seems like an odd hill to die on for a man who's appointed himself the Grand Protector of women's right to 'fairness and equality', but it's in keeping with how patriarchy and its adherents work to maintain narrative control. Men like Morgan have always claimed a biological authority to define women's realities for us; if they can determine what constitutes real equality, it allows them to define what constitutes real oppression. They may have found their latest target in trans identities, but the practice of delegitimising us and our rights to self-determination is evergreen. As feminist discourse modernises and evolves, patriarchy works overtime to infantilise us; our feminist foremothers were clearly sensible and justified in their scope, but Women Today™, with their never-ending demands for *more more more*, are childish, petulant and greedy.

Morgan isn't the first man to reference the suffragettes as an example of *real feminism*; in fact, he's assumed a posthumous disgust on behalf of Emmeline Pankhurst for what he calls the 'man-hating, bomb-threatening brigade' so many times you'd be forgiven for thinking they'd stood shoulder to shoulder at the front line of the printing press, churning out politely worded requests to pretty please consider giving the sweet ladies a bit of a say. That Pankhurst was arrested three times, tortured while in jail and publicly ridiculed as exactly the kind of man-hating, bomb-threatening *nuisance* Morgan sneers at now is a fact conveniently ignored by him and all the other men who want to pretend their hostility towards the women's rights movement arises not from a refusal to relinquish unearned power but the fact women haven't asked nicely enough.

The ret-conning of history never happens by accident, especially not where social justice movements are concerned. Those who claim the authority to construct the present also believe themselves entitled to rewrite the past and their role within it. So it is that women marginalised by their contemporaries, tortured by their jailers and mocked by the ruling class are now pointed to as examples of the *correct* version of female freedom fighter, whose *sensible* activism was warranted because the oppression she and her brave comrades faced was *real*. Yesterday's feminists had something substantial to fight for and against, and how do the women of today honour their memories? By showing their tits on the internet, labelling everything 'sexist' and *sending men to jail* just because they said hello in the workplace!

Men like Morgan insist on a definition for womanhood not just because it indulges their transphobia, but because it facilitates their paternalism. Women can't be allowed to define ourselves—what we want, what we need, even who we are. We must be defined by men, who in turn patrol the borders of those definitions, deciding not just who among us gets to enter reality but who gets to *stay*.

But what does that have to do with marriage? Two words: reproductive productivity. See, love as a necessary precursor to marriage is very recent. Before the starry-eyed young folk of the nineteenth century decided love might be kind of a big deal, the primary goal for any marriage was to build a bigger empire by merging families (and wealth) and then adding to the flock. When transphobes ask all these rainbow-brained wokesters ruining society to answer the head-scratching question of *what is a woman?* they're not looking for nuanced dialogue or to expand their own thinking. They just want to force people to admit that you *cannot* be a woman unless you have the only thing that makes a woman valuable in the first place.

A womb.

For a group of people who love to claim sole credit for the building of the world, (cis) men rusted on to patriarchal thinking must find it super annoying that the one thing they can't do is build life. Diminishing women's reproductive role and knowledge is fairly standard practice by now, but not even the theft of obstetric control has fully changed the fact that their precious heirs have to come out of a woman. Wombs are easy to master. It's everything that surrounds the womb that men struggle to understand. Women are fucking *nuts*. Honestly, it's crazy that something as important as the perpetuation of male lineage has been left up to us!

For millennia, men have devoted themselves to the exploration of our brains, our bodies, our reproductive systems, our capacity for logic, our maternal instincts, our proximity to ungodly behaviours, our proximity to saintly ones, our inherent carnality, our inherent innocence—where women are concerned, men have left no stone unturned in their quest to discover who we are, how we came to be, and why it is just and right that we accept our natural subservience to them. That there has never been any real evidence to support the claim that women are inherently inferior or even altogether *different* in capacity is irrelevant; even today, the results of scientific studies looking at gender differences are more likely to emphasise insignificant variables than the far more common correlations seen across the gender spectrum.

It says a lot about patriarchal reality that even demonstrable and overt denunciation of women's capacity isn't enough to taint the perceived intellectual importance of those men given the authority to construct it. Today's male podcasters (when will they shut up?) might have found a new platform from which to broadcast their views on women and how we're all dumb bitches who need to stop pretending to be as good as men, but these are hardly original thoughts. We can (and should) dismiss them as the mouth farts of cringecel dumdums whose knowledge of women holds about as much weight as a bucket made out of air, but these are also not new ideas. Nor have they been drawn from the outskirts of history, passed down along that extremely niche line of statistically anomalous men we're told make up the 0.0005 per cent of Bad Guys (when 99.9995 per cent of them are brilliant and decent and good and would never, not in a million, trillion, bazillion years, ever do anything to hurt a lady #NotAllMen). They aren't the first to insist that women defy our true nature by trying to be 'like men', or to believe the thing we need above all else is to get married and start popping out babies. No, when the male podcasters of today talk about women's physical, rational and emotional inferiority, they're giving a direct shout-out to the father of western logic himself, Mr Aristotle.

Aristotle wasn't entirely bad, I suppose; he did at least think that society fared better when women were as happy as men. But given he also held strongly to the belief that women were 'feeble-minded', it's unclear if he consulted any women, happy or otherwise, to find out what that meant. It seems obvious to me that women in Ancient Greece would share the same concerns as women today: that they might be lucky enough to die of old age instead of being murdered in their beds, and also that men stop fucking telling them to smile. Witnessing the turgid procession of the philosopher-to-podcaster pipeline, however, we can safely assume that Aristotle's views on the whole thing were pretty similar to those shared each week on *Mastering the Feminine* with your host Kermit McDermit (not a real podcast but probably also a real podcast). Namely, that women were happiest when siloed off in the domestic space and turned into broodmares.

The self-appointed gurus of today who blather on about how women lean too much into 'their masculine' are just regurgitating the nonsense Aristotle (oNe Of ThE gReAtEsT tHiNkErS oF aLl TiMe!) posited about women almost two and a half thousand years ago.

But here's your Logic Daddy for you. Aristotle believed women were deformed and inferior versions of men, aberrations created as a result of weak semen. According to the *father of western logic*, babies were created when a man's semen and a woman's menses collided. In order to bear a son (the default human), a man's semen had to be cold enough to cool down the woman's hot menses. If he shot a load of weak jizz into her, though, the heat of her menses would overpower it, leading to a half-human—a *girl*.

As half-humans, women's only useful purpose in Aristotle's eyes was to act as incubators—which was pretty much the consensus of all the other male experts, too. Boy boffins in Ancient Greece knew how volatile the uterus could be, and how it single-mindedly 'hungered for intercourse and pregnancy in a way that was always beyond the control of the woman it resided within'. Aristotle's own teacher, Plato, had claimed that a womb would become 'vexed and aggrieved' if left unused, a belief no doubt inspired by the Greek physician Hippocrates (the father of modern medicine), whose own rigorous scientific research led him to discover a malady he called 'suffocation of the womb'.

Suffocated wombs—a condition caused when they had too much blood in them or, conversely, were arid and dry—caused all manner of disorders in adolescent girls and women, especially if they became dislodged and began migrating around the body. To prevent this, the male physicians recommended tethering the uterus. How could this be done? By the well-known curative powers of a deep dicking, silly! An early marriage (can't get schwing without a ring) and lots of sex would ensure that these wombs—the 'animal within an animal', as the famous physician Aretaeus would call it five hundred years later—would be satiated and stable.

Experts!

A brief overview of the spooky-wooky history of wombs:

The spectre of the malevolent womb and the dark powers it wielded over weak lady types was popular among the Ancient Greeks, and was taken up with gusto by people across the world for centuries after. It was basically like the feta of the ideas marketplace—hard to find at first, but once everyone realised how tasty it was you could get it down the local Coles, Right up until the sixteenth century, pretty much everyone just accepted that wombs were extraneous to their owners. Without proper supervision (from men, naturally), these snarling beasts could act like a portal between the Dark Lord and his coterie of unstable women, whose insatiable cunts now had the power to unleash hell on earth. Two thousand years after the Greeks were prescribing marriage and pregnancy to prevent wombs from going on a Contiki tour, the Catholic Church was issuing the same edicts—except this time it was to prevent women from 'unleashing their original sin'.

Things didn't get much better in the seventeenth century and beyond. Wombs still exerted too much control over the person who housed them, but instead of wreaking physical havoc, the male experts claimed it was women's *mental* wellbeing that was harmed. Women all over the shop were diagnosed with hysteria, an accusation still used today to dismiss women's inconvenient feelings as erratic insanity.

And from where does the word 'hysteria' derive?

Hystera. The Ancient Greek word for uterus.

Of course, we now know that uterine activity can cause both physical *and* mental distress to a person. The conditions being examined from antiquity onwards by men who had only their own suppositions and biases to work with weren't imaginary, but nor were they the result of errant wombs rampaging around the body. The chronic pain and mental distress felt by women was most likely due to things like endometriosis, adenomyosis, menorrhagia, premenstrual tension (PMT), premenstrual dysphoric disorder (PMDD), and symptoms of perimenopause and uterine cancers—conditions which are *still* not always treated or even researched properly, because maladies reported by women are too often dismissed as figments of our imagination. Even today, it takes an average of eight to twelve years to be properly diagnosed with endometriosis. And because the health system is informed by racism as well as sexism, this medical neglect impacts Black women more profoundly than it does white women, despite the fact research has shown they experience more severe symptoms.

Guess what one of the 'cures' still peddled for endometriosis is? (I'll give you a clue: they came up with the answer two thousand years ago.)

Having a baby!

Fucking philosophers, man.

It's little wonder the male philosophers of yesteryear (and last year, and this year, and probably every year from now until the end of fucking time) have felt entitled to wade so confidently into the lakes of womankind and loudly declare what's what. They're experts, innit?

Patriarchy has made it possible for men with privilege to retain control over who gets to claim expertise, with the path to becoming (or at least to being considered) an 'expert' deliberately limited to those most likely to serve the status quo rather than disrupt it. Throughout history, access to formal education (a class-based concept in itself) has been denied to women, people of colour and the poor. Even now, in an era when everyone technically has the right to pursue academic qualifications, the system is still designed to favour the few while disadvantaging the marginalised. (For more on this, I highly recommend reading Australian writer Bri Lee's incisive exploration of academia, *Who Gets to Be Smart?*) Access to education determines not just who gets to be thought leaders, but what is dismissed as irrelevant in the establishment of that thought practice. Consider the evolution of the medical profession, which has historically harmed more than its fair share of women through the application of shoddy standards, deliberate malpractice and a general disinclination to trust women's testimonies in favour of diagnosing psychological unrest. Despite women forming more than half of the world's population, there are still too many people willing to accept without question the idea that men have proven themselves naturally more capable not just of treating everyone in general medical practice, but of specialising in fields like obstetrics and gynaecology. Beginning with Hippocrates and moving right through to the present, gynaecological concerns have been scrutinised, diagnosed, pathologised and (occasionally) treated almost exclusively by men. Not all women have vaginas and/or uterine organs, but it's fair to say that gynaecology is overwhelmingly concerned with cis women. Doesn't it strike you as bizarre, then, that the physicians for most of this history have been cis men whose understanding of what they would call 'the female body' has been theoretical at best and downright illogical at worst?

Bizarre, yes, and offensive. But only a man unencumbered by the irrational mood swings and nonsensical thought patterns of silly ladies could possibly access the kind of calm logic and innate scientific instinct needed to unlock our mysteries. *Obviously.*

I'm not suggesting a cisgender man can't be a good obstetrician—but I also don't care to make space in this argument for those who might be. Like, I'm glad you're providing patient-led health care and keeping women safe, Kevin. That's great for them. I'd give you an award, but you've probably received a ton of them already.

The thing is, if Dr Kevin does a good job now, it's not because of the legacy of his profession. Cisgender men did not demonise and punish and ultimately ban women from practising midwifery as *experts* (I mean, who do you think managed the 'women's business' before men anointed themselves the leaders of it?) because they wanted so badly to make it *safer* for us. Commandeering women's business as a means of controlling the women themselves has always been a particular tactic of patriarchy, and childbirth has been no different. When you think about how readily we've accepted cisgender men as the master builders of a reproductive process they've had zero personal experience in, it's absolutely bonkers.

But the elevation of men as the experts on women's fertility didn't happen by accident, nor as a result of their superior skills. As Barbara Ehrenreich and Deirdre English wrote in *Witches, Midwives and Nurses: A history of women healers*, the supplanting of women as the experts on their own bodies was an act of both gender and class warfare. The gendered nature of the attacks are obvious—denying women authority in matters even (and maybe especially) pertaining to women is a tactical move by the patriarchy to shore up Aristotle's assertion that women are inferior, and therefore in need of men's guidance. But women who practised as healers during the Middle Ages also posed a threat to the nobility, because they provided a service to the peasantry that was collective and community-based. The nobility took seriously the risk of a 'rebellious lower class' rising up against them, and the provision of medical care not only kept more of that group alive and kicking but also fortified the belief that they were worthy of the same care available to the aristocracy. Investment in the development of a male-dominated, formalised medical profession designed to replace both the legitimacy and the authority of the women healers removed power over health care from the peasantry and returned it to the ruling class. As Ehrenreich and English argue, the establishment of 'professional' medical industries was directly intended to enforce class hierarchies and protect privilege—just the same as marriage does now—while exploiting women as the labour force that maintains men's power. By the end of the sixteenth century, obstetric practice was limited to people who'd had a university education—and the law denied women access to higher learning. Not only were women denied the right to formally 'learn' how to deliver care they'd been overseeing for *millennia*, but they could also be prosecuted if they tried. Kind of like how abortion care providers in America now face possible prison time if they help to end pregnancies safely.

The removal of women as healers may have begun in earnest during the Middle Ages, but men made sure to hold the door shut for almost a thousand years after that. By the early 1970s, more than 90 per cent of doctors in the United States were men.

That's an extraordinary disparity, and of course it gave them a terrifying amount of power to not only further pathologise women's bodies and mental health, but also to prescribe cruel treatments without fear of opposition. Women who advocated too strongly for themselves, particularly when it came to pregnancy and childbirth and even the right to do these things *by themselves*, would be recorded in their medical notes as being 'uncooperative or neurotic'. Alongside this, a reality was constructed in which male expertise on bodies, medicine, science and brains was the default, with women's attempts to contribute anything to these fields considered laughable at best and an act of insurrection at worst. The spheres of influence belonged to *men*. Women thrived in the domestic space, our natural domain! The fragility of our reproductive systems has always been unable to cope with the strain brought on by too much thinking. It was unseemly for women to deal with bodies, and dangerous for us to be given power over life and death. What could we possibly offer to the emerging (exciting!) world of science?

Not our brainpower, any man could tell you that. That's why we need fathers and then husbands—so they can tell us what's real (their authority), and what's real stupid (us).

———

Men don't listen and women can't read maps.
Men are more visual, women more about communication.
Men don't see mess, but women love to clean.
Men are more logical, women more emotional.
Fuck, these reductive statements are stupid.

Few things rev people up more than the opportunity to share unqualified neurobabble about how mEn's AnD wOmEn'S bRaInS aRe DiFfeReNt. It's appealing to think there might be some neurological reason for the chasm of behavioural differences that exist between the sexes. If science—which we know is never wrong!—could be used to prove that men really *are* better at being paid more and women excel at picking up clothes, then men could stop feeling so bad about benefiting from the massive social advantages they've deliberately engineered for themselves, and women could stop expecting them to change.

Alas, although an avalanche of research has been produced in the last fifty years attempting to prove that We! Are! Different!, there's never been any convincing evidence. Sorry to burst your bubble, Kermit McDermit, but brains are brains are brains—and when shaped under the same conditions, neither neuroplasticity nor academic aptitude differs between people on the basis of gender alone.

Like all stories about patriarchy, this is an old one, too.

At the start of this chapter I mentioned Piers Morgan's penchant for referencing Emmeline Pankhurst, as if championing her almost a century after her death somehow buys him credit for the changes in women's political freedom that she, along with countless other women, helped to bring about. Pankhurst was just one of many political activists who were fucking shit up at the time, and they were *not* treated kindly by the men whose patriarchal systems they were trying to destroy. (Remember Olympe de Gouges, who was executed at the guillotine for hurting Robespierre's feelings?) The ruling class of men didn't want women fighting for political suffrage or liberation from the domestic sphere. For more than two thousand years, they'd been getting away with prescribing marriage and babies to fix our Lady Problems, and that suited them very nicely, thank you very much. But things had advanced a bit, and the problem now became how to convince women of a certain class that marriage and reproduction was *natural*, and therefore necessary to their moral wellbeing. Once upon a time, you could just take all the naughty women, strap them to a chair and throw them in the river to see if they were a witch. Science called for a different burden of proof.

Say, fellas! What if we could prove once and for all that women are dumb as fuck and incapable of holding a logical thought in their little lady brains? They'd have to give up this 'independence' nonsense then and accept their place in the order of things.

It's wild to realise that all the way up to the turn of the twentieth century, scientists were still largely in agreement that intelligence and the capacity for rational thought could be determined by the shape and size of a person's skull. Women's heads were small with cutesy-wutesy brains as tiny as a plum. Okay, not quite a plum. A small cantaloupe maybe. Whatever the fruit, it was definitely smaller than a man's! Ergo, women were nitwits.

CASE CLOSED.

Well, not quite. Although the initial premise seemed sound (women's heads are smaller, therefore they have less brain matter packed in there), the accepted correlation between size and strength came unstuck when scientists realised they also had to take dimensions into account. Basically, you can't just compare brains in terms of disembodied size; you also have to measure their size in relation to the body. Experiments had disproven the theory that intelligence could be determined by the mass and weight of a brain, and craniology too had been debunked. What next?

Perhaps concerned about the embarrassment of persistent backtracks, some scientists decided that leaning into a more benevolent view of womanhood would be wiser. It wasn't that women were biologically *inferior* to men; maybe we were just *different*. The embrace of biological essentialism—especially in regard to women's 'natural' inclination towards mothering and caregiving and aptitude for domestic tasks—provided a more foolproof way to discredit the newly stirring wave of feminism that saw women of the time pushing for greater access to public space and influence.

This was around the same time menstruation—the womb's wallpaper!—began to be cited as a reason for women's diminished capacity. In a speech to the Royal Anthropological Institute in 1869, James McGrigor Allan declared that the 'crisis' of menstruation caused women to 'suffer under a languor and depression which disqualify them for thought or action [and that] much of the inconsequent conduct of women, their petulance, caprice and irritability, may be traced directly to this cause'. Demonstrating once again that misogyny is the least original form of comedy, he warned against allowing women proximity to any kind of power while in such a fractious state: 'Imagine a woman, at such a time, having it in her power to sign the death-warrant of a rival or a faithless lover!'

Yes, best not to give the bleeder access to the nuclear codes—what if she's *on the rag*?!?!

To close on this little chapter in the sprawling history of Men Making Shit Up To Benefit Them And Then Calling Themselves Experts, here's one of those 'fathers of' moments again. Just like Aristotle before him, Charles Darwin, the celebrated 'father of evolution', also believed that women were intellectually inferior to men. The lack of actual evidence for this was irrelevant. He was an expert, and he felt it to be true. Who was anyone else to argue?

Darwin conceded it was possible for women to demonstrate *some* degree of intelligence. But according to Charlie boy (who also believed in the evolutionary supremacy of the white European race), if a woman showed even an inkling of a man's aptitude for thought, it was due to an anomaly of inheritance; to wit, she'd got it from good old Dad. (Aristotle might have it that some of the cold sperm won out after all—but only a scooch of it.) In keeping with the diabolical reframing of women's inherent purpose—indeed, the asserted truths of *what women are*—that were being used at the time to counter women's political activism, Darwin was gracious enough to concede that, in one area, women had superior thoughts to men: the realm of domestic morality.

———

To this day, baseless theories and objectively misogynistic *feelings* about men's and women's inherent differences continue to be peddled in order to deny women full access to our own power. In denying women power of our own, patriarchy has made it that much easier to convince us that aligning ourselves with men is the answer. In this system, women's power—and therefore, our value—comes from being *chosen*. We're worthy, because a man wants us. Our lives mean something, because we put our wombs to good use making babies for those men. To want something outside of this is deranged, twisted, *wrong*—we must be mental, hysterical, self-loathing. How could we possibly know what's best for us? We're *women*! We need men to translate the human experience for us. I mean, you don't have to look far to see the legacy of invented male expertise still ejaculating its cold, inferior jizz all over the public sphere. But all of the claims men have made to expertise and authority are built on nothing more than their ability to enforce a reality that shifts according to their own needs.

The impact of this misogyny and the repeated efforts to wrestle women and our skill sets into the lace-trimmed iron shackles of the domestic cage cannot be overstated. Even in 2023, women who advocate for ourselves against the medical system are labelled with words like 'hysterical', 'neurotic' and 'difficult', or diagnosed with personality disorders designed to undermine our experiences and destabilise the confidence we have *in our own fucking perception of reality*. Women who violate religious codes dictating how we should and shouldn't behave, what we should and shouldn't do with our bodies, and what we should and shouldn't aspire to in our lives are being met with the brute force of patriarchal governments determined to remind us who belongs to whom. And those of us who set about asserting our own realities and perceptions, and whose efforts to do so in turn show other women they are capable of authoring perception, are met with the full force of opposition one would expect from those desperate to maintain the reality that has served *them* well for millennia.

Men are not the experts by default. They have become the *performers* of expertise by colluding systematically, over and over again, to prevent women from participating as fully realised humans in the world. We can't be builders ourselves, despite building the world in our bodies. We're more suited to being *helpers* and *followers*.

What would the world look like if this history had more of *her* stories in it? Why is a woman's value in the world still determined by whether or not she's shown herself deserving of having a body at all? All these wombs wandering about, unused and therefore wasted! These *arrogant* women, believing themselves to be above their role! Thinking they can have a life on their own terms, instead of recognising that the only purpose to women at all is to act as glorified post boxes for men's important packages to be transported through the world. We can't *choose* to abstain from that, because they won't fucking let us. Claiming a legacy for ourselves would give us too much power over *theirs*. And so we're out here, more than two thousand years after the fucking 'father' of modern medicine coined the term 'hysteria' to pretend women's forced reproductive service was some kind of benevolent paternalism, and we're still fighting for the right to control *our own fucking bodies*. Abortion rights are being systematically destroyed all over the United States, not just by male legislators but also by the gender traitor foot-soldiers, who buy power for themselves with freedom taken from other women. Women the world over are reminded again and again that our lives will amount to nothing unless we lean into our (fabricated) biological purpose and commit ourselves to *nurturing*. But even this we can't do alone—oh no, single-mother families are the most *dangerous* of all the families! All those children grow up to be criminals and layabouts, because they've missed out on the steadying hand of an authoritative father figure! Get yourselves married, girls, as soon as you can and put those wombs to work the way God intended!

What is a woman?

We may never know. Because we were never given the opportunity to find out. Men discovered reason, and used it to justify their fear of women's power. Our bodies demonstrated control over life and death, and so that power needed to be pathologised as something volatile and dangerous, something over which we had no control. Virginia Woolf once observed that women are 'the most discussed animal in the universe', with countless numbers of male-authored (of course) books devoted to the zoological exploration of them each year. These infinite, endless discussions about *what women are* have magically always drawn the same conclusion: that we are the necessary conduits through which men express their genius, unburden themselves of lust and pass on their genetic seed. This is our role, the thing we were made to do, and we should be grateful for it. The opportunity to become a wife leads to the opportunity to become a mother, and we need to undergo this process in order to temper our hot menses and hysteria with the docile blessing of reproduction. Mothers give birth to the children. That is what Sky Daddy created us to do.

Because only fathers can give birth to the world.

SOMETHING NEW

'Jane, I take your place now, and you must go lower, because I am a married woman.'

—Jane Austen, *Pride and Prejudice*

5

PUT A RING ON IT

'I've been dating since I was fifteen!
I'm exhausted. Where is he?'

—Charlotte York, *Sex and the City*

The first online proposal I can remember seeing involved a Bruno Mars song, a slowly moving Honda CR-V and a revolving door of dancers, all of whom were connected to the couple in question. It was Portland, Oregon, and a man named Isaac Lamb had enlisted a cohort of friends and family to help him propose to his girlfriend, Amy Frankel. As Frankel travelled backwards while sitting in the open boot of the SUV, a flash mob performed an impressively rehearsed dance, lip-syncing the lyrics of 'Marry You'. As the song nears its conclusion, Lamb appears in front of Frankel and drops to one knee.

'You have already given me a lifetime of happiness,' he tells her. 'Will you let me spend the rest of my life trying to give you the same? Marry me?'

Frankel accepts happily, the couple embrace and the crowd goes wild. It's all over in less than six minutes, but the influence of this particular video on the proposal business will last for years.

Shortly after securing his girlfriend's agreement, Lamb uploaded the video to YouTube. Perhaps he expected it would only be watched by his friends and family, but the views kept climbing, and within a few days the proposal had been watched at least twelve million times. Three days after posting, Bruno Mars tweeted his congratulations to the pair, adding, 'I don't think I could have made a better music video for this song.'

Amassing a huge amount of views in a short space of time (not to mention capturing the attention of a celebrity) seems small fry in the era of TikTok, when a thirty-second clip can rack up millions of likes in a matter of hours, propelled along by an algorithm uniquely trained to feed content into people's willing faces. But this was 2012, and social media was still in its relative infancy. The advent of TikTok was four years away, and even its predecessor Vine hadn't been launched yet. To say this marked a permanent shift in the culture isn't really an exaggeration; Lamb and Frankel were perhaps two of the first ordinary people to field multiple offers to appear on morning television (all expenses paid, naturally) just for doing something a little bit whacky and posting it online. They settled on NBC's *Today* show, where Ann Curry asked Lamb if he wanted to apologise to men everywhere for 'upping the proposal ante'. Much laughter ensued.

The video is joyful, there's no doubt about it. It's hard to fault the effort required for a DIY Busby Berkeley number, especially when done in the service of L-O-V-E. I watched it again ahead of writing this chapter and I wasn't surprised to discover that I still found it genuinely moving. I might dislike marriage, but I'm a sucker for a good musical number.

Since Lamb's video propelled him headfirst into his proverbial fifteen minutes of fame, the cataloguing of everyday moments has become par for the course. Everything is content, whether it's a father braiding his daughter's hair (possibly the greatest guy who's ever lived!!!) or a wife demonstrating how useless her husband is at putting away leftovers (hahahaha girl me too, this is just like Chad!!!!)—social media has reinvigorated the marriage business most of all, not to mention drastically expanded the target demographic for those aspiring to become part of it. And it all starts with a ripper proposal, every last detail of which has to be meticulously planned for the benefit of the faceless people watching. In the modern age, it's not enough for someone to get down on bended knee in front of a beautiful sunset or drop a ring into the bottom of a champagne flute. How *embarrassing*! Such a proposal could never take the world by storm—and taking the world by storm is exactly what proposals these days are meant to do. It's a dog-eat-dog world out there, and competition is tough. Those making the proposals are no longer just competing for the approval of the people to whom they're proposing; they're also pitting themselves against millions of other would-be spouses scattered around the globe, all of them looking to capture that special something extra that makes their (professionally) filmed moment stand out above all the others and hopefully transition them into a post-wedding career as a heavily sponsored 'content creator'.

The rise in ostentatious and elaborate proposals isn't merely light-hearted romance. With the options now to create destination proposals, hire professional photographers to capture the 'spontaneous' moment and even enlist the services of paid proposal planners, it leads me once more to the question that keeps coming up the further I delve into the institution of marriage and the garlands of bells and whistles draped across its doorway.

Who is all of this meant to be *for*?

———

Elaborate proposals have become so firmly entrenched in the cultural mythology of modern marriage that anything less than parachuting your beloved into a field of sunflowers specially planted for the occasion while a choir of trained parrots sings Michael Bublé songs in harmony is considered unromantic. Leaving aside the logistics of such a thing, this commitment to high-end production values seems especially baffling when you realise that most couples have at least some idea that marriage is on the cards. According to *The Knot*, which is less a wedding website and more a well-oiled machine harvesting the crops of people's marital aspirations, almost half of all couples have already discussed what kind of proposal they want to be 'surprised' with, and a full three-quarters were involved in selecting their ring (more on those bad boys later).

Despite this, the suggestion that couples might consider proposals a bit outdated these days, given they're less likely to come as a surprise, can spark confusion at best and horror at worst. It's not enough to sit down and have a mature adult discussion about marriage, carefully weighing up the pros and cons, establishing clear ground rules on how you plan to raise any children you might have (not to mention how to address the gendered economic fallout that comes from having them), and then let your loved ones know what you've decided. That's not a good story! WHERE ARE MY SUNFLOWERS?

Well might people point to 'romance' as a defence for the continued tradition of proposals, but it's worth asking why the private decision to marry requires public approval. Mutual discussions of intent held prior to making an engagement official may be the norm now, but the need to demonstrate that these choices have been made in service to passion rather than practicality suggests a lingering anxiety about how people come to marriage in the first place. Ellen Lamont, author of *The Mating Game: How gender still shapes how we date*, suggests that marriage's shift from being an economic choice to one made with regard to 'love and personal fulfilment' creates a different kind of social pressure to secure what is seen as a 'good match'.

Basically, people want their proposals to send the message that they have great sex, and tons of it.

Underpinning this anxiety about public perception is the matter of who does the asking. In same-sex couples, this is obviously a moot point. But despite the supposed feminist progress the marriage institution has undergone, heterosexual pairings still conform overwhelmingly to men getting down on the proverbial one knee. This is despite the fact women are still much more likely to at least *prompt* the proposal by initiating discussions about the future of their relationships.

In 2019, *The Knot* found that a whopping 97 per cent of men reported proposing to their partners. And rather than find this uncomfortable, Lamont notes a majority of women not only prefer this state of affairs but consider the alternative—proposing them-selves—to reflect negatively on their own value. She chalks this up to cultural stereotypes that frame women as desperate and men as noncommittal, which probably has nothing to do with the proliferation of sitcoms and romantic comedies and how they've both conspired to destroy women's self-esteem and frame our assertiveness as unattractive. Single ladies may be sad as fuck, but even they're not as pathetic as a woman who has to browbeat a guy into marrying her!

Lamont calls this adherence to traditional gender roles the desire to 'play the girl', both within the privacy of a romantic relationship and as a means of proving something to the outside world. These 'ritualised moments', as she refers to them, are where otherwise progressive and empowered women often really lean into gender norms, in the hopes of reassuring people that what-ever external success they may have carved out for themselves, it hasn't eroded their much more important feminine value. Perhaps this is another explanation for why proposals themselves have become so intense—the bigger the gesture of love, the more currency a woman can claim in an economic system that places being chosen at the top of the hierarchy. So successful has the pathologising of successful, financially independent women been that many of us have learned to apologise for it or at least try to conceal the extent of our formidable attributes. A friend of mine is a leading paediatric neurologist but when she meets men, she tells them she's a nurse. That isn't meant as a slight on nurses, who are among the hardest and smartest of workers. But my friend has observed that the same eyes that glaze over when she mentions being an expert in brains will light up at the thought of her mopping men's brows and healing them with a sweet smile. There's a reason you won't find 'sexy paediatric neurologist' as an option at your local costume shop. As the bitingly clever satirist Dorothy Parker once quipped, 'Boys seldom make passes at girls who wear glasses.'

But according to Lamont, most women who want the *appearance* of being passively proposed to are also actively involved in the behind-the-scenes planning of what they want that proposal to look like ('surprise-ish', one respondent calls it). If proposals are performed at least in part for an audience either real or imagined, then stage-managing every aspect of them is a way for women to ensure the show gets rave reviews—especially when they don't trust their useless 'best friend' to get it right.

Clearly, 'playing the girl' means doing a bunch of the work, too. Welcome to marriage, baby!

———

'I woke up all night thinking it was a dream.'

So wrote Kourtney Kardashian on a series of photographs posted to Instagram in October 2021. Against a sunset backdrop and surrounded by roses (artfully arranged into the shape of a heart, with a centrepiece of roses merging the letter T with the letter K) and candles, an intimate audience of millions were invited to share in the moment the eldest Kardashian daughter's boyfriend of ten months, Travis Barker, dropped to one knee and asked her to be his wife. The photographs (professionally taken, of course) include a laughing Kardashian, head tilted up towards Barker, eyes half-closed and ring finger casually on display. The proposal's highlights are captured via images of the pair sitting on the ground together, walking along the beach, kissing in front of the setting sun and then, finally, the all-important close-up of the ring.

The proposal was a 'complete surprise', a Kardashian source told *People* magazine. 'Travis told everyone that he planned to propose, but everyone was great at keeping it a secret.'

Sure!

Leaving aside for a moment the fact that *nothing* happens in the Kardashian clan without everyone—and that means *everyone*—carefully knowing which staging mark Kris Jenner has assigned to them, the performance of a 'perfect' proposal necessitates the pretence that the bride-to-be has absolutely no idea what's about to happen. Despite being clearly styled for the occasion, we are meant to believe that Kourtney Kardashian has, through some marvellous stroke of fortune, been given what all women are told we must want—a man publicly declaring his romantic devotion to us in front of the world, and us just wonderfully, gratefully *surprised* by the whole thing.

Speaking of fortunes, Kardashian's engagement ring was reportedly purchased for a cool one million dollarydoos. I know this because everything about the ring—from the estimated number of carats to the thin, white platinum band and the designer—was discussed breathlessly across tabloids, gossip sites and bridal forums. As far as I can tell, there was scant commentary about the obscenity of spending such an exorbitant amount of money on a piece of jewellery. After all, this isn't the point. The point is the public performance of love and commitment, and what this tells us about the value of the woman being honoured with it. Once upon a time, Travis might have presented Kourtney with one hundred cows. But only because she's *worth it*.

Western society loves to credential itself as more 'enlightened' in regard to women. Cultures in which marriages are arranged are sneered at, while the women who still come with a price on their head are pitied. We would *never* diminish love in that way, or women! But what is the celebration of exorbitantly priced, ostentatiously designed rings if not a nod to age-old dowry systems that tell the world (or at least the world you operate in) how much money a man is willing to spend in order to claim you, the most valuable jewel of all, for his collection? This obscene display is made even worse by how the selection process is framed as a competition between women. The cultural message that tells us to beware of being 'left on the shelf' is built on capitalist, patriarchal ideals. It isn't enough just to be chosen. You have to be chosen *first*, by the highest bidder, and in a way that will make everyone else envy you. A woman's value must be demonstrated by the ornate objects her beloved is willing to adorn her with, be they material possessions like engagement rings or carefully orchestrated (and highly photographable) moments that say to the world, *This is what she deserves.*

To use a detestable phrase circulated by self-appointed relationship experts, a 'high-value woman' can expect to be endorsed by the material quality of the circumstances surrounding this public declaration of love; the more ostentatious it is, the clearer it becomes that she has managed to land a 'high-value man'. The Kardashians have a great instinct for the capitalist market, and part of this performance is of themselves as powerful, savvy businesswomen. But not even they are willing to contradict this format, understanding as they do how essential it is for their economic success to embody all the hallmarks of the romantic fairytale—to be the very best at 'playing the girl'. Being chosen by men isn't anathema to the image they have of themselves as highly powerful women; it's a core part of it.

Now, you might not care about the Kardashians, and I completely endorse this sentiment. To me, they represent all the worst things about choice feminism and the individualism that rules the marketplace. I object to being force-fed information about them at every turn (and apologies, because I'm doing the same to you!), and I truly believe the world would not suffer if they were all banished to a desert island with enough food to sustain them forever but no means of communicating with the outside world or possibility of leaving. They're repugnant in every way, channelling a form of consumerist prosperity theory whereby they want us, the lowly public, to believe that everything they have and hoard has come to them not because they engage in morally bankrupt behaviours so as to amass piles of money and privilege on the backs of other people, but because a higher power has recognised them as being *worthy* of this blessing.

But while all that may be true, the problem is that their behemoth presence persists. They're canny enough to understand that the influence they wield is at its most powerful when it presents their success (or at least slivers of it) as a possibility for us all. And so they pretend to be Normal Moms, posting TikToks and Instagram videos showing them doing Normal Mom things like making snacks and embarrassing their children by filming themselves singing in the car, and this is meant to give the audience just enough of a hint of relatability to make the gilded edges of the rest of their lives seem within reach; to make us think that, behind the private jets, designer wardrobes and incomprehensible amount of expensive cosmetic interventions, they're really not so different from the rest of us peasants.

As we'll see in the next chapter, the modern practice of large-scale weddings evolved out of the newly established (white, European) middle class wanting to emulate the practices of the nobility, even if just for a day. But while such aspiration might have once been sneered at as gauche by those with inherited wealth, a new kind of *noblesse oblige* operates in the age of social media. The Poors still aren't allowed to touch the skirts of our overlords—but we are certainly welcome to look as they swish around in them and collect our emoji praise.

In this respect, marriage proposals shared online can function as a means of demonstrating one's social mobility and class in a way that feels inviting as opposed to showy. If the Kardashians are a kind of American monarchy, the displays of their wealth and privilege are carefully designed to be consumed by a fawning public desperate to 'keep up' with what the celluloid royals are doing without feeling isolated by its abject unattainability. In a world where reality blends seamlessly with fiction, Kourtney

Kardashian kneeling on a beach while her boyfriend presents her with a ring that costs more than twice the price of the average American's house isn't a garish display of wealth and vapid self-indulgence—it's a love story fans can celebrate, while gazing on wistfully either in hope that it might one day happen to them, or regret and self-recrimination over the fact it didn't.

The upshot of maintaining this bullshit and calling it 'romantic' is that it keeps women from becoming too comfortable with the notion of our own independence, presenting it as superficially appealing but not enough by itself to make us *truly* happy. This isn't a mistake; it's the fucking point. We're being asked to believe that Kourtney Kardashian—a member of reality television royalty, founder of Poosh, mother to three children and with an estimated net worth of US$65 million—is in her heart of hearts no different from the rest of us (or at least what so many of us have been told we should be): just a girl, standing in front of a boy, asking him to love her.

———

A history lesson on rings, if I may.

In almost every engagement announcement shared across socials, you'd be hard-pressed to avoid seeing what the ring looks like. Pop culture has immortalised 'the rock' as being one of women's primary obsessions, with this usually being one of the first questions asked of the newly engaged both onscreen and off. A ring's design can make or break a proposal, with would-be brides gleaning inspiration from all quarters. In their (extensive) section on rings (how to choose them, how to repurpose vintage items into them, a guide to every type of diamond—honestly, it's some of the most boring reading material I've ever come across, and I've read Jordan Peterson), Brides.com has a segment called 'Get The Look' that will help you to imitate the rings of celebrities like Jennifer Lopez, Hailey Bieber and the late Queen Elizabeth II.

There's a long and storied history behind the 'engagement' ring, whose first recorded appearance dates back to the Ancient Romans. They believed the fourth finger of the left hand contained a vein (the *vena amoris*) that led to the heart, which is why people traditionally reserve this finger for their engagement and wedding rings. Although this theory has long since been disproven, it's a good example of how traditions are formed and why they persist. So attached to betrothal and marriage has it become that some folks seem weirdly shocked at the thought of using that finger for anything else. Personally, it's always annoyed me to think a part of my body could be reserved by other people on behalf of a person I haven't met yet, which is why I use that finger specifically for masturbating and casting spells on men who annoy me.

Although engagement rings largely serve a ceremonial purpose these days, there were good enough reasons to have them back in the days when marriage and sex were both legally used to constrain women. A ring signified the *intention* of marriage, which in some ways worked to protect the rights of women who might be drawn into sexual relationships with men under the promise of matrimony, only to find themselves abandoned after the fact. The Visigothic Code—a set of laws that brought Romans and Germanic people together under one rule in the mid-seventh century—emphasised greater rights for women than had previously existed; they could possess property and their own money, but they were also afforded more protection if they found themselves being ghosted by fuckbois whose promises to marry them disappeared at the same time as their hard-on, taking the woman's virtue with them but potentially leaving behind a now-illegitimate child. The Visigothic Code declared that, even in the absence of a written agreement, if a ring was given and accepted as a pledge of betrothal, then 'the promise shall, under no circumstances, be broken'.

The maintenance of a woman's 'virtue' (read: hymen) has always preoccupied people intent on controlling women's sexuality and freedom. Even today, it isn't uncommon (although it *is* absurd) to see people comparing 'used' women to inanimate objects, like sticky tape that's lost its grip (which is when a vagina is used so much it becomes tacky—if only the same could be said for boring stereotypes!), locks that can be opened by multiple keys (a vagina that yields to countless men rather than opening for just one) or an unlocked car just begging to be stolen (a vagina walking around in a short skirt, attached to someone who may or may not have been drinking—but #notallmen!).

Yet despite the continued existence of retrosexist views on women and sex (not to mention the enforcement of these views in particular cultural contexts), the issue of premarital sex in 2023 is considered largely settled. Not so throughout most of history, when paranoia about bloodlines and women's chastity coalesced to place the burden of sex on the shoulders of us gals. Hundreds of years after the Visigoths sought to protect (some) women from being caught up in men's nefarious deeds, Jane

Austen underscored the harm that could be done to a woman *and* her family if her lust should be allowed to get in the way of her sense. When the fifteen-year-old Lydia Bennet runs off with noted cad George Wickham, it's only the promise of their engagement that offers hope for the preservation of her reputation. With no confirmed engagement in sight, the Bennets fear the worst: that all of respectable society would know one of the Bennet girls had been living 'in sin' like a common trollop. Had Mr Darcy not stepped in to save their reputations, the fallout would have been catastrophic; the remaining Bennet sisters would be consigned to spinsterhood and poverty, because no man would associate himself with such a rotten family. As the simpering, obsequious Mr Collins declares in a letter feigning sympathy for the Bennets' misfortune, 'It would have been better had she died.'

With this historical context in mind, the importance of an engagement ring seems obvious. Despite the personal wishes of the United States Supreme Court, we haven't yet returned to the era when women's sexual histories can be used to cast us out of society entirely—but those justices are appointed for life, so give it time. So why does the symbol of a ring—particularly when they continue to be overwhelmingly worn by only one half of an engaged couple—still carry so much weight? And if not for *literal* virtue-signalling, why has the ring itself become an object of such scrutiny?

It may be that the proposal itself has assumed more social capital than what comes next. A recent survey of almost nine hundred women in Hong Kong conducted by the diamond company De Beers found that, while most of those women were happy to have smaller weddings, they considered a carefully staged proposal to be of paramount importance and necessary to ensure a positive experience overall. In fact, 81 per cent of women surveyed considered the ring to be the most important detail, and 94 per cent wanted to be involved in choosing it, with the youngest demographic of those women the most concerned about the ethical origins of their diamonds. Marriage, but make it progressive!

De Beers is hardly unbiased here. They're the most famous diamond merchant in the world, employing more than twenty thousand people, with mining operations in Botswana, Canada, Namibia and South Africa. They're also responsible for reinventing what an engagement ring represents for a modern audience. Most people these days would consider diamonds and engagement rings as synonymous with each other, the diamond itself being an indicator not just of quality in the ring but also the purchaser. But in the post-Depression era, the number of diamonds sold in America declined rapidly. As Richard Shotton writes in *The Choice Factory: 25 behavioural biases that influence what we buy*, 'on the eve of World War II only about ten per cent of engagement rings had diamonds'.

It wasn't just economics responsible for waning demand. Engagement rings in general were going out of fashion with young people. This was bad news for a diamond cartel like De Beers, so in the late 1930s, as the world was gearing up for another global war, they determined to Make Diamonds Great Again. After putting a call out to advertising agencies to help create some 'propaganda' for them (true story), they began working with the agency N.W. Ayer & Son. A year was spent conducting market research, and in 1939 they launched an advertising campaign to 'educate' the public about the four C's of quality diamonds: cut, carats, colour and clarity. (I have no idea what any of those things mean, but they're sufficiently important that 75 per cent of respondents to the aforementioned survey considered them essential to the proposal.)

This was just the first step in a calculated corporate campaign designed to shore up consumer trust (there's four more C's for you). In 1947, N.W. Ayer copywriter Mary Frances Gerety coined the advertising slogan 'Diamonds are forever', emphasising the durability of the stone as a symbol of love that would never die. The tagline was initially met with hesitation from Gerety's mostly male colleagues (shocker), but Gerety had the last laugh—not only has it become one of the most enduring corporate slogans in history, but in 1999 it was also named the slogan of the twentieth century by *Advertising Age*. At the same time, N.W. Ayer publicist Dorothy Digman—who ran the De Beers account—continued to elevate the glamour of diamonds in the public eye. Pre-empting today's online influencers, Hollywood stars were sent diamonds to wear on red carpets, and Digman coordinated much of the product placement that began appearing in movies like *Gentlemen Prefer Blondes*.

With the notion of 'forever' being now firmly embedded in the public's mind, what kind of financial dowry—sorry, 'spend'—was expected in order for a man to prove that commitment to his beloved? Well, with the lingering pressures of the Depression still in mind, De Beers suggested a full month's salary. The average annual salary for a man in 1950 was US$3605 (in 2022, this is about the equivalent of $43,000). By the 1980s, De Beers doubled down with the tagline: 'Isn't two months salary a small price to pay for something that lasts forever?' By this point, the average male salary had jumped to $24,195 (or $66,740 today), $4000 of which De Beers wanted consumers to. believe was the appropriate amount to spend on a ring.

And boy, were they certainly seeing their slice of the pie. As Shotton points out, 'sales of diamonds in the United States alone rose from $23 million to $2.1 billion between 1939 and 1979'. This figure has only continued to climb: in 2021, De Beers recorded a total revenue of $5.6 billion, a whopping 66 per cent increase on the previous year and its global pandemic-related tightening of belts.

Despite the enormous financial success enjoyed by De Beers since their partnership with N.W. Ayer, there was another reason engagement rings—and, more specifically, diamonds—were able to make a comeback in mid-twentieth-century America. As Margaret F. Brinig explores in her legal paper 'Rings and Promises' (1990), the abolition of 'breach of promise' acts first established in Indiana in 1935 and continued in sixteen states across the next decade played a significant role in enticing young women back to the idea of a ring. Much the same as the Visigothic Code had done in Western Europe in the seventh century, breach of promise acts offered some degree of protection to women whose chastity— and marriageability—may have been compromised by broken betrothals. If a man were to put a woman's future stability at risk by breaking both hymen *and* engagement, his ex-fiancée could sue him for damages.

Good for her!

Legal restitution for withdrawn proposals were not historically uncommon, and continue to appear in some form all over the world. The first successful case was *Stretch v. Parker*, all the way back in 1639, in England. The practice continued to be prevalent enough in legal terms that *Australia's Marriage Act 1961* included an end to breach of promise provisions (note that the government saw fit to end women's right to restitution a full ten years before any Australian state thought to end men's right to conjugal authority), but laws protecting the rights of would-be brides remained on the books in England and Wales up until 1971, after a 1969 case that saw Eva Haraldsted sue prominent footballer George Best. In the United States, certain legislatures still allow for jilted lovers to file breach of promise claims. As recently as 2008, a forty-six-year-old woman successfully sued her former fiancé after he backed out of their engagement. RoseMary Shell had agreed to take a US$50,000 annual pay cut to relocate from her Florida home to Georgia, where Wayne Gibbs owned a construction company. But after Gibbs dumped Shell, leaving nothing but a note and $5000, Shell took him to court. Gibbs was ordered to pay her $150,000.

Given the security breach of promise provisions offered women otherwise subject to draconian morality codes regarding their sex lives, their removal posed a particular risk. Engagement rings may have been waning in popularity prior to World War II, but they soon re-emerged as a form of both financial and social security for women, aided in part by the enormously successful campaign run by De Beers. An engagement ring was considered the property of the woman to whom it was given regardless of whether or not the wedding eventuated, and a diamond in particular went some way towards providing the financial restitution previously offered by breach of promise laws.

Of course, in a modern context most of these issues are moot. A woman's sexual history might still be scrutinised to grotesque degrees (and certainly judged in a different light from a man's), but these days it's generally accepted that women have sex before marriage and sometimes lots of it. No amount of conservative punditry and its hot takes on 'loose women' with 'high body counts' is likely to succeed in declaring sex itself as the reason why women are making themselves unmarriageable, no matter how confused Ben Shapiro seems to be about the connection between a 'wet ass pussy' and women's pleasure.

So, why are engagement rings still considered so important to the performance of marriage? At this point, it's surely just the flawed understanding of tradition and 'romance' (not to mention diabolically clever corporate marketing) that encourages women to want to brand themselves as claimed. Decades of seeing proposals play out on television and in movies has imbued *the rock* with a significance it doesn't deserve, and that only contributes to the notion of marriage for women as a competition for economic and social advantage. If your ring isn't as big/expensive/pretty/ tasteful as someone else's, doesn't this mean your prospective spouse is just a bit . . . shit?

It's always a bad idea to associate moral quality with material objects, especially when we're using those objects to broadcast something about ourselves to a viewing public. But this is just another example of how the wedding industrial complex works to eke every last dollar it can out of symbolic gestures considered 'essential' to the marriage process.

Ironically, neither Mary Frances Gerety nor Dorothy Digman ever married. According to J. Courtney Sullivan, author of the book *The Engagements* (which is in part a fictional retelling of Gerety's life), Gerety had never been particularly romantic, preferring to 'stay up late with her dogs and write copy'. She'd moved to Philadelphia, intent on carving out a career, and she stayed there until her death in 1999. Dorothy Digman, meanwhile, lived with her mother. The two women responsible for reinventing the engagement ring for a twentieth-century audience had more important aspirations and goals than becoming someone's *wife*. I can only imagine this became more pronounced to them through the cultural shifts of the 1950s and 1960s, whereby married women were expected to glean all their satisfaction out of whitegoods and Valium. Instead, Gerety continued to write the copy for De Beers for the next twenty-five years, enjoying what would have been considered an illustrious career for a woman at the time, despite it still being an uphill slog. To give you some idea of just what she was up against, to mark N.W. Ayer's twenty-fifth anniversary of working with De Beers, the ad agency gave each of its male executives a gold watch. Gerety was not included in the gesture. Mind you, these were the same men who used Gerety and

Digman as a kind of pre-internet Google for questions regarding women's wants and desires. So absurd were the lines of enquiry that Digman began documenting them, which is how we now know that mid-century ad men knew so little about their wives or women in general that they needed to ask, 'Would a woman find it strange or objectionable to find a horse head on a bed?'

But perhaps Gerety and Digman continued in some way to influence De Beers even after their deaths. In the early 2000s, De Beers launched its 'Raise Your Right Hand' campaign. The increase in divorce rates, coupled with a decrease in marriages, prompted the diamond company to target the robust economic status of an emerging demographic: the single woman. Make no mistake: this was cynical feminist rebranding at its finest. According to the copy, if your left hand was for 'we' then your right hand was for 'me'. Heart versus voice. Commitment versus independence. The modern woman no longer needed to wait for a *man* to buy her a diamond; for a cool few thou, she could buy one for herself and display it proudly as a sign of her strength and autonomy. *Women of the world, raise your right hand!* Women may still have little in the way of adequate pockets, but the corporate urge to rummage for the coins we keep in them continues apace. In 2021, De Beers launched its 'I Do' campaign. Working with advertising agency Omnicom, the mining company called for female purchasers to celebrate 'commitments to ourselves, to one another and the wider world'.

Propaganda indeed.

———

If women can buy our own rings now, not to mention houses or flats in which we can live in peaceful bliss, what compels so many of us to keep falling for the lie that we need to be given these things by a man in order for them—and us—to be worth something? Perhaps it's down to how each of these performances is received. 'Playing the girl' keeps us in thrall to conservative gender roles, and there's some degree of unburdening that comes from that. The story might be boring as hell, but the script is easy to learn. We needn't worry about forgetting our lines, for there aren't that many of them. Mostly, it just requires us to make ourselves smaller than we are, giggle in the right places and gaze up at the man come to deliver us from the weight of having to make decisions for ourselves. 'Being the woman' is trickier, in no small part because it means standing before audiences who so often hate what you've done to the character.

Years ago, my friend Dawn shocked me when she said yes to a man she'd only been dating for three months. The words of caution voiced by her friends and family didn't help. If anything, they helped to create a narrative that this love was worth fighting for *because* it came at such a personal cost. Nothing is more compelling to a twenty-five-year-old with no problems than the ability to hold court about how your parents don't approve of your fiancé.

The engagement lasted quite some time (he was younger than her, and had no money or initiative), but they eventually married in a lovely ceremony that his parents let everyone believe they'd paid for. They lived together amicably enough, but it was clear that one of the roles Dawn was occupying in addition to 'wife' was 'mother'. The marriage finally ended after Dawn met someone else and realised that you only have a finite time on this earth, and it shouldn't be spent having sex with a man whose greatest ambition in life was to grow his collection of *Star Wars* figurines. When she told me she was leaving her husband, giddily in love with someone new and feeling herself to be seen in a way she hadn't experienced previously, I congratulated her and then, wanting to sate my curiosity, tentatively asked why she had said yes to him in the first place.

'Because I thought no one else would ever ask me,' came the honest and heartbreaking reply.

I find myself wondering how much Lamont's idea of 'playing the girl' affects women's decisions when it comes to marriage. Behind the joyful proposal stories we're privy to these days, there must be at least some women who feel trapped by the fear that this might be their only chance to headline a story we've been told repeatedly is the only one that matters. Marriage (or finding 'the one') is still framed as the ultimate goal, and its importance is further drummed in by the sneering disdain directed at unpartnered women. Deep down, Dawn knew the man she had said yes to wasn't her perfect match; but she also believed her options were limited and that girls like her (at least in her mind) had to accept the love that was on offer rather than wait for the kind of love they had once dreamed might come their way.

This is the problem with treating marriage as a reflection of a woman's value rather than something she might decide to do in addition to all the other experiences her life will provide. If the world tells you you're worthless without the love of a man (and then mocks you as some kind of maladapted weirdo if you disagree), then you learn to do the work of patriarchy by hating yourself if it doesn't quite work out. This doesn't just significantly damage a woman's self-esteem; it also makes her a target for abusive predators with a keen nose for vulnerability, and more likely to overlook red flags, cruelty or just her own lack of attraction or interest in a partner. He might not be the greatest guy in the world—but he's the one who's there. If she wants a turn at playing the girl, she'll have to get used to absorbing disappointment.

I suggested as much to my friend Clare one afternoon while lying on a table in her tattoo studio. As with most of the conversations I've had during the course of writing this book, the talk has quickly turned to marriage and its various pitfalls. Like me, Clare finds the concept of marriage weird and oppressive. Unlike me, she was once very close to being trapped in it.

Clare was engaged at the age of twenty-six. (She refers to this as 'so young', which of course it is—but I also remind her that, once upon a time, unmarried women of twenty-six were considered 'old maids'.) Clare wasn't super enthused by the proposal. She knew the relationship wasn't great ('He was hot,' she told me, 'but he wasn't very nice and we fought all the time') and she didn't especially want to get married. But she said yes anyway, and told herself that maybe getting married would magically solve all the problems in their relationship.

The cultural messaging around proposals runs so deep that it stands to reason finding yourself caught up in one might produce some conflicting feelings. A lifelong antipathy to the marriage state might disappear the instant a man goes down on bended knee and presents you with both a ring *and* a culturally acceptable story you can tell at parties. Sure, you never wanted to get married—and you almost certainly don't want to marry *this* guy—but maybe going along with an engagement and everything that quantifies it feels a bit like ticking off an item on a bucket list of things women are meant to do before they die. Like learning how to walk in high heels or amassing a collection of colourful bath bombs. Choosing to accept a proposal is a bit like buying a dress on sale that you don't really want but you worry you might regret leaving on the rack later on.

That was certainly true for my friend Bridget, whose ex-boyfriend proposed to her on a plane while crossing the Atlantic. They'd only been going out for eleven months, and not only had she never professed a desire to marry him, but she'd also actively stated her fierce opposition to marriage on numerous occasions. Still, when they crossed the international dateline and the captain came over the loudspeaker to ask if she would marry Derek, she found herself crying and saying yes. The passengers cheered (naturally—everyone follows a script with these things) while Derek placed the ring he'd bought a month or so earlier onto the fourth finger of Bridget's left hand, signifying to the world that she was now off limits.

Of course, Bridget had no choice but to say yes. At their heart, proposals are an act of entrapment, and there's nothing quite so inescapable as a tin tube 30,000 feet above the ocean. But what I found most interesting was the fact that Bridget's happiness in the moment was at odds with how she'd felt about marriage her whole life.

'When he put the ring on my finger, I had this sense that I was experiencing something really romantic,' she said to me recently, the two of us drinking a bottle of cheap Aldi fizz on her balcony. 'It's like . . . it's a *proposal*, you know? And I guess maybe it just felt in the moment like I was becoming part of a traditional narrative of what women are supposed to want.'

You might think I'm being melodramatic in saying proposals are an act of 'entrapment'. Maybe the ones delivered in public are, sprung on you in front of ten to fifty of your closest friends or perhaps even your entire graduating class. But surely proposals staged privately and with thoughtful gestures are just . . . romantic? Especially if they're welcomed by the intended spouse-to-be, or even expected. Say, Clementine, aren't you being just a little bit too curmudgeonly and pessimistic? You haven't said anything *good* about proposals in this whole chapter!

Well, hear me out.

Modern marriage is, at its core, a government contract. It's a way for the government to keep track of people's domestic partnerships, and to use those domestic partnerships as proof of society's fundamental commitment to conservative monogamy. Married couples receive certain financial benefits as both reward for getting married and enticement into marriage. This exchange isn't born out of benevolence. The state doesn't give a shit if its citizens are spiritually happy, especially not its lady citizens. Marriage serves both an economic and social purpose, which is why the institution continues to be fiercely protected and women in particular are intimidated into embracing it. While many women around the world now benefit from no-fault divorce laws, divorce itself is stressful, time-consuming and often cripplingly expensive. As far as legal contracts go, marriage is almost stupidly easy to get yourself into and incredibly tricky to extract yourself from. And again, it's purposely designed this way.

So why, given the legal ramifications of marriage and all that the contract entails, do people not treat the decision with the businesslike pragmatism it deserves?

Because if people—and again, women in particular—really looked at the implications of that decision, many of them might choose not to do it. They might have a party, sure. But signing a legally binding contract? Pass.

Bridget's excitement at being initiated into Engaged Woman World (EWW) was short-lived. So short, in fact, that even as the applause of fellow passengers was still echoing around the economy cabin, her gratitude was already shifting into terror.

'The flight attendants had brought us each a glass of champagne in flutes from business class,' she told me. 'Derek had gone to the bathroom, and I remember looking at my hand as it gripped the stem, that ring winking back at me. The excitement I'd had just moments before suddenly disappeared, and all I felt was intense dread in the pit of my stomach.'

Bridget never married Derek, luckily. She left him for someone else a year or so later, and then broke up with her a few years after that. She currently lives with a primary partner in an ethically non-monogamous relationship in an apartment where each of them has their own bedroom.

On the balcony that day, I asked her how she feels now about that proposal.

'It's weird,' she says, 'because so many people who really do love me were in on it. Two of my best friends helped him choose the ring! My parents knew about it. He actually asked my *father* for permission to propose, which is so gross. I mean, to be fair, my mum did advise him against doing it on a plane, and my dad was clear that the only one who could give permission for me to marry was me. But all the people who knew me best—who *knew* that I wasn't really a marriage person—were still able to be drawn into this big "romantic" gesture, because we're still so sucked in by the idea that this is what women want.'

I guess this is what it comes down to for a lot of people—that a woman's personal desires and aspirations are always up for negotiation, especially when flattered by someone's ostentatious public declaration of love. Think of the videos you've seen of men following women onto graduation stages, usurping moments of academic achievement and forever altering her memories of what the day was really about. She might be a qualified doctor (maybe even a paediatric neurologist!), but what's more important is that she's *engaged*. Forget about that degree—show me the ring!

And it's not just professional achievements that are disrupted in this way. Other moments are stolen from women's lives, taken without permission but always with the expectation that the recipients be grateful for the intrusion. Think of the clip that went viral in early 2022, showing a weeping woman being proposed to in the middle of her father's funeral. Her would-be husband later explained that he wanted to give her something to help ease her grief—and doesn't that just tell you everything you need to know about how some people see marriage as the be-all and end-all of a woman's aspirations?

For my friend Jackie, this moment of theft happened at her fortieth birthday party. The evening was meant to celebrate her forty years of life and all the incredible things she'd done and survived to get there, but a proposal from her girlfriend that she had neither asked for nor wanted to put her on the spot in front of all her friends and family, had turned the night from *hers* into *theirs*. Their two children (from separate relationships) were even enlisted to help with the ruse, with her three-year-old daughter presenting Jackie with the ring.

Jackie wasn't all that interested in becoming a wife, but what could she say? Asking someone to marry you in front of a roomful of people is like blocking all the escape routes, which is precisely the point. So Jackie said yes, and a few years later they became one of the first same-sex couples in Australia to be legally married. A few years after that, they became one of the first same-sex couples to file for divorce. Being gay didn't protect them from all of the negative aspects of marriage, nor did it prevent dynamics of power and control from being used within that marriage. The manipulation didn't begin with the manner of that proposal (or the fact her child was co-opted into it), but it certainly made it harder for Jackie to leave.

Others have fared even worse, with rejections leading to retaliation. Consider the case of Svetlana Orlova, who was ambushed on live television in Spain in 2007. Orlova had been invited to appear on *Patricia's Diary*, a daytime show with two million viewers. Imagine how she must have felt when her ex-boyfriend, Ricardo Navaro, appeared on set, dropped to one knee and said, 'I want you to marry me—you are everything to me.'

Orlova said no. Later, Navaro—who'd already been subject to a restraining order for domestic abuse perpetrated against Orlova—murdered her by stabbing her in the neck. Orlova paid the price of saying no with her life, a fate delivered to all too many women—including, and maybe even especially, the ones who say yes, given the statistical risk of homicide women face from husbands.

Those who can say no without fearing they'll be killed still can't guarantee escaping punishment of some kind. Public proposals posted online undoubtedly also come with risks. Imagine the absolute thrashing that would be directed at a woman if one of these viral clips ended in her turning the man down. The comments would be filled with derogatory remarks about her looks, about what a *mean bitch* she is, about how she'll grow old and lonely and die surrounded by cats. She would most likely receive physical threats, too, because she had the temerity to reject a man. We don't have to imagine too hard, because we see women chastised for rejecting men all the time. The superficial narrative that extols a proposal as one of the greatest moments of a woman's life also promises endless sympathy and support for the men who are gallant enough to bestow this gift. Politely declining causes humiliation for a man *who was just doing what you women always say you want*. And as we well know, humiliating men is a war crime.

Of course, some women do escape the whirlpool. For Clare, the path to freedom was less fraught than Jackie's. She called off the wedding after a conversation with her aunt helped her to realise that she didn't have to go through with it just because she'd said yes and just because he was there.

'She took me out for lunch one day and basically told me that I could have whatever kind of life I wanted,' Clare said. 'It was a revelation, because even though I had always thought of myself as independent, I'd never really heard that message before: that not only did marriage not have to be the primary goal for a woman, but that we could actively reject it and do whatever we wanted.'

Badass aunts. May we know them. May we have them. May we be them.

As for Dawn, she's finally found love with someone wholly committed to her happiness and who champions her every day— herself. The shiny new man who saved her from the boring one turned out to be cruel and emotionally abusive, hiding the worst of his traits until after she'd married him and had a child. He found her insecurities and drilled down into them for years, but he underestimated how much strength a woman can find when she realises that playing the girl doesn't have to mean being the foil in some man's story; it can also mean being the hero of your own. Dawn left him, and now she lives her best life with determination, joy and unparalleled love.

Being chosen didn't save her life. She did that all by herself.

———

Not all of us will learn how to be our own hero, or if we do then the road to get there might be treacherous. This is what happens when we raise generations of girls to believe that playing themselves to suit a story necessarily involves allowing other people to direct you.

I used to think that women who accepted marriage proposals had always aspired to the idea of being someone's wife, and that they had therefore only ever concerned themselves with the small problem of *whose* wife they would become. While that might be true for a lot of people, in the course of writing this book I've found myself swayed by another possible explanation for the overflow of brides-to-be sharing their good news (and rings) across carefully curated social media platforms: mass inertia in the face of cultural and romantic expectation, and fear of what happens when you try to write a different story for you to play the girl within. Perhaps this is what I find most sinister about marriage proposals, and the artifice behind staging them.

Simply put, how can you comfortably say no to handing away the rest of your life when the only script you've ever been presented with has always called on you to say yes?

6

THE HAPPIEST DAY
OF HER LIFE

'I have in me the germs of intense life. If I could live, and
if I could succeed in writing out my living, the world itself
would feel the heavy intensity of it.'

—Mary MacLane, *I Await the Devil's Coming*, 1902

When I was nineteen, I worked for a period of time in a pub in
the Adelaide Hills. The pub itself wasn't particularly special, but
its position on the top of the range gave it an enviable west-facing
view across the city. Because of its capture of the sunset market,
it was a prime spot for weddings. Fridays and Saturdays would
be booked out months in advance, with the occasional Sunday
thrown in for good measure. Couples could select from a range
of different package deals. Those who opted for a sit-down dinner
over canapés could choose to serve either two courses or three.
Beer, wine and soft drinks was the standard choice for drinks,
except if the client was rich (when it might extend to spirits) or

Christian (in which case the only spirit allowed would be that of the Lord).

I hadn't been to many weddings in my life, and I can't say that the experience endeared them to me. It wasn't just because marriage had never been a particular aspiration of mine; it was that, almost without exception, every single wedding I saw was exactly the same as the last. The same table settings, the same food, the same terrible wedding music, the same grotty behaviour from inebriated groomsmen and invited uncles, all of whom always managed to find an opportunity to squeeze past the young waitresses close enough to press their dicks into our backs. This was in the early 2000s, when cigarettes were still cool, and large groups of people would congregate on the pub's balcony to blast thick clouds of smoke into the air as they contemplated which bridesmaid or cousin they'd try to finger or give a blowie to in the bathroom later on. At some point, the DJ would play 'Teenage Dirtbag' and everyone would race to the dance floor, where someone—usually the best man, who by now had sunk about half-a-dozen pints—would attempt to do 'the worm'.

It was a grim scene. But the thing that got me the most was how so few of the brides seemed to be really enjoying themselves. They were always too afraid to eat anything, in case an errant blob of sauce or meat spilled on the white gown they'd been starving themselves for weeks to fit into. And so they'd sit on half a glass of sparkling wine, knowing that any more than this would bypass their empty stomachs and go straight to their heads. These same concerns were not shared by the groom, who'd be pissed before we'd finished handing out the first course. This would become even more obvious when it was time for the speeches, almost none of which were given by women and certainly never by the bride herself. Over the course of about a year and a half, I heard countless men say exactly the same things to and about the women they had just pledged to spend the rest of their lives with.

I love how supportive she is. She takes such good care of me. She's got a great sense of humour, because she always laughs at my jokes.

Not one of them seemed able to say anything they actually *knew* about their wife. Only that she was beautiful, and they appreciated how she made their lives better.

Often, the bride's father would also stand up and say a few words. These were usually about how proud they'd been to walk their 'little girl' down the aisle, and how they knew Michael or Sam or Matt or Ben would 'take good care of her'. Occasionally, they'd make some crack about how they were glad she was someone else's problem now. This would always be met with chuckles, but the true guffaws were reserved for when the best man shared a hilarious story about that time Michael or Sam or Matt or Ben had fucked a girl and then left a giant shit in her toilet as a joke, and how great it was that he now had a wife to keep him on the straight and narrow.

After the speeches, as everyone got even looser, the bride and groom would walk around the room and thank everyone for coming. I always found this part perplexing. You've dropped thousands of dollars on a build-your-own wedding in which dozens of people you felt forced to invite were given as much cheap plonk as they liked *and* a plate of chicken or beef (sometimes fish), and you're supposed to walk around and thank *them* for coming?

But nothing about these carbon copy festivals of hetero-sexuality depressed me as much as the bouquet toss. It usually happened about three-quarters of the way through the reception, shortly before the bride and the groom took their leave and headed back to their hotel to have what I can only imagine would be horrendous sex or, for the sensible ones, a hot shower and straight to sleep. You could always tell when it was about to happen, because the lights would be turned up ever so slightly to avoid the risk of collisions between women made temporarily myopic by booze and crazy with wedding fever. Realising their moment had come, the unmarried (and intent on changing this) ladies would gather in the centre of the room, where the bride was standing on a chair. Arms raised at the ready, they'd wait as the bride counted to three and lofted the bouquet over her shoulder. A scuffle would ensue as the participants jostled for the prize. In particularly boisterous groups, two or three women might even find themselves on the ground wrestling for it. On these occasions, it wasn't uncommon to hear male onlookers (who by now had surrendered their ties and top buttons to the party gods) whoop and holler. Eventually, a winner would be determined, and she'd stand clutching the trampled-on flowers triumphantly, enjoying the rapturous applause. The other women would gather around her, dejected but putting on a brave face. *Well done! You'll be next!* At this point, the winner's boyfriend (if present) might begin to look a bit sick.

As I said, I hadn't been to many weddings as a guest myself. This hasn't changed all that much in the years since, because most of my friends are unmarried. But on those rare occasions when I was invited, I always refused to participate in the bouquet toss, and found it embarrassing and irritating if pushed to by other people. A bit of fun or not, the ritual of competing with other women in order to attract the romantic hand of fate seemed completely humiliating. I'm a competitive person by nature. I like to win. I'm not proud of how I behave when playing cards or board games with my friends. I would elbow another woman in the face to grab those flowers, just to come out on top. I could see the bouquet toss becoming ugly if I were to step into the ring. But the thought of being confused for someone who cared about being next in line rather than just proving I could have made a good linebacker was disgusting to me. Jostling to be the next selected for marriage was pitiful enough; being perceived as caring about that was a bridge too far.

But it's tradition! people cry. *It's fun! Don't be such a killjoy!*

'Tradition' has always been the go-to defence for maintaining sexist rituals associated with marriage, the practice itself being the most obvious example. But tradition is a shapeshifter. Turn it one way and you'll find something people are willing to defend furiously as a cultural tie to our ancestors. Turn it another, and it's recognised as something so horrifying we feel blessed to be rid of it.

You know—like wedding DJs.

———

Let's talk about tradition.

During the Middle Ages, it was considered normal—and even expected—that a bride's virginity be confirmed. This was sometimes done prior to the wedding, with a midwife using her fingers to feel for the presence of a hymen (which was a bit unfair for us sturdy girls whose hymens might have made their departure while riding a horse or just engaging in some vigorous stretching). It might also have been confirmed post-coitus, with the public display of bloodstained bedsheets. For the aristocracy, whose virginity was more closely monitored to prevent illegitimate claims on inheritance, it wasn't uncommon for a priest to watch as the newly married couple (who may have only met that day) disrobed and copulated.

Fun times!

Although some cultures still demand blood ceremonies be performed to satisfy the patriarchal need to claim a woman's sexuality as the property of men, such a 'tradition' would be baulked at by many of the people who invoke the same word to romanticise practices they like. *It's just how it's always been done* might be true (or at least seem true) for things like throwing rice at a newly married couple, but few people would defend the Victorian practice of throwing old shoes with as much rigour as James Crombie of Aberdeen, whose twenty-four page treatise titled 'Shoe-throwing at weddings' (1895) argued, 'Pelting a bride and bridegroom with old shoes when they start on their honeymoon is a custom we are all familiar with, and in which many of us have participated.'

Interestingly, the bouquet toss is one of those 'traditions' that isn't as old as people think. As with most of the rituals that accompany weddings, it emerged out of weird necessity rather than any kind of ancient commitment to party planning.

Remember, for most of human history marriage was one of the only pathways available to a woman to improve the economic circumstances of her and/or her family. This was especially true for women in the British upper-middle classes who were subject to coverture. If there was no son to inherit the family property, the estate in its entirety would be entailed by law to the nearest male relative. And although it was common for brothers to house spinster sisters, distant male relatives were neither expected nor obliged to shelter women who hadn't managed to secure a suitable marriage. Women could be thrown out of homes they'd lived in for decades by men they'd never met and who'd never set foot inside the house prior to inheriting it.

Although the concept of love as a precursor to marriage began to gain popularity in the 1800s, it couldn't quite outstrip the economic need for marriage in the absence of all other options. Superstition led women to believe that touching the bride during the wedding ceremony would bring them luck, and bring a suitor their way. The apocryphal story is that, after one too many bridal gowns were ruined or torn by women angling to be next in line, brides began to throw their bouquet instead.

Et voilà! A tradition was born.

It being less necessary now for women to marry for economic reasons (the operative word being 'less'), the toss has come to represent something more needy and distasteful. It's an indulgence of the social anxieties we're supposed to have about unmarried women, which is that we're a problem in urgent need of solving so we don't spend the rest of our sad, empty lives burdened by the stench of desperation and the futility of having nothing to do.

The fact that there's no real equivalent for a wedding's male guests (the garter toss is hardly the same thing) is revealing. Men might be enticed to engage in a beer-drinking contest or some kind of wrestling match to prove who is the strongest and most virile, but never to discover who'll be next month's lucky groom. That would be considered pathetic. *Girly.* The actions of a beta cuck! Men fight with other men in order to win the respect of men everywhere. And although that might sometimes involve fighting over a single woman, these displays are never intended to suggest they might want love or marriage for themselves—even though they're the ones most likely to benefit from it.

Peel back the layers on other wedding practices and you'll find some equally retro motivations. Warding off demons, bandits and even the prospect of physical altercation were all cause for concern on a wedding day, and measures were taken to mitigate against each. For example, we can date the use of bridesmaids and groomsmen all the way back to Ancient Rome, where the law required ten witnesses to be present at every wedding. As Roman law didn't consider women to be humans, only property belonging to fathers, brothers and husbands, these witnesses had to be men. The group would accompany the bride to the wedding to protect her from any thieves intent on stealing her dowry (and don't you just love the idea of having to *pay* a man to marry you, only to become his property?). Having safely navigated the risk of theft, the wedding party had to contend with the threat of malevolent spirits targeting the bride and groom. To confuse them, the group—which now included ten bridesmaids—would dress identically to the marrying couple so the spirits would be unable to distinguish them from each other. These days such a prospect might horrify an enthusiastic bride whom, it is explicitly understood, must be *the* standout on her special, special day. Funny how some traditions can be abandoned while others, like bridesmaids all being poured into five versions of the same ugly dress, are steadfastly maintained!

Centuries after Rome required men to stand as wedding witnesses, groomsmen were employed for different reasons. In the sixteenth century, the Germanic Goths decided that it was easier just to kidnap a woman rather than go through the rigma-role of negotiating their price with whichever man was thought to be her owner. If the abduction was successful, the groomsmen would stick around for the ceremony in case the woman's family tried to reclaim her *or* another group of Really Cool Guys tried to steal her for themselves. Rather than standing next to the groom, the best man was positioned next to the poor woman whose luck had suddenly taken a terrible turn. And the reason grooms traditionally stand on the right-hand side of the wedding altar? Because this was the best position from which to draw their sword or a weapon in the event of a fight. As time went on and the Church began to wield more power over the wedding ceremony, this staging continued—but now the bride was expected to stand on the left to symbolise that Eve had been formed out of Adam's left rib.

Weddings are full of retro practices romanticised as 'tradition'. But although we can trace a lot of these customs back to historical eras in which people were more willing to believe in evil fairies than in women's right to freedom of choice, many of them are modern fabrications. As Jia Tolentino explores in her excellent essay 'I Thee Dread', what western culture has been taught to view as traditional is very often recent capitalist invention. As Europe moved out of the Industrial Age and towards a modern era, the potential for *love* (which had also been reinvented as marital tradition) to be monetised proved too alluring to resist. Marriage had always been about economics, with the money exchanged in service of keeping the shop *closed* to outsiders. The birth of the wedding industrial complex happened at a time when marriage itself was ceasing to be a purchasable item, but the individual status it conferred could be carefully curated via the right dress, tastefully designed invitations and artfully taken photographs.

And suddenly, everyone was open for business.

I live a short walk from Melbourne's unofficial 'wedding district'. Every weekend, women come here from all over the city, trying to find the perfect dress in which to exchange vows. Tulle, satin, sequins, beads—whatever you're looking for, you can find it in one of the dozens of stores that line the main road. The cafe I visit most days is next door to one of these, and I've watched many a purposeful bride-to-be and her mother sipping on flat whites while flipping through wedding scrapbooks looking at dresses. Whatever she chooses, it has to be *perfect*.

If I were to ask you to picture a traditional western wedding gown, you'd probably think of a flowing dress in some variation of white or cream, made out of satin, silk or a similarly delicate fabric. Although the fashions have changed over the years, the notion of a white wedding dress has been embedded in the collective conscience. Surely this is just how things have always been done?

But in fact the association of a bride with white is less than two hundred years old. For most of the last millennium at least, women just wore their best dress, whatever the colour. Even for the middle and upper classes in Europe, a wedding gown was more likely to be made of black silk for the very practical reason that it was easier to keep clean. Buying a dress that would be worn only once was beyond the economic means of most women.

It was Queen Victoria who instigated the trend of what we now associate with 'traditional' wedding dresses, when she appeared in white at her nuptials to Prince Albert in 1840. Royal protocol dictated that she should have worn the crimson velvet robes reserved for all matters of state, but Victoria was deeply in love with her betrothed (who also happened to be her cousin—notice how few people want to bring that tradition back!) and wanted the ceremony to reflect this. She declared she would make her vows to him as a wife and not as a monarch. Her commitment to the performance—and to Albert—even saw her promising to obey him, which was a radical and politically dicey move for a queen to make. But she insisted, and chose to represent her devotion to the Man Who Would Be King (but only as a consort, much to her dismay) by wearing a gown with a white satin court train. To symbolise her virtue and fertility, the train was bordered with orange blossom. Such a gesture had never been made by a British queen, but marriages based on love rather than political or economic expediency were beginning to take off (how progressive!), and the romantic devotion suggested by Victoria's sartorial choices was enthusiastically embraced by the public. What can only be described as 'wedding fever' swept the country, and brides from near and far raced to follow in the fashionable footsteps of the young queen.

Relationships among the well-to-do these days come with their own set of rituals, from soft and hard launches of paramours on Instagram to professionally documented proposals and then the inevitable posting online of the carefully curated wedding. But what we want to think of as an authentic expression of love is more often than not the time-honoured practice of Keeping Up With The Joneses. Modern brides might look to the styling choices of their favourite designers, models and celebrities and think themselves fresh and cutting edge, but aspiration isn't a modern invention. The trappings of elaborate weddings didn't arise because people suddenly discovered love and wanted to throw a party for it. Instead, they were born out of the desire for a newly established middle class to mimic the lifestyles of the extraordinarily rich and royally famous. Sure, you might not be a queen or a member of the aristocracy—but with the right dress, you could pretend to be one for a day.

While it might have previously seemed a craven indulgence to invest in a one-off gown, the willingness to do so became part of the wedding performance—and make no mistake, weddings are performance from start to finish, designed to elevate social status while feigning humility. A beautifully constructed, steamed and pressed gown made in a variation of white or cream didn't just signal its wearer had both taste and an intact hymen, it also suggested she might have her own lady's maid. After all, only someone with a domestic staff would risk wearing a dress more likely to show off the signs of wear and tear, not to mention wine and food splashes. For those with the economic means to do so, a delicate dress like this could be purchased with the knowledge it would only be worn once before being removed to a chest or trunk to be either retained as a keepsake or worn a quarter of a century later by a daughter. (No doubt the modern practice of 'dress trashing'—in which brides photograph themselves wading into the ocean or deliberately spoiling their expensive gown as part of the wedding ritual—would scandalise people for whom the idea of a 'special dress' was considered sacrosanct. It scandalises me, to be honest. Throw the man out, not the dress!)

There were no photographs of the newly married queen and her prince, but news of the lavish dress spread quickly via newspapers and society gossip. It was a cultural game changer, and solidified the radical new idea that marriage could be made even more powerful if it were entered into because of love and not just economic or diplomatic pragmatism.

But while the monarch *did* adore her beau, she was also motivated by the duty of her station. The introduction of machines to the textile industry had revolutionised the speed with which clothes could be made, yet it had all but destroyed the trade of individual artisans. The British lace industry was facing annihilation, and Queen Victoria understood that the role of the monarch is to safeguard one's subjects against poverty. Dismantling blood rule and redistributing unearned wealth would seem to be the obvious way to do that, but Vicky went down the influencer path instead. She chose a cream satin handwoven in Spitalfields and a large piece of Honiton lace, whose delicate beauty she wanted to put on prime display. And what's the best colour to show off lace?

White.

Queen Victoria's lace veil and *un*traditional white gown was just the start of the wedding revolution. As news of her fashion forward bridal wear spread, more and more women opted to wear white on their wedding day as a signifier of both their virtue and their elevated status. (Demonstrating the circular nature of fashion, contemporary 'offbeat' brides often opt for outfits in any colour *but* white. I guess one woman's Honiton lace is another's pair of Converse sneakers.)

But this new generation of brides didn't just imitate the dress. Against her own wishes, the ceremonial aspects of Queen Victoria's nuptials also precipitated a shift away from smaller marriage ceremonies attended mainly by family and towards more festive, elaborate and *expensive* displays. According to journalist and biographer Julia Baird, Queen Victoria's royal wedding cake weighed a whopping three hundred pounds (one hundred and thirty-six kilograms), and was served at a wedding banquet that involved a 'a frenzy of nodding, curtseying, beaming and handshaking'. The bride herself disappeared early (no doubt wanting to get to the business of getting *down* to business), and evidently wasn't disappointed by the delights that awaited. She wrote of the evening: 'Albert [and his] excessive love and affection gave me feelings of heavenly love and happiness I could never have hoped to have felt before . . . Oh! This was the happiest day of my life!'

Queen Victoria and Prince Albert might have set the standard for both weddings and love marriages, but the success of the latter is exceedingly rare. As the pre-eminent marriage historian Stephanie Coontz writes, 'People have always loved a love story. But for the most part, our ancestors did not try to live in one.' I can't imagine most women experiencing a marital devotion so deep that they ask to be buried in their wedding dress, but the hope they may find it is surely what drives people to continue trying.

The propaganda machine responsible for selling marriage to a modern public has been so insidious and diabolically clever that it can be difficult to deprogram those who've bought in. The idea that marital unions built on love have underpinned human evolution since the moment we crawled out of the sea may be historically inaccurate (and easy to disprove), but it continues to hypnotise people. We're an inherently fanciful lot, and most people don't want to abandon the dream of one day finding their soulmate. Despite my steadfast opposition to marriage, I can understand why people might struggle to renounce the fantasy. When I was six or seven, I spent an afternoon spinning plates on my head because my sister told me this would shrink me so I'd become small enough to play in my doll's house. I finally accepted that it wasn't going to happen, but there's a part of me that wishes such whimsy could be real. It's nice to believe in magic.

The wedding industrial complex took the desire people had to believe in magic—specifically, that of soulmates—and turned it into a multi-billion-dollar money spinner. It's easy to persist with the myth that romantic love is essential to human happiness, because the reality of it occurs in private while the idealised view is that it has no end. Weddings (or at least the ones presented as aspirational, which is almost all of them) are designed to be ephemeral public displays, and built on myth-making which crumbles at the first sign of fact-checking. Once you see how *strategic* the whole operation has been, it's hard to believe how easily we've all fallen for it.

All this time, our 'something old' has really been 'something new'.

———

Almost two hundred years after Queen Victoria donned a gown that launched a million imitations, business is in full swing. Despite recessions, pandemics and even a downturn in marriages overall, the economy is one of the biggest winners when it comes to saying 'I do.' In 2016, the wedding industry in the United States—home to the largest economic spend on weddings in the world—registered a staggering US$72 billion. And although this figure dropped to around $55 billion during the first year of Covid-19, by the end of 2022 it had surpassed $60 billion. Now that people can travel again, destination weddings in the US alone account for around a quarter of all nuptials, and are worth $16 billion a year. Globally, the wedding dress market is worth an estimated $2.8 billion.

As of 2021, the average individual cost of a wedding in America was $28,000 (which jumps to $34,000 if you include the engagement ring). In Australia, that translates to roughly $36,000—more than 60 per cent of the average salary of people aged between twenty-one and thirty-four. The UK isn't far behind, with an average spend of £17,000 (approximately A$30,000). And in case you're looking at your bank account and feeling impoverished, don't worry—the couples spending big don't necessarily have money either. According to a 2022 survey conducted by the Australian government's Moneysmart website, 82 per cent of couples use all or part of their savings to pay for their wedding and 60 per cent take out a loan. More worrying is this: almost one-fifth of couples pay for their wedding using their credit card.

It's hard to fathom what kind of party would be worth going into an insane amount of debt for, and I say that as someone who generally loves a good knees-up, especially if it includes constantly revolving platters of mini arancini. In lieu of a wedding (and to contradict the oft-touted reason for having one as 'we did it for the party'), I planned a fancy shindig for my fortieth birthday. I bought a slinky dress, hired a beautiful venue on the river in Abbotsford, chose some canapés and even designed a welcome cocktail to complement the all-you-can-drink package. As parties go, it wasn't inexpensive. But it was still about a third of the price of a wedding, with the added bonus that I didn't have to budget for an eventual divorce. What could $20,000 more possibly buy?

Maybe not that much, as it turns out. Not after the dreaded 'wedding tax' has been added.

Like the gender wage gap or Brad Pitt's rapid decline into creep territory, the wedding tax is one of those things people generally don't like to admit is happening even though it unequivocally is; the idea of a punitive tax sounds bad and cynical, which are two things the wedding industry prides itself on at least pretending not to be.

In 2019, a writer named January Jones put the wedding tax to the test when she began planning her own nuptials. Seeking estimates from a number of different event vendors, she found that quoted prices experienced a hike when the W word was mentioned. An ordinary blow wave went from $100 to $250, a DJ from $600 to $1000 and the cost of dry-cleaning two similarly described dresses from $30 to $280. But the steepest increase was reserved for the venue, the cost of which went from $6000 for a standard party to a whopping $25,000 for a wedding reception.

Why would a vendor supposedly in the business of celebrating love exploit it for profit?

Because they can!

See, a wedding isn't like a regular party. It's a *cool* party. And no matter what the divorce and remarriage rates say, it's a party people want to believe they'll only get one chance to deliver with maximum impact. So when a service provider or vendor finds out that the little get-together you're hosting isn't for a birthday or graduation but for a *significant* occasion like the legal entwining of two identities for the benefit of community validation and government tax breaks, the price will mysteriously double or even triple. Despite the fact wages in general aren't increasing alongside wedding inflation, darned if people aren't willing to pay a premium to host and then broadcast their dream day on social media—which, ironically, is where most of the inspiration and impetus to construct said dream day has come from.

So insidious is the industry that many a bride has reported the use of emotional manipulation to upsell anything and everything in service of the Big Day. *But you only get this once*, the person providing the table settings implores. *Don't you want it to be absolutely perfect?*

Of course she does, because anything less than *the* most perfect day will be a crushing disappointment. That's how she found herself agreeing to spend an extra $5000 to have the *special* tablecloths made out of French flax linen instead of the standard cotton ones that were a fraction of the price.

Why are these decisions mostly left to the bride? Because that's her job, silly! Like a horrifying portent of a future spent buckling under the weight of the mental load, women are the ones overwhelmingly put in charge of planning the day that marks the end of their freedom. To be fair, this is often viewed as a welcome responsibility—because how could that big goof she's marrying (her best friend, she's so lucky to have him!) possibly be trusted to get the tableware right?

Thankfully, she has help in the form of that aforementioned billion-dollar wedding industry. Phew! When it comes to planning a wedding, today's bride has a slew of publications, websites and digital vision boards from which to glean inspiration. But one of these stands out in particular, for sheer longevity if nothing else: *Brides.*

The definitive online wedding guide, *Brides* was launched as a print magazine in 1934 with the title, *So You're Going to Be Married.* Its emergence into the market occurred, not-so-coincidentally, when a bunch of savvy business owners and diabolical corporate geniuses decided the best way to reinvigorate a post-war, post-Depression economy was to persuade young people to care about weddings. For almost a century, *Brides* has weathered economic slumps, numerous name changes, the shift from print publishing to an exclusively digital presence and the broadening parameters of who can marry at all to continue doing what it does best—delivering beautifully photographed wedding fantasies and ideas for unique canapés to an audience of breathlessly optimistic romance fiends. Who best to turn to, then, to glean some understanding of what's involved in planning such an event?

And boy, does it seem to involve A LOT.

According to award-winning wedding planner, Nicole-Natassha Goulding, it should take a year or so for a couple to plan their wedding. (She says 'couple', but with the notable exception of some same-sex weddings and fashionably in-touch cis-het men, I would be prepared to wager very few Standard Blokes are devoting much time to the consideration of whether or not fairy-lights in a forest clearing have become too mainstream. For argument's sake, though, we'll pretend that 'couples' are indeed orchestrating their big day, in the spirit of true equality, and ignore the anecdotal evidence provided by celebrants, wedding vendors and brides themselves that shows the vast majority of this work is being done by women because 'they're just better at it'. You know, like laundry and being normal human beings!) A year allows enough time for couples to secure their wedding vendors, lock in a venue, find the perfect dress, select the members of the wedding party, plan the honeymoon and send out their save-the-dates. It also enables the happy duo to have some serious conversations around what kind of wedding they want to have, and what budget is necessary to help them achieve it. To keep on top of it all, Goulding suggests starting a wedding planning binder or an Excel spreadsheet.

Reading Goulding's advice is exhausting. I can't imagine having the time, interest or organisation skills necessary to make a list of party-related obligations let alone assemble an entire binder full of them. To be fair, I'm not exactly a 'planner' and nor have I ever concerned myself with the merits of bonbonnière. I'd have to learn how to use both Excel and a physical binder to be able to use them even halfway correctly, and even then I'd probably just wake up on the day and hope to wing it. It's not that I find *lists* themselves boring and mundane, it's that I can't imagine using them to document seating charts or menu suggestions.

But not for the first time while writing this chapter, I find myself wondering if I'm being mean-spirited. Is this internalised misogyny? Am I baulking not just at weddings, but at the assumption that only *girls* care about weddings? In every other aspect of my life, I'm a fierce defender of girls loving things that other people hate or deride. I froth for make-up and frills. My favourite colour is pink. I call everything 'cute', especially suits worn by men working in the corporate sector. In middle age, I've discovered a fondness for elaborate cushions. I bristle at the insult implicit in people sneering at feminine interests.

Yet I can't defend wedding planning in the same way, because it seems to me to uphold the convenient stereotype that positions marriage as something women are desperate to pin down and men work hard to avoid. It frames the wedding as being *for her*, which makes it seem like a kind of public award ceremony to congratulate her for having a boyfriend, something for which invited guests must give her a prize. If the stereotype is that men generously concede to marriage in order to satisfy the desperate yearning of women, the subtext is that she should at least show her gratitude by taking on all the work involved. You know, just like she'll be expected to do as his lucky, lucky wife!

I'm not the only one who sees it like this. An episode of the podcast *Sounds Like A Cult* explores the feverish mentality of weddings, and posits that one of the reasons so many men do little to nothing to plan their nuptials is precisely *because* it reinforces the idea that the wedding is 'her thing', which paves the way later for him to cash in on something for himself. She got to have that huge, expensive party—it's only fair that he be allowed to buy himself a motorcycle!

Regardless of your own thoughts on party planning, the fact remains that the majority of this work is done by one person. And rather than enjoy this responsibility or even insist on it, when surveyed most of these women report wishing for a greater level of involvement from their future husbands, because—funny story!—working as a team makes people feel loved. It is literally that simple, yet so many men still fail to meet or care about the target.

It seems likely to me that the majority of men who absent themselves from wedding planning do so because they believe on some level that they've already done their part. They proposed, didn't they?! Why should they have to plan something when *she's* the one who cares about it, and they've been kind enough to give it to her? Surely all that's expected of them is to just turn up and go through with it?

Whatever, Clamington, that's just more man-hating hyperbole from the misandrist witch!

Well, you'd be surprised by the things men say as they prepare for marriage. There's one group of people with extensive knowledge of this, and they're more than happy to talk.

You should know, by the way, that your celebrant almost certainly hates the man you're marrying.

———

The moment I announced that I'd be writing this book, I began receiving messages from celebrants keen to share their insight and experiences. Unfortunately, the outlook is pretty grim. Whether they're new to the game or have years of experience under their belt, the general consensus among them backs up what I've already said: not only do people spend far too much money on a single party, but for the most part there will always be one person in the couple who's doing most of, if not all of, the work. And yes, this includes same-sex marriages.

It should be clear by now that I'm mostly concerned with how marriage entrenches gender inequality between men and women while advertising heteronormative goals to queer people, so let's reflect on the chasm of difference between the contribution to wedding organisation made in these dynamics. Although the celebrants I spoke to acknowledged that equality of labour was possible when men *wanted* to take an active part in coordinating the day, the vast majority of men had little to no responsibility aside from turning up (and even then, it's touch and go).

These stories read like fabricated excerpts from *Manhater Weekly*, but I assure you they're all true (and I wish that magazine was, too). In one particularly depressing example relayed to me, the groom managed to shirk his *one* task until it was literally almost too late. Listen—I cannot stress to you enough that if you discover your husband-to-be has waited until the morning of your wedding to BUY HIS SHIRT, then you should take this as a clear indication of just how close to the bottom of his list of priorities you are. This is not a man who will be getting up in the middle of the night to care for his own baby, nor is he someone who will consider it part of his purview to empty dishwashers or scrub toilet bowls. What he will do is expect you to have sex with him despite his lack of effort where you're concerned—though he won't mention this in the Tinder bio where he claims nobly to be staying in his marriage 'for the kids' and not for the domestic labour he enthusiastically exploits.

The laziness displayed by so many grooms, both overt and casual, isn't just limited to logistical demands. Part of any celebrant's journey with a couple is to ask them separately to reflect on what it is they love about their partner. Ideally, their answers will be incorporated into the ceremony as both a sweet surprise for the two people marrying and to add a personal touch for the guests. Again and again, I've been told that women are much more likely to speak proudly about their partner's many attributes and interests, while men are more likely to talk about what kind of domestic tasks she's good at (in the best-case scenarios) or make fun of her (in the worst). For a lot of men, it seems that the concept of love is fairly indistinguishable from a cleaning service.

Now, I've heard some dastardly accounts of men's behaviour towards the women they claim to care for, but even I was shocked by some of these anecdotes. One celebrant recalled a woman who confessed that her future husband—who was already doing nothing to help with organising the wedding—couldn't even be bothered filling out this standard questionnaire, and so she'd had him dictate his answers to her while she wrote them down. She must have felt some degree of humiliation when explaining to the celebrant why the man she called 'the love of her life' was so disengaged from her humanity that he couldn't summon the energy to say a few nice things about her on a pro forma, but women are masters at making excuses for men and their abject uninterest in us and the things we care about.

The worst part? This was his *second* marriage.

This story reminds me of the woman who once told me, with no small amount of embarrassment, about the parenting book she'd bought when she was expecting her first baby. The book was about how to be a good father—but she knew her husband would never read it, so she read it instead and shared with him the parts she thought were useful.

Unbought shirts and ignored forms aside, few things come close to highlighting just how much women have been brainwashed into accepting *anyone* so long as he has a pulse more than the story about a man I shall refer to as Piss Boy. When asked what he loved most about the woman unfortunate enough to be marrying him, he replied that she didn't get upset with him when he drank too much and pissed the bed.

Well might you gag on reading that, but what I find most difficult to wrap my head around isn't the wetting of the bed itself (honestly, my opinion of men is generally so low that this doesn't even surprise me); it is the absolute shamelessness that made him able to report this routine behaviour to a third party with no reflection or self-consciousness at all. Men will confidently state that women having unshaved pits and pubes is a crime against hygiene, and yet have the brazen audacity to treat everything around them—shop walls, pot plants and even their own beds—like an acceptable place to empty their bladder. I guess it's easier when you're not the person charged with cleaning it all up—and we can all agree that even if Piss Boy isn't telling his partner to wash those sheets, she knows that without her intervention he'll just let them dry and keep sleeping in them.

These are the small humiliations that women learn to swallow with a smile, having been programmed by patriarchy to believe that being pissed on by a man while asleep is still better than having no man to piss on you at all.

But the thing about small humiliations is that they bite back. And the more of them you have, the hungrier they become. Every dismissive word, every casual insult, every moment in which it's made clear to you that you don't matter, not really—they all feast on you from the inside out. Your needs will never be considered equal to those of the person you've been told you're so lucky to have, the person who considers *you* lucky to be the one he uses as a footstool each night, and those little servings of disregard and scorn will gorge and gorge until there's nothing left of the things that once made you feel good about yourself. When that happens, it's so much easier to make you believe you owe him even more. Because now you're not just lucky he married you—now you're also lucky he hasn't left.

How many women do you think have stood there on their wedding days, so proud to have secured the thing they were told would be the difference between happiness and despair? How many believed the person they were marrying truly would love and care for them through thick and thin? How many thought this was the start of something amazing, a life spent in partnership and continually evolving love, only to realise later how wrong they were? How many of them recall that girl with the shining eyes and the hope in her heart, standing there in her carefully chosen dress with her perfectly styled hair and thinking that her life, her *real* life, was about to begin, and wish like hell they could scream loud enough across time and space to make her do the one thing that might save her?

Run.

7

HONEY, YOU'RE HOME

'I would strongly advise every woman contemplating sexual union of any kind, never to live together with the man you love, in the sense of renting a house or rooms, and becoming his housekeeper.'

—Voltairine de Cleyre, excerpt from a speech given in Scotland, 1897

I grew up in the nineties, when movies were obsessed with depicting frazzled women rapidly ageing out of their fertile years, career girls with sheer stockings and high heels who were becoming increasingly agitated about when they would meet The One so their life could finally begin.

This fixation on securing a man must have been galling for the women who'd done their service in the feminist trenches of the 1970s. Having fought so hard for the right to leave marriages, to gain rights for single mothers, and to work and earn money for oneself, I can only imagine how frustrating it must have been to see so many of their successors desperate to return to that nuclear home and its white-picket cage.

But those of us who've survived the romantic disappointments of youth forget how persuasive the propaganda machine is, or how seductive the promise of love can be. These were the girls who'd grown up tugging at their increasingly distracted mothers' apron strings during feminism's second wave, delivered finally into a womanhood where they'd been told they could 'have it all', not yet realising that this phrase wasn't coined by feminists to celebrate the gains made by the women's movement, but by men looking to undermine them. Having fallen for the ruse that there was an 'all' that could suddenly be had, modern liberated women would soon discover that emotionally stable, financially independent, socially confident men do not find those attributes similarly charming in a woman, and would deal with the disappointment of this realisation by blaming the feminists who had lied to them about it.

That was your first mistake, girlies! Listening to those bloody man haters! Look how they've gone and made you all *miserable*! Back to the kitchen with you, where you belong.

Did feminism tell women they could 'have it all'? Or was that just something the broader culture settled on to define feminism's purpose, the underlying message designed to make it all sound a bit greedy, a bit domineering, a bit . . . mannish? It seems to me that feminism told women that they should have options and agency, and not be enslaved to the exploitation and demands of men. Bit different, really.

This kind of bait and switch has long been the mechanism by which the defenders of patriarchal rule seek to discredit feminists and the battle for women's liberation. By establishing feminism as the ill-conceived system under which women suffer a deficit of happiness and wellbeing, conservatives intent on preserving patriarchy can more easily tout its credentials as the state in which women's liberation has already been secured. *It's not that we want you women to be unhappy!* they'll insist. *Quite the opposite! We just know better than you what you need in order to* be *happy.*

Then there was the obvious problem of feminism's superiority complex. Because doesn't women 'having it all' mean that men will have less? How can that be fair?! That doesn't sound like a movement for equality to me. That sounds like . . . female SUPREMACY! Men shouldn't have to lose just so women can gain; we'll never solve the battle of the sexes as long as we're in competition with each other; men and women have different skills and therefore different strengths, blah blah blah blah BLAH.

The cynical response to the scraps of freedom women had taken for themselves was exactly as Susan Faludi predicted in her searing polemic, *Backlash*. Published in 1991, *Backlash* articulated in forensic detail all of the mendacious lies and selective arguments the status quo and patriarchy would use to reframe women's liberation as a step backwards for women, from married women agitating for property rights in the nineteenth century to suffragettes fighting for their rights to political agency in the early years of the twentieth century, and then finally the artificial hand-wringing spawned during the second wave over how all of this *freedom* would cause irreparable harm to women's biology, happiness and overall success.

This false concern is a favoured weapon in the fight to keep women from reaching our full potential, as is the pretence that it's not the liberation per se that men hate, but merely the questionable methods used in pursuit of it. You have to remember that the significant successes clawed out by feminism over the last century were done in the face of enormous hostility and violent opposition, not happily dispensed by good-hearted men willing to reward us because we chose the right time of day to ask. Every generation of men has worked their hardest to hold back the rising tide of women's emancipation—not that they'll ever admit this.

One of the most crucial tasks we can undertake as women is to unearth the history of ourselves that has been hidden. Listen to its whispers. Kill the things that you've been taught to believe in, starting with the version of womanhood men have written for us. That is for their reality, not ours.

———

Amid a modern-day nostalgia for a so-called 'simpler time', few things carry more weight than the idea of the traditional family unit. Nestled in suburbia, where the streets are lined with trees and every house boasts a white-picket fence, this era of 'traditional family values' seems to be remembered most fondly by people who weren't there. Still, to hear them tell it, this was a time of great prosperity and even greater happiness. A time when men were men and women thanked them appropriately (and daily) for their service. Everyone had a place and a purpose, and they took pride in fulfilling the duties of their station.

For men, this involved donning a hat in the morning and going out to work in the bustling marketplace of innovation, new technologies and bold ideas. As the family breadwinner, Ron or Jerry or Dick did what he had to do in order to provide for the family depending on him back in the suburban dreamscape. In exchange for his heroic efforts, his wife maintained the home, the children and, most importantly, herself.

These were the roles they were born to play: Dick out building the world in the great beyond, with Jane ensconced at home, building a salmon mousse. As any online historian trained in the field of Making Shit Up will remind you, this is how men and women *have always been*. From the moment our primordial ancestors crawled out of the sea, men have heeded their biological imperative to take charge. Men—who were big and brave and very, very smart, even when they were just wee little fishy things—slithered on ahead to make sure the coast was clear, paving the way for us weak girlies to follow in their wake. As humans evolved from sea boogers into lumbering bipeds, women continued to rely on men for everything—food, protection, comedy—because the notion that we might have something to contribute to humankind's collective survival was obviously absurd. While men hunted for sustenance, we waited by the door to the cave, our lips smeared in berry juice, to greet them on their return.

This ancestral history—which is absolutely, undoubtedly, unquestionably true—is the reason women shouldn't be allowed to work, earn money, drive cars, vote, run for political office, have opinions, disagree with men or *God forbid* remain single. Because we were not *built* to do those things. We were built to be wives and mothers, and to live in nice little enclaves taking care of the needs of men, whose superior (sorry, different) biological make-up right from the very beginning established them as the winners of the bread, and women as the bakers. Feminism can try its hardest to fight biological design, but it's a losing battle. That's why women are so damn *tired* now! Because on top of being naturally geared towards doing all that unpaid, thankless, boring domestic work, they've been told they should go out and have a 'career'. Those silly duffers!

No, what we need is to go back to the Way Things Were. Men have known it all along. That's why they've worked so hard to save us from our dangerous ambitions. Let's be serious: it's not natural for women to work, just like it's not natural for us to have body hair between the ages of whenever men start wanting to fuck us and whenever men stop wanting to fuck us. All this freedom has made us desperately unhappy, and who do we have to blame for that? The bloody feminists, that's who. Men have been out here since forever just trying to do their best by us, and how have we repaid them? By demanding the right to take care of ourselves and have a bit of a go at this 'world building'—as if it's that easy!

The family unit has been absolutely destroyed as a result, and things have gone pear-shaped for everyone. The economy's fucked (feminism's fault for stealing all the jobs from men). Single-mother homes are on the rise (also a result of feminism, because God knows it can't be men running out on their responsibilities). On the other hand, women aren't having anywhere near enough babies, inevitably leading to a catastrophic decline in the population—which is always thinly coded racism for what white supremacists call 'replacement theory'. On the *other* other hand, women are having too much sex, which is ruining their ability to pair-bond (science). The truly nasty/damaged ones even make money from it, shaking their bits on the internet for every man to see (if he pays for it)! Don't they know that men (our protectors) make a clear distinction between the common whores they'll pay to jerk off to and the saintly women good enough to be given marriage for nothing? Good luck finding a husband, Madison! Enjoy that California bungalow you bought outright with all your OnlyFans cash, BECAUSE NO MAN WILL WANT YOU NOW!

In our misguided quest to be considered fully formed humans, women have gone and thrown away everything that made us *happy*. As the beating heart at the centre of the traditional family unit, it was our job to stay on task in order to maintain the circulatory system of the most important of all society's building blocks. Now it's collapsed, chaos has ensued, anarchy is here and we still have to do laundry! This is why they kept us from having any power in the first place—give us an inch of the castle grounds and we'll topple the whole kingdom.

It makes for a good story. But as with most stories told in patriarchy's defence, not a single word of it is true.

———

Ask any (white) man named Steve what the earliest human societies looked like and he'll probably describe some version of that hunter-provider myth. Until well into the twentieth century, most anthropologists and evolutionary biologists agreed with him. In 1975—coincidentally, the same year unmarried, single women in the United Kingdom won the right to have their own bank accounts—the sociobiologist E.O. Wilson compared the financial district of Wall Street to kinship groups living in the African savannah at the dawn of humanity, writing: 'During the day the women and children remain in the residential area while the men forage for game or its symbolic equivalent in the form of money.'

The idea that women have been little more than amorphous slugs feasting on the labour of men has always been a popular one, mainly because it gives legitimacy to the reprehensible erasure of women's vast global contributions to the building of civilisation. Even now, in a period of time routinely pointed to as having secured all the rights to equality women could ever need or want, people still blithely subscribe to this myth as if it a) has any basis in reality, and b) doesn't make them sound like a gigantic twat. Crack even the mildest of jokes about men and you'll be accused of hateful *missssandry*, but it's apparently 'just stating the facts' for Kevin and Randy over at the *Edgelord Podcast Hour* to declare that women were peripheral to evolution because MAN HUNT MEAT.

It's just so depressingly *easy* for people to repeat unfounded garbage, especially when it suits their purposes. I say 'people', because it's not just men who invest in this nonsense, but women, too. Remember the wise words of journalist Celeste Headlee, who once said, 'It's the job of some women to buttress patriarchy, and they're nicely rewarded for their efforts.'

When we think about men's construction of reality, this is a prime example of it. The people (men) given the privilege of *imagining* history and then writing about it were guided solely by their own sense of what seemed possible. We need only think of the supposedly definitive guide to humanity's evolution to see where the selectivity really comes in. *On the Origin of the Species* was published in 1859, a full twenty-three years before the United Kingdom passed the *Married Women's Property Act 1882*. When Daddy Darwin (our 'father' of evolution) asserted women's biological inferiority, he wasn't an outlier in an otherwise progressive society; his views were very much supported and informed by the society he lived in, which held that women were less than men in almost every respect, save for the very specific claim they had (thrust on them by men) to being the moral guardians of the home.

The idea that women have an inherent maternal instinct that supercedes all others was invented in the early twentieth century by psychologist William McDougall. It appeared alongside a list of similar unfounded theories of human instinct in his 1908 book *An Introduction to Social Psychology*. This is the kind of nonsense that gets passed down from generation to generation until it quickly becomes accepted as immutable fact.

What people ignore when they repeat this particular claim of sex-based supremacy (as well as developments in scientific inquiry) is how it contravenes the behaviour of other animal species. As the feminist scholar Carol Gilligan points out, no other life form on the planet is segregated by sex in this way. Sure, you could argue that humans have evolved to make decisions based on social concerns—but this in itself discredits the idea of a biological beginning in which men did everything and women did nothing. Either humans have always conformed to the model of male breadwinner/female homemaker (which seems unlikely, given that the model is an absolute anomaly in the animal world) or humans *evolved into* a society in which men wielded their physical strength to suppress women's power and force us into submission. It can't be both!

And yet, the widespread acceptance of the male breadwinner/ female homemaker origin story remains. This is despite the fact numerous palaeontologists throughout the twentieth century not only challenged it, but found evidence to disprove it. In her definitive history of marriage, Stephanie Coontz points to an anthropologist's observations of a mid-twentieth-century African hunter-gatherer society. In this group, adult women 'typically walked about twelve miles a day gathering food, and brought home anywhere from fifteen to twenty-three pounds [seven to eight kilograms]'. A mother carrying her child in a sling covered the same distance and returned with the same amount of food. Women have always gathered, just as they've always hunted— because groups that work and live communally all contribute to the survival of the tribe. As Coontz points out, humanity's earliest diet didn't include an excessive amount of meat for the sheer fact it was easier to source food from plants, eggs, insects and the sea than it was to hunt large game. The fantasy men have of their Stone Age selves as ripped dudes tearing the flesh of an animal apart with their bare hands is ludicrous. You're an accountant, Jeff. Are you going to bore the wildebeest to death?

Gilligan also argues that early human societies wouldn't have survived if they lived as patriarchy dictates. It was through relational cooperation that evolution was made possible, a fact demonstrated by Aboriginal nations in Australia—and they would know, given they collectively make up the world's oldest surviving civilisation.

Marriage didn't emerge out of a human need for duplex living. Its primary purpose throughout history has been to maintain power. In early civilisations, the power being protected was more likely to do with that of large-scale kinship groups. Growing an economic base assisted in the survival of the whole. As time went on, the beneficiaries of those economic structures were able to operate in smaller units. For example, the development of agricultural methods enabled individuals to amass a much bigger stock of wealth for themselves rather than the broader group. It was this, rather than any kind of innate biological imperative, that created masculine paranoia around the legitimacy of their heirs. If you'd worked that bloody hard to get this whopping pile of land and all the money it brought, you developed an urge to keep it in the family. 'Marriage'—and originally even that just meant sexual relations between members of the same tribe or as a form of trade to secure friendships and therefore peace with other tribes—was traditionally about survival *of the group*. The changing nature of economics and small-scale living shifted its priorities, until it became about securing family wealth.

It remained this way for centuries, with marriage—however disempowered and brutalised women were within it—understood as a business arrangement whose intention was to grow and preserve a family's economic wealth. Sure, people had always fallen in love. But love as a necessary precursor to the legal union was considered unnecessary. In fact, people were warned against seeking love as part of the matrimonial contract, because the volatility and transient nature of love could only threaten rather than strengthen it. In the early nineteenth century, young people (who, like feminists, are always blamed for ruining society—high five, young people!) began to romanticise the idea of a marriage based on love. A new form of 'companionate marriage' emerged, one that horrified older generations who, having had a bit of life experience, clearly understood that houses built with sand are prone to collapse into the ocean.

Annoyingly for the young folk, it turned out their elders weren't all that far off the mark. The rise in companionate marriages led almost immediately to a rise in the divorce rate. And we're not talking about the 1970s here, when feminists won the right to no-fault divorce. We're talking the *1870s*, when 0.3 out of every thousand marriages ended in the big D. Sure, it was still lower than would be seen a century later (in 1970, five out of every thousand American marriages ended in divorce), but this was largely due to the fact that a legal divorce was harder to obtain (unless you had a lot of money) and was still considered taboo. That didn't stop some women (at least, those who had the means) from doing what they could to free themselves from unhappy unions. In turn-of-the-century America, the phrase 'going to Sioux Falls' became code for 'getting a divorce', because South Dakota was the easiest (if also the most expensive) place for a rich, white woman to escape the bonds of a marriage she didn't want. As the late-nineteenth-century anarchist and marriage abolitionist Voltairine de Cleyre so cleverly said, 'I don't need to prove to you that marriages make people unhappy; we have the divorce rate for that.'

Much to the chagrin of misogynists everywhere, I guess it turns out that feminism isn't responsible for the divorce rate after all—it's freedom.

And that's progress, baby.

———

Characterising male breadwinner/female homemaker family units as 'traditional' might appeal to the chronically ill-read, but it's little more than misplaced nostalgia for a time that never really existed. Central to this nostalgia is the Feminine Woman who, much like nineteenth-century English poet Coventry Patmore's saccharine image of the 'angel of the house', floats around in the background of life. She knows never to put herself in the centre of the action—the speaking parts of the play are always for the men—but her delicate grace and unimpeachable morality has seen her placed on the highest of pedestals, and the light she emits from there does the important work of illuminating all their stories.

Called upon by her biology to endlessly nurture the people around her, the Feminine Woman lives only for others. If she can be said to have any needs at all, they exist only in the sense that she must be *needed*. The more she sacrifices of herself, the happier she is. Having ambitions beyond the domestic sphere is a sign of something untoward in women. She will either be too mannish or too arrogant, or both—a combination which ought to be considered a crime against humanity (and certainly is, depending on who you ask).

So deeply entrenched has the figure of the Feminine Woman become that people today—usually, but not exclusively, men— still speak of her as the natural embodiment of womanhood. She is how women have *always been*, notwithstanding the parts of history inconvenient to this narrative, when women were by their very natures sluts, witches, crones, shrews, infantile and constantly out for revenge. But while those tropes still remain very much in play, the Victorian era's creation of the Feminine Woman outstrips them all—because unlike those tropes, which reflect at least a nominal diversity of women's character traits and our very real (and sometimes admirable) capacity to act in our own self-interest, the Feminine Woman doesn't exist at all. She's a blank slate for whatever morally superior virtue men want to project onto her: an innocent virgin, a doe-eyed young bride, a submissive lover who allows herself to be guided by experience, an encouraging wife and finally, above all, a doting mother.

One of the many (many) sins of feminism has been the cold-blooded annihilation of this much-admired figure, to the detriment of women everywhere. Without the Feminine Woman to guide our own moral centres, we have been left rudderless, without direction and disconnected from our true selves. Feminism has filled our heads with nonsense and left us adrift on the Sea of Unhappiness, unable to find our way back to the one thing that will restore equilibrium not just to our spirits but to the world itself: devotion to others instead of ourselves.

That there's no biological evidence to support this claim of a caretaking martyrdom unique to women is irrelevant, as is the fact it's only been in circulation for around two hundred years. After all, 'everyone knows it', which is enough to make it an incontrovertible truth. When Rodney Fuckerbag turns the lilac lights on in his kitchen and films himself offering 'life coach' advice to men who'd rather steam iron their own ballsacks before talking to a woman like a human being, he'll undoubtedly waffle on at some point about this 'loss of femininity', and how it's feminism that's caused us to abandon our true nature and wallow in misery. Fuckerbag's grandmother knew what it meant to be a 'real woman', and she *loved* it. But the blue-haired, hairy-pitted frightbats of today seem to be doing everything they can to repel men (yes, correct) and *it's just brazen destruction of the traditional family unit*!

An incomplete list of the things feminism is responsible for, according to Rodney Fuckerbag:

Women being ugly
Women having too much sex
Women rejecting marriage
Women entering the workforce
Women being depressed and unhappy

The Feminine Woman would never dream of doing any of these things, which is how we know they must be the fault of a nefarious outside force (feminism!).

Let's look at each of these claims in turn—not for the purpose of legitimising them, obviously, but to give you, the reader, more of a solid historical basis from which to tell Mr Fuckerbag that he's a dickwad.

FEMINISM MADE WOMEN UGLY

In reserving the right to construct reality, men also reserve the right to decide who's allowed access to that reality. Patriarchy has always closely guarded the parameters of acceptable woman-hood—acceptable womanhood being first and foremost the kind that caters to male authority. Feminism actively works to dismantle patriarchy, rules and all, which makes the women who subscribe to it ugly by patriarchy's standards. Ugliness is therefore one of the greatest sins a woman can commit against patriarchy and the men within it, because it diminishes her use to the system. And she'll be considered ugly regardless of whether or not her appearance conforms to ideals of beauty, because men still believe that to call a woman ugly is the ultimate burn.

FEMINISM MADE WOMEN FUCK TOO MUCH

Current discourse among the maladjusted misogynists of the world—and I use the word 'discourse' extremely lightly—is disturbingly fixated on the idea of a woman's 'body count'. That is to say, how many people she's slept with. Proving once again that all ideas are recycled, especially bad ones, women who sleep with *too many men* are dirty, defiled, gross, damaged and deserving of absolutely zero respect. You can fuck her, sure—but you wouldn't want to actually *date* her.

The fact that the men holding forth on these issues think they'd even have a shot is hilarious, but why let reality get in the way of a good male power fantasy? Women who've had too much sex ~~might know you're bad at it~~ can't be allowed to live freely, because they're 'damaging their ability to pair-bond'. This is on the bingo card of things dumdum men say with unwavering confidence, because they heard other men say it and thought it sounded good.

I'd love for feminism to take credit for unleashing women's sexual appetites, but it's unfortunately not true. For a start, we have all those dead witches and their penis trees to reckon with. But secondly, if women have ever not fucked freely, it's because the risks to their livelihood were too great. Pregnancy, damaged reputations, scandals—patriarchy has made it impossible for women who have something to lose to explore sex without putting themselves in harm's way. And I say, 'women with something to lose', because of course we're just talking about a certain kind of woman here—in fact, with all of these bullshit FEMINISM HAS DESTROYED! claims, we're only ever talking about a certain kind of woman. She is almost always white and almost always middle class and above. Throughout history, men have never given a single shit about the women whose virtue and humanity they consider well below their own. Black women subjugated by racism, enslavement and dehumanising ideas about their own carnal natures (drawn from eugenicist 'fathers' of science, who proclaimed the intellectual and moral supremacy of whiteness) have had neither their rights to their own bodies upheld nor their rights to their own babies, and even today are much more likely to be subjected to the violence of the legal, judicial and health-care systems than white women. Sex workers, poor women and disabled women have similarly been denied humanity and control over their bodies, and are rarely—if ever—protected from the determination some men have to assume it for themselves. The only people afforded this dubious kind of 'protection' are white women of a certain standing—because these are the women whom men want to reserve for *wifehood*, when they've finished 'running through' the women whom they see as being practice grounds for their own carnal urges and entitlement to fuck 'too much'. So what they mean is: 'The unnamed, as yet invisible woman I plan on marrying must not fuck at all, because when I commit to taking on a wife, I want her to be in pristine condition.'

Bad news for you, weenies. Women fuck. And women started fucking freely long before late-stage twentieth-century feminism got their hooks into them. The 1920s was a hotbed of women's sexual conquests, erotic awakenings and girls getting up to well-deserved mischief. Your 'traditional' 1950s woman was most likely the daughter of someone who knew what an orgasm was.

Maybe that's what really scares you about the sexually liberated women you despise.

FEMINISM MAKES WOMEN REJECT MARRIAGE

As the conservative Christian media mogul Pat Robertson said before he went to hell, 'Feminism encourages women to leave their husbands, kill their children, practice witchcraft, destroy capitalism and become lesbians.'

Correct!

I mean, all of that does sound perfectly reasonable and exciting. But I don't think old Patty Cake felt that way!

Suffice to say, men are still *very scared* about women rejecting marriage and devoting ourselves to lives entirely of our own making. Give a man a fish and you'll feed him for a day. Teach a man to fish, and he'll still find a way to blame women for wanting to feed themselves.

The truth most men don't want to face up to is that feminism can't make women do anything. If women are rejecting marriage—and they are, overwhelmingly—it's because *men* have proven to be completely subpar. YOU ARE NOT A GOOD OPTION. Get it?

But it's so much easier to blame a political movement, especially one that *has* succeeded in teaching women to see through the patriarchal reality that's been constructed around them. Feminism teaches women to value themselves, and to seek solidarity and community with each other. It teaches women that we matter in the world. That we have identities and inner voices that deserve to be heard, especially by ourselves. Beyond this, feminism encourages women to work towards dismantling oppressive systems and ending violence—and hey, if more women are rejecting marriage and the men who expect to be waited on hand and foot within it, then maybe that's telling you something, fellas.

Again, though, these things are not new. Women have always rejected marriage. They may not have succeeded in escaping it, but women have fought against the institution for as long as it's existed. It has always been a cage—feminism has just helped women see they're trapped in one.

FEMINISM MADE WOMEN WORK

The idea that second-wave feminism of the early 1960s and ensuing decades created working women is common, and because of that we can also say it's a testament to the insufficiency of our education systems. Women have always worked—all second-wave feminism did was expose the nature of the conditions under which women worked, and advocate for equal opportunities with men within that labour system.

Why does this fiction of the labourless woman persist? In part, it's because people are wilfully ignorant and totally uncurious about history. It's also because, once again, it depends on the *kind* of woman you're talking about. Even some feminists mistakenly attempt to highlight historical oppression by saying things like, 'Well, that's just because women weren't allowed to work.'

Wrong!

Women have been integral to industry. And not just as unpaid domestic labourers (although this is true, too), but as paid workers. The money might have been terrible (deliberately so) and the opportunities much scarcer than those available to men (also deliberate, but occasionally in our favour—not being conscripted in wartime was pretty good, to be honest), but women of certain socioeconomic backgrounds have *always worked*. What do you call the paid domestic staff working for upper-crust toffs, scrubbing floors from morning until night? This was and is work, and it shouldn't be effaced to make for a narrative that only includes the most privileged women among us. And what about the young single women in the late nineteenth century who went to work in textile factories in search of freedom and financial independence? The textile export industry was what kept America afloat at the turn of the century, and we have young working-class women to thank for that!

But the image of the Feminine Woman and her devotion to domesticity persists. And it erases one key historical moment in the *establishment* of that Victorian-era house angel. To understand how she evolved, we really need to look at the impact of the Industrial Revolution. There's no doubt the industrialisation of the world's labour force led to some pretty amazing advances in technology and manufacturing. Of course, none of them seemed to involve an adequate number of pockets for women—but on the plus side we have elasticated waistbands now, so that's something. But the mass migration from localised work into factories led to seismic shifts in the way communities (and families in particular) worked and operated. Prior to the Industrial Revolution, people in Europe and colonised America lived in agrarian societies. The aristocracy might not have worked all that hard, but everyone outside of it—men, women and children—certainly did. Whether as butchers, bakers or candlestick makers, everyone had a job to do that kept society ticking over. As I've already noted, modern conservatives love to fantasise about history as a softly lit dreamscape, when women eagerly embraced the roles of wife and mother while hubby hi-hoed off to work each day, though the reality was a lot less *Leave It to Beaver* than this.

But here's the thing. Even during the *Leave It to Beaver* heyday of the 1950s, women worked. And that included middle-class women. In fact, between 1940 and 1960, there was a 400 per cent increase in the number of American working mothers. In total contradiction to the oft-cited nonsense of 'traditional marriage' and its sparkly-eyed, apron-wearing wives just so *thrilled* to be using their new oven for the first time and waiting for hubby's car to pull into the drive, married women actually accounted for the greatest number of women working in paid employment during the 1950s. Why? Because there were so many more of them than there were single women, and the postwar boom had delivered a raft of jobs deemed 'too feminine' for men to do. Things like clerical work, care work and service work. Y'know, girl shit.

On top of that, the GI Bill had promised a pension to returned servicemen. But despite it being one of the biggest welfare programs in American history (in fact, almost all welfare programs demonised in America today began as welfare for 'respectable' white people), it wasn't enough to actually 'provide' for a family as a single income, so married women and mothers worked to supplement it.

Say, that looks an awful lot like women providing and protecting!

The postwar boom had injected huge amounts of money into economies all across the world, but nothing lasts forever— especially not economic boom times. In the 1970s, the days of wine and roses gave way to the biggest economic recession seen since World War I, leading to yet another influx of women entering the paid workforce. Families could no longer survive on one wage, and so women rolled up their sleeves and did what they could to pitch in.

This is what really grinds my gears about the stupidity of the conservative wing nuts and the embarrassing little trad wives who get paid big bucks to speak out against women earning incomes for themselves—it's that they actually don't know what they're talking about, and they're too fucking *lazy* to bother educating themselves. While feminism may have responded to the conditions of the work women were finally able to do (but in many cases had no choice in), it didn't create the capitalist conditions under which this work was deemed necessary for survival. What feminism and its tireless, brave, hardline and fucking ferocious advocates did was fight for laws to protect women from sexual harassment, wage discrimination, maternal discrimination and unfair dismissal. Feminism also fought for women to strive for greater status in the workforce—to be paid an equal wage and to have the opportunity to lead. To suggest that in going to work to *save* their families somehow *destroyed the family unit* is a fucking insult designed to conceal the truth behind the claimants' fury—that women unleashed from the boundaries of the home found that they actually *loved* being out in the world. That work brought them satisfaction and purpose. That they liked having their own money. And that, within a few short years of this labour shift occurring, more women than ever before began to report they would continue to work even if their financial situations didn't demand it.

That was fifty years ago, and nothing has changed. Men just do not pull for their families the way women do. That's what feminism has exposed, and that's why women are leaving men. If you're feeling overwhelmed when trying to balance work and domestic tasks, I've got news for you: it isn't because feminism's failing you—it's because your loser husband is. Women do not leave men who step up. They leave men who drag down.

FEMINISM MAKES WOMEN DEPRESSED AND UNHAPPY

Men love to blame feminism for women's unhappiness, I guess because it's easier than accepting their own shortcomings. In a way, maybe it's true. Feminism *does* increase a woman's chance of unhappiness, largely because it's impossible to unsee what feminism exposes. Once you know how artificial patriarchal reality is, you can't go back to believing in it anymore. Once you see how much men hate you, or at least see you as interchange-able with other women performing their role, it's hard not to feel demoralised about the conditions of your life. Women have always been made unhappy by seeing the extent of men's exploitation of them. But that's never stopped men from doing it.

Depressed women weren't created by feminism, just as the workplace wasn't. If that were the case, there wouldn't have been any need for all those asylums men threw us into. Women's domestic depression is much older than Germaine Greer and equal rights at work. To understand why, we again need to go back to the Industrial Revolution. The creation of a marketplace that existed beyond the domestic sphere succeeded in permanently shifting the home from its traditional role as a place of public production and recasting it as a place of private refuge. Prior to the Industrial Revolution, people—and that included married couples—worked at home. The domestic space itself was a place of work, and there was no real distinction between that and home. The creation of two separate marketplaces changed all that.

For most women, work went on as normal. There was probably a lot more of it, with no home staff to cover domestic duties that would have ordinarily formed part of the day. But for the newly established middle class (mostly white women, the protected species of conservative societies everywhere but only as long as they commit to upholding them), the sudden absence of production was felt keenly. Far from nurture and maternal instinct being the gas that keeps women going, there was suddenly *fuck all to do*. And the glut of activity and purpose hit them hard.

As Barbara Ehrenreich and Deirdre English write in *For Her Own Good: Two centuries of the experts' advice to women*, the inertia suddenly thrust upon women used to being active, purposeful and *productive* had a terrible effect. Hotly debated among (male) physicians as *the woman problem* (what to do, what to do!), it gave rise to fierce depressions, long stints in bed and feelings of listlessness that couldn't be shaken. Charlotte Perkins Gilman shared her own experience of this in her 1892 domestic horror story, 'The Yellow Wallpaper'. Almost a century later, Betty Friedan catalogued American women's spiritual malaise in her 1963 book, *The Feminine Mystique*, exposing the dissatisfaction of women who had been encouraged to aspire to homemaking as a sign of status only to find it empty of all meaning. In the 1960s, Valium (aka 'Mother's Little Helper') was introduced to the American market, and for the next twenty years it would be the most prescribed medication in the country, just as laudanum had been prescribed (in excess) almost a century earlier to treat the wandering women, with their wandering wombs.

Feminism didn't invent burnout, capitalism did, just as patriarchy entrenches the view that domestic work is women's responsibility regardless of whether—and perhaps especially if— she is also bringing in an income. It's true that women are tired. But that's not because they were somehow tricked into working. Women are tired because they went out to work to alleviate the financial pressure weighing on men, but men did not recipro- cate in the home to alleviate the domestic pressure inflicted on women. Can women have it all? We certainly get the lion's share of the work, and none of the freedoms men claim for themselves.

Welcome to marriage. Look around. What do you see?

Honey, you're home.

SOMETHING BORROWED

'Hope is the thing with feathers—

That perches in the soul—

And sings the tune without the words—

And never stops—at all—'

—Emily Dickinson, *The Complete Poems of Emily Dickinson*

8

YOUR FATHER'S NAME

'A wife should no more take her husband's name than he should hers. My name is my identity and must not be lost.'

—Motto of the Lucy Stone League, founded in 1921

A few months after my sister married her second husband, I noticed that she'd changed her last name on Facebook to match his. I was repulsed, and messaged her immediately. *What the fuck are you doing?!* I demanded to know, exercising my right as a little sister to be completely obnoxious.

'Relax,' she replied. 'I was just trying it out.'

'You're not going to keep it, are you?' I asked, leaving no doubt as to my opinion on the matter.

'God no,' she said. 'I only did it because ___ has been hassling me about it.'

I'd noticed that her husband (now ex, thankfully) had liked the post, which had turned my stomach. I found him intolerable at the best of times, but there was something especially irritating about his public claim to her identity. She had a name already, and it happened to be the one we both shared with our dead mother. The thought of her abandoning it for some . . . *man* . . . was galling. Thankfully, the experiment was short-lived. After she reverted back, she told me her husband had thrown a mini tantrum about it, complaining that her refusal to take his name meant she wasn't committed to the marriage. If we could harness male fragility and turn it into an energy source, we could finally build that sun cannon in the desert.

Where marriage is concerned, the issue of names carries an absurd amount of weight. But if you ever want to throw yourself into a completely pointless fight, preferably with strangers, can I recommend you take to the internet to post an utterly benign statement about how the practice of becoming Mrs Goofball after marriage is anachronistic and questionable. I guarantee you that your day will be spent fielding defensive replies from women either angry that you've undermined their *choice* (the individual provision of which is apparently the singular focus of feminism) or insistent that you recognise *their* reasons for doing so were exceptional. If it's a dopamine rush you're looking for, this is where you'll find it.

For women who continue to be compelled by the cultural narrative that marriage promises (but rarely delivers on), the question of whether or not she'll take 'his name' will be frequently raised. Despite living in a post-feminist world in which gender oppression is merely the whisper of a bygone era (at least according to the men who bombard my inbox each week), the cult-like practice of women taking their husband's name after marriage remains relatively steadfast. As recently as 2022, American data revealed between 70 and 80 per cent of women in heterosexual marriages changed their names. The reasons cited vary, with the most common including a dislike for one's family of origin, an overabundance of names that are apparently terribly difficult to spell, respect for a husband's cultural ties, or just a general ambivalence to one's own moniker. But by far the most common reason is this: *It was important to us that we all be a family, and I wanted to have the same last name as my children.*

Now, I'm not suggesting there's no truth to any of these factors, but let's address the elephant in the room: the reason most women rush to be Mrs Goofball isn't because they hate the sound of their own last name or they're sick of repeating it over the phone (how often does that happen to any of us really?) or even that 'it's just easier': it's because marriage as a patriarchal institution still holds enormous cultural sway (and performing each and every one of its most public rituals is a way to make the marriage seem stronger and more romantic than it actually is), and because *men like it.*

That's not a judgement, merely a fact. I'm as susceptible to this messaging as anyone else; a recent conversation with an old boyfriend reminded me (humiliatingly!) that I once romanticised the idea of branding myself as part of *his* family rather than retaining a foothold in my own. I was telling him about this book, becoming increasingly agitated as I described the expectations of fealty still placed on women who marry men. He sat there patiently while I ranted, recounting the history of coverture, citizenship and how insulting it was to hear the administrative defence that 'it's just easier', not to mention the insult of women just absorbing the idea that their children would automatically be blessed with the name of a man who'd had to give up nothing to grow them and most likely would give up even less to raise them.

I finished with the emphatic declaration that *I would NEVER take a man's name.* Not me—never in a million years!

'You know, Clem,' he responded, 'I remember a time when you said you would take my last name if we ever got married.'

I stared at him, horrified. 'That can't possibly be true.'

'Yep,' he said. 'You said you'd take my name, but that if we had kids and one of them was a boy, you'd call him Ford.'

I opened my mouth to deny this, and then paused. We had dated seriously when we were in our early twenties, which is basically the same as saying we'd dated when we were fetuses. It *did* sound like the kind of bollocks I might have said when I was a newly gestating human and enjoying the feeling of watching myself be in love. I'm sure I would have framed it as progressive at the time, probably preparing to brag about it in the same way people do their alternative weddings.

Oh, our wedding? Well, of course we wanted it to be really unique. *We had a selection of food trucks and our celebrant wore roller-skates, and we arrived at the ceremony in a kayak made out of cheese.*

I imagined myself as a young woman, thinking about being introduced as Clementine Goofball, proudly declaring to the new world I had stepped into that I was loved. These were the days before social media had really taken off, but I'm sure I would have been thrilled by the prospect of being able to announce this new identity via a coy name change to my Facebook account—the same thing I'd felt so disgusted by seeing my sister do. Of course, being a feminist and a Cool Bride, I would have made sure everyone knew I'd be keeping some semblance of my former self in the already-chosen name of my future (male) child.

How humiliating! I'd buried the memory so as not to be reminded of the cringiness of youth, the same way one might burn an old diary or a folder full of black and white photographs titled, 'Feet'.

'Well,' I said to my former lover, 'aren't we lucky we didn't get married? Because that makes me feel absolutely disgusting.'

He laughed. 'Very lucky,' he agreed.

Romance propaganda can impact us all, it seems, even those of us who've sworn off marriage. Had I married my then-boyfriend and thrown myself into the performance of being Somebody's Wife, I would have found myself a divorced thirty-something with a name that no longer had resonance for me but that I might have felt trapped into keeping just so that I could say, 'This way, I still have the same last name as my son, Ford Goofball.'

How many women make 'choices' about their lives, relationships and identities that aren't really choices at all but a line or direction in a cultural script they've been watching play out over and over their whole lives? When we're young, the imperative to be chosen for marriage is more than just aspirational—it's the confirmation that we're *somebody* in the world. We're bombarded with the message that to be a woman alone is to be nothing much at all. We're merely detritus adrift on the ocean and constantly in search of a shore on which to wash up so that we might be useful for whoever finds us there. Becoming a wife and a mother is what elevates us into our higher purpose which, ironically, so often involves us becoming the lowly foundations on which men are supported to achieve *their* purpose. This, we are told ad infinitum, is the only way we can achieve true happiness.

Even now, those of us who resist this messaging are met with backlash that ranges from simple confusion ('but don't you want to be happy?') to dismissal ('you'll change your mind one day') to enticement by virtue of personal comparison ('it's possible to find a good man; my husband is amazing!'). Dare to express these sentiments online and you'll be swiftly reminded that women *don't get to decide what's good for us*. It's as if a tractor beam sweeps out across the city the moment a woman pops up to say, 'Not for me, thanks!' Men, enraged by the thought that a woman might not consider a lifetime of domestic service an appealing option, will roll up to scream abuse at her. Cats, wine, misery, old age, nursing homes, no visitors, ugly, no one wants you, who hurt you, see if us men care, you women are the ones who need marriage, selfish, pair-bonding, body count, dried up past thirty, spinster, enjoy your sad shitty life in your one-bedroom flat you old hag—I mean, you can really take your pick from the bingo card of Things Men Say To Women Who Don't Want Them.

I get that people make choices and want to defend them. But no choice is made in a vacuum, and it's essential that we question *this* choice and how it operates to construct a reality for women in which we are always expected to diminish ourselves 'for love'.

Your name won't be the only part of yourself and your identity that you give up in your marriage, but it's definitely expected of you. Navigating the path that will best ensure your survival within a system that wants to undermine and diminish you may be an effective way to secure some kind of power, but it isn't liberation—no matter what name you choose to put on it.

———

Well, that's all very well and good, you might be thinking. But *I* took my husband's name, and I don't feel oppressed by it. I wanted to do it! It was my *choice*. And isn't feminism about choice?

First, feminism is not about choice. Feminism is about liberating the world from patriarchy, the primary victims of which are women. Making choice the basis for a political framework is an unworkable approach to real political change, because it makes everything defensible and nothing subject to critique. 'Choice' is a meaningful and essential goal when it comes to dismantling how women are *oppressed*, but not all choices are the same.

For example, all people with the capacity to become pregnant must have reproductive choice and agency if they are to be free. Access to abortion health care is a liberator, and insisting on people's right to access this choice is a fundamental tenet of feminism. If women are oppressed on the basis of reproductive capacity—and arguing this is a moot point, given that we are and always have been, as demonstrated by the historical fear of wandering wombs, the witch trials targeting midwives, anti-abortion legislation and enforced reproductive service—then wresting back control over our reproductive capacity is integral to ending that oppression. The choice to continue a pregnancy is also essential to feminist liberation; forced sterilisation is still used as a tool of reproductive violence, as is the forced removal of children at birth or beyond because the state has decided *it* gets to control which of the women they force to have children are allowed to *keep* children.

But while some choices liberate people from oppression, others impose harm, especially when they necessarily involve the subjugation of another person. If I 'choose' to become a fast fashion influencer, making money by partnering with companies like Pretty Little Thing or ASOS, does that make my choice feminist? And in claiming that this choice is feminist, by virtue of the fact that a woman (me) is benefiting from it, does that make it an *unfeminist* act to critique that choice? Of course not! Fast fashion wreaks untold damage on the world, not just environmentally but also in its insatiably capitalist exploitation of workers (80 per cent of garment factory workers are women) and communities in the global south. The women who work in those factories for a pittance, with no guaranteed workplace safety and high incidents of abuse and sexual harassment, churning out the clothes that help to line the wardrobes of consumers (not to mention the pockets of influencers) aren't liberated by Kourtney Kardashian or Hailey Bieber's entrepreneurial skills. The use of 'choice' as a defence against feminist critique is harmful because it renders all feminist critique null and void. Choice alone isn't feminist just because a woman made it. That's incredibly infantilising, and suggests that women should be cheered on for every little thing we do, even when it's relentlessly prioritising our own privileges.

I'm not saying that taking your husband's name has the same impact as exploiting garment workers. Obviously the two are incomparable. But I do think it's fair to say that participating in the capitalist institution of marriage and all its bells and whistles— *including* the practice of being romantically 'blessed' with a man's name—feeds that capitalist machine. Marriage is overwhelmingly an exercise in consumption, from the ring to the engagement party to the wedding and all its disposable products, and then everything that comes after it (because a family needs a car or maybe two, and a four-bedroom house and brand-new things for the kiddies and annual holidays and and and . . .).

Apart from anything else, we should be robust enough to consider why it is we make the choices we do, and how we come to the conclusion that they're the things we want. How many women who insist they *chose* to change their name can really say they would have made that choice if they hadn't already been socialised into a system that has not only expected women to be the ones to do so but for centuries actually legally enforced this?

Leaving aside for a moment the fact that, for the vast majority of human history, marriage itself has not been a choice women were able to make freely. The law of coverture was formalised as a legal doctrine in Britain in 1753, when a judge named Sir William Blackstone (another male expert!) wrote that 'the very being, or legal existence of the woman, is suspended during the marriage, or at least is consolidated and incorporated into that of her husband: under whose wing, protection and cover, she performs everything'.

Under the legal principle of coverture, a woman had no identity. When a girl was born, she was considered the legal property of her father. As her owner, he could decide what happened to her—including who would become her next owner, aka her husband. To symbolise the new acquisition to his property port-folio, a man would 'give' his name to his wife. This is just a fancy way of saying that she was forced to take his name, because the law dictated that she wasn't allowed anything for herself. Not her money, not her clothes, not even her own kids. This last point is particularly grotesque. Long before the introduction of no-fault divorce, women could find themselves trapped in marriages that were abusive not just because they had no legal right to their own freedom but because they had no legal right to *their own children.*

This was the way of the world, an accepted part of civilised human life. Men owned women, and they branded them with their names to let other men know the state of play. When we speak about 'choice' now as a legitimate defence in the choosing of a 'family name', we can't and shouldn't ignore the history of the practice. We can't and shouldn't ignore the countless now-invisible women who *didn't* have that same choice, but instead had it forced upon them the way they were also expected, right up until the late twentieth century, to endure their husbands forcing themselves on them as part of their 'conjugal rights'.

Because this is the thing: although the legal aspects of cover-ture started to run out of puff with the introduction of the *Married Women's Property Act 1882*, the legacy of the practice can still be felt even today. Every time the bank sends you a letter addressed to 'Mr and Mrs Goofball', this is coverture. Every time your in-laws or family members insist on addressing you by your husband's last name, even if you didn't actually take it, this is coverture. When a lending institution insists on putting your husband's name as the primary borrower and yours as the co-borrower, this is coverture. When mechanics or tradespeople ask to speak to 'the man of the house' in order to confirm that he has, in fact, approved your requests, this is coverture. When medical professionals refuse to perform tubal ligations without the permission of husbands, it's coverture. For fuck's sake, even *single* women who seek tubal ligations or hysterectomies are often told to think about the invisible future husband who's being denied a say over the womb he partially owns.

Men who kill their wives believe in their hearts that these women *belong* to them. That's a legacy of coverture, too.

Every little act that treats a woman like she's the property of her husband, even though the law technically says otherwise, is the remnant of centuries worth of a legal doctrine in which women *were* unequivocally considered to be the property of their husbands and as such entirely without the right to assert anything of their own identity.

Yeah, but marriage today isn't about ownership! It's about the merging of souls, two people becoming one unit, a *family*.

A good, strong family needs a good, strong name. And, hey . . . yours is just your father's anyway. What's the big deal?

It's just your father's name.

Honestly, if I have to hear this argument one more time, I think I'll scream.

Let's unpack this. In fact, let's unpack all the arguments around 'choice', starting with this, the most annoying one.

YOU'VE GOT YOUR FATHER'S NAME ANYWAY, SO WHAT'S THE DIFFERENCE?

For at least the last one thousand years in the western world (bearing in mind that many parts of the world follow matronymic naming protocols) most women up to now have been given their father's name at birth. We can talk in a moment about changing that practice, but for now let's just accept that it's generally how things go.

Do you know who else has their father's name? Men. But they have something else that women, as a general rule, are not blessed with—they have the privilege and luxury of owning that name for themselves. No one looks at a boy child and imagines a future for him in which he and the blank slate of his identity go into the world to find their forever home. Men own their names from the moment they're given to them, with the expectation being that they'll go and find someone 'worthy' to bestow it on. When people say, 'What's the big deal? It's just your father's name anyway,' they don't think they're telling you to choose between keeping your own father's name or your husband's father's name, because your husband's name isn't on loan to him in the same way yours is. The moment they're born, boys enter a proudly patriarchal lineage in which they 'carry the name on'. It's theirs. They own it. Now go out and make me proud, son! They may be one in a long line of many, but they also get to be front and centre in the families they assemble *beneath* that name.

It's not the same for women. I may have been given the name 'Ford' when I was born, but in the eyes of some people I will never *own* that name in the same way my brother does. He doesn't have his father's name; he has *his* name. And if his wife had chosen to take it when they married (she didn't, because she's cool), she would have had *his* name, too, not his father's.

Why is the choice between your father's name and the name of some other guy? It's *my* name. I was born with it. I have made my way in the world with it. Why don't I get to own it the way a man does? The idea that women have transitional identities stands in opposition to the reality that we are whole, rounded creatures who exist in our own separate right. To marry would already take my freedom from me—I'll be fucked if I'd ever let it take my name, too.

IT WAS JUST EASIER TO CHANGE IT

Actually, the easiest thing to do in any situation is usually nothing. Keeping your own name means avoiding annoying administrative tasks across a range of different bureaucracies, because keeping your name means *you don't have to do anything different*! What people mean when they say 'it was just easier to change it' is this: it was just easier to conform to what was expected of me than to have to keep explaining to people why I didn't want to change it; or it is easier for me to say that than to have to admit to *you* that I have bought into the whole romantic fantasy of being *given* a man's name.

Changing your name might be easier than dealing with the onslaught of criticism from people who think women are supposed to do so in order to legitimise their role as a wife, but it *isn't* actually simple for a woman to change her name rather than not. What is true is that this 'choice' is easier for her than it is for her husband, both socially and legally. In 2013, a Florida man found himself being charged with fraud for impersonating another person on his driver's licence—because he had changed his name to his wife's after they married. Lazaro Dinh (who took his Vietnamese wife's last name as an 'act of love' and a way to honour her culture) was told that Floridian law didn't allow him to do this. In fact, only nine states in America allow a man to change his name on marriage the way a woman can, while other states deliberately discourage the practice by requiring additional paperwork and charging exorbitant fees.

Can choice really be choice when it isn't provided to all genders equally? Even though it seems rare to find men like Dinh who have 'no particular emotional ties to [their] last name' and are willing to change it, most will find themselves up against some kind of obstacle if they attempt it. That might be in the form of additional administrative hurdles, but it's just as likely to be in the reactions of their friends and family. What kind of man would take a *woman's* name? And not just her name, but her father's name! *Another man's* name! GAY. We know who wears the pants there! Give her your balls, too!

If the issue of names in marriage were truly a choice *and* if it were really that easy, we would see more men opting to take their wives' names. After all, it's not as if men don't also hate their fathers, have difficult-to-spell last names or want the same last name as their children. But no, they are not making this 'choice' in the same numbers as women—and this disparity makes it rather less of an equal choice and rather more of a gendered practice.

IT'S TRADITIONAL

Nah. It may form part of Anglo-Celtic tradition now (in many eastern and Arab countries women keep their names after marriage), but it wasn't always so. In fact, it didn't even become 'a thing' until the twelfth century—and it wasn't until around four hundred years later that marriage was presided over by a member of the clergy. 'Tradition' is not quite as unwavering as people think.

MY NAME IS REALLY DIFFICULT TO SPELL

Around 90 per cent of the time, I have to spell 'Clementine' for people. How often am I required to tell people my name in the first place? Not that much. Beyond admin shit, people usually need to know my name for things like coffee orders. But I would never change my first name just because people ask for it to be spelled or pronounced to them, so why would it make sense to have to do that for a name you barely need to tell people?

I'm willing to concede the grammatical burden of a name like Kruczynski or Wojciechowski, but it's unlikely that all the women scrambling for a reason to justify giving up their name are of Polish descent. Meanwhile, does no one ever marry a Polish man? What do those women cite as reasons for *taking* his supposedly difficult-to-spell last name?

Listen, there *are* legitimate reasons to want to hide your last name from people. I would never judge someone for concealing a cultural identity that puts their physical or economic safety at risk. But that's not about marriage—that's about oppression. And honestly, a lot of the people I've seen use this argument are white and Anglo as hell.

WHAT'S THE POINT OF GETTING MARRIED IF YOU'RE NOT GOING TO CHANGE YOUR NAME?

Really? Is this why we fought for same-sex marriage rights? So straight women (or women marrying men, at least) could change their names? Please, do not insult our intelligence! If the willingness of one person to change their name is a threat to the institution of marriage, why was so much energy spent defending it from the *homosecksyualays*?

'Of course they can't get married, silly! How would we know which one was supposed to be the girl?'

Once again, it assumes an obligation on the part of women to fulfil their end of the marriage bargain—to become, if in name only, aligned to her husband as a part of *his* identity.

MY FATHER WAS A PIECE OF SHIT AND I DIDN'T WANT HIS NAME

This is a completely fair and reasonable point of view to take. You shouldn't have to bear the name of anyone who harmed you or made you feel unsafe, unloved or unsupported. But why wait for marriage to address this? I mean, what do unmarried people do when they hate their fathers? You don't have to wait for a partner to come along to give you permission to change anything about your life—not your job, not where you live and certainly not your name. Create something new, just for yourself. Make your *own* family line, with you at the very start.

I WANTED TO HAVE THE SAME LAST NAME AS MY KIDS

This one both breaks my heart and enrages me. Because now that we *have* actually got rid of coverture (technically, anyway) we are no longer required by law to give men naming rights over children—to give men the legal right to declare their *ownership* over children. So the fact that so many women cite this as a reason for changing their own names is evidence that coverture remains deeply ingrained in us all.

Listen, if you're the one going through the pregnancy, you should claim automatic naming rights. It's your body that's working hard to build an entire human from scratch. It's your body that will be placed under enormous stress in the building of that human, and your body that risks injury, trauma and, in some cases, permanent disability in the birthing of that human. You are the one most likely to provide the majority of care to that child when they're born, and certainly the one who'll be held to account for any of that child's extremely normal, child-like behaviour in public as it grows up. You're the one who'll handle the mental load for that child and who'll do most of the boring shit for that child. Crucially, you're the one whose career and earning capacity will be severely curtailed by that child and who'll be discriminated against when you try to return to work. You're the one people, including your husband, are more likely to say should 'stay home with the kids' rather than going back to work because 'her salary barely covers the child care'—as if you and you alone have to prove economic benefit to the family as a whole in order to earn the right to return to your profession. And for all that effort and risk, you're supposed to turn around and automatically give some *guy* the right to brand YOUR child with his name, just because he had a three-second dick spasm in a vagina that might now have a prolapse?

Personally, it's not that important to me to have the same last name as my child. In fact, he and his dad and I all have different last names, and it's never been a problem. (We're also in a separated co-parenting relationship living in different houses, and I've never felt like more of a family.) But if you're saying it's so important to you to have the same last name as your children that you'll change your own name for the privilege, it tells me that you *do* care about this connection.

So why doesn't he? Why doesn't your husband care enough about having the same last name as his kids that he'll change his name to yours? If he really cared, surely he would consider it. But the fact is, men just aren't expected to think about it at all. And they're certainly not expected to do it, because that would be emasculating. She takes *his* name so the world can see who the boss is; how embarrassing to reverse the order of that hierarchy and admit to the world you're just your wife's little bitch, right?

Doesn't sound so good when we put it like that. Doesn't sound like much of a choice.

———

As I wrote this, I thought about the young girl I was and the romantic dreams I'd forgotten about. At first it made me sad to think that, despite the confidence she had in her mind and potential, she might have felt her existence as a woman to be so marginal that it had caused her to live on the periphery of life. Her interior life wasn't enough all by itself to give her value in the eyes of the world, so much so that she thought being thrust into the role of somebody's wife might have given her more of a shot. I don't think she felt like her life would be meaningless without marriage; at least, that's not my memory of it. She had aspirations beyond it, that's for sure, and she had a voice that she wanted to use. But on some level, I think she also felt that being part of this cultural ritual would propel her into a sphere of acceptance that marked her as worthy. She would no longer be the dorky schoolgirl who'd been on no dates, the strapping young lass who never felt comfortable in the kinds of sweet dresses teenage girls wear while they're testing out the edges of their womanhood. All the boys who'd ignored her in her life and the girls who'd seemed agitated by her personality—these things would all be made okay by the realisation that she'd found *her person.* Someone to claim her as his, and he as hers. She could take his name and then people would know. They would know.

How I wished I could tell her and all the other girls trying to construct a reality for themselves outside of the glittering, artificial promises of this one that these things are all an illusion. That what once seemed like adventure so often turns out to be conscription. I want to line them all up and say: Darlings, marriage cannot possibly have the power to change who you are in the world; it cannot make you beam brighter than you already do, or make you somebody better than you already are. You have blood, bones and a beating heart—and you have those things with or without a ring on your finger.

But it turns out I didn't have to tell her. Because the other thing I felt—the thing I still feel—is gratitude. I'm so glad for that girl, because despite the come-hither call of the wedding march and the temptations it offered, she ultimately didn't do it. Not with that man, and not with anyone else. She must have known on some level that it was all bullshit, and that a single day in a person's life isn't enough to make up for the slow chipping away of the life that comes afterwards. I'm so glad that she worked her way through to becoming me, and that she wrote the blueprints for all these thoughts and ideas that I'm so insistent on sharing now. She wasn't meant to be somebody's wife, branded by his name because to keep her own would be seen as wilful and suspect. *Why would you even get married if you're not going to take your husband's name?* the people would ask. *Is he okay with that?*

Do you mean, is he okay about you keeping the name you grew up with? The one you were known by before you became Somebody Real? The name that schoolfriends will look up years down the track, only to find you've disappeared into the mist, just another ghost in an endless procession of other women whose names and identities and lives were never given substance of their own, but passed between men, as if this was what would give them form at last?

Age paves the way for us to know ourselves first and foremost, outside of the roles we once thought would help others to identify us. The romance promised not just by marriage but by all the little trinkets that adorn the gilded cage is an ephemeral lie: the ring grows tight on the finger, the bonbonnière from the wedding stale and old. And the name, that new name you were so *lucky* to be given, turns out to be just another thing that helps to keep you from being the girl you were born to be.

9

CHELSEA MOURNING

'In the beginning, Woman was truly the Sun. An authentic person. Now, Woman is the Moon. Living off another, reflecting another's brilliance, she is the moon whose face is sickly and wan . . . These days the things women do invite only mockery. How well I know what lurks behind this ridicule. And still I am not one bit afraid.'

—Hiratsuka Raichō, *The Seito Manifesto*

To paraphrase one of the most successful opening lines of all time (in a novel dedicated to the pursuit of marriage, no less), it is a truth universally acknowledged that a single woman in possession of great freedom must be celebrated and revered.

Just kidding!

That woman is gross and ugly and she must be destroyed before she infects other women with the disease of Independent Thought.

Where did she come from, this incomparably putrid bog monster? Presumably she began life like any other girl, spreading sugar and spice and everything nice wherever she went, all the while dreaming of the day she'd marry her fairytale prince and live happily ever after. This is what all girls want (well, all the *normal* ones, anyway!), and we know this because we've read it in books written by men, seen it in art made by men and heard it in passing conversations held between men for, oh, just about all of human history. As we all know, men are never wrong or self-serving, so it must be true.

Keen-eyed sociologists that they are, men understand that women who sit outside of this genre of girlhood must be damaged in some way. Why would a woman shun the glorious blessing of being a wife (or give up on trying her damnedest to become one) unless there was something fundamentally wrong with her? A chronic history of trauma, perhaps, such as the accumulated devastation of being ignored by men (the worst kind of pain)? Scientifically speaking, the absence of male suitors will send a girl deep into melancholy, then resentment, and eventually hateful, violent fury. Deprived of the warm glow of a man's interest and thus stripped of life's purpose, this unearthly demon now spends her days worshipping the hideous gods of feminism and all their snake-tongued lies, that pesky uterus once again gone bouncing around her unloved body as she numbs the intensity of her hunger for male affection with a series of industrial-sized dildos, pharmaceutical-grade drugs and the regular updating of her blog, *Why Men Should Die.*

This is a very scary, absolutely not made up, totally true-to-life depiction of single women everywhere. Ridding the world of their evil is a serious business, which is why so many extremely smart and totally rational men have taken on the challenge. Like everything our pioneering brothers do, men are brilliant at it and extremely efficient.

You look like you're having an independent thought, the clever boys say, very cleverly. *Is it because you're a fat cunt with daddy issues?*

You have to understand, they don't *want* to speak to women like this. They're the Good Guys! They're only doing this because they care about us and are worried about what will happen to all of us single hobbits who have nothing, absolutely *nothing*, to give our lives purpose or meaning. We could have had a ring—one that made us *invisible*!—but instead we let some old gay wizard convince us to throw it into the fires of Mount Doom. That's the woke agenda for you. And so the men will keep warning us about it, screaming at us from behind television screens and keyboards until their throats are hoarse. This is how much they care about our happiness.

You want them to recycle comedy routines involving cat ownership and substance abuse? You got it! If it's rock solid statistics you're after, head to the reddit/mensrights group and you can learn all about how the world was created by men—every last *inch* of it—and women should shut their pie holes and start showing some respect. The devil works hard, but men who need their clothes washed work harder . . . and these warriors for justice will not rest until the last remaining hold-out in the Sad 'n' Single club admits that a queen is nothing without her king.

If it's male attention these sick, twisted banshees want (and they do, of course they do) then by the power of Grayskull, it's male attention they're gonna get.

———

I saw a meme on Instagram recently, a picture of an ant with the caption: 'A single ant can live up to 29 years.' Someone had written underneath it: 'What about a married one?' Cue endless comments, mostly from men, collapsed in hilarious guffaws about how *clever* this was and how *accurate*. Marriage! It destroys a man's will to live!

The insistence that marriage (or even committed domestic partnership) is something men run from and women chase isn't just intellectually insulting, it's also deeply hypocritical. As any woman who's ever dared to celebrate singledom (or even just be fine with it) can tell you, when it comes to women *rejecting* marriage, no one seems more desperate and furious than the men who claim to enter into it unwillingly. Men have always found ways to punish women who defy social conventions and dare to walk their own path, but the rampant misogyny that proliferates online has allowed for a particularly vicious critique of happily unmarried women. The fact that such behaviour only confirms women's suspicion that life with the 'world builders' isn't all it's cracked up to be is conveniently ignored; women need men, END OF STORY, and if they know what's good for them then they'll bloody well do what they're told.

It's in this expectation of servitude and pleasure that men as a class have continued to assert intellectual authority over women's lives. As the Enlightened Scientists of the Victorian era discovered, it isn't that we're *inferior* to men (not necessarily, anyway); it's that we're *different*. We don't have the same lofty goals as men, nor do we share their aspirations for world building. We're homebodies—literally! We want to be taken care of and to find a good strong mate with whom to have children, because procreation is our biological calling. We know this is true, because men said so.

Those of us who don't yearn for these things—for husbands and babies and houses in which to nurture everyone but ourselves—aren't evidence of a different kind of woman, and therefore proof that women can be as multifaceted as men. Rather, we're evidence of a *woman gone wrong*. A woman whose very nature has been damaged somehow, perverted by feminism and all the horrible, no good, very bad lies it's told us about what we can do and be in the world. Succumbing to feminism won't liberate us from the mythical 'patriarchy' and the men who supposedly run it; it will (and in fact already has) harm us by encouraging us to mimic them. Let's face it, women are irrational and crazy. FACT. We don't even know who we are, let alone what we need. We're like self-driving cars, but in the early testing phase when they're still ironing out all the glitches. This is why we need men to be the drivers: to tell us what to do, what to think and how to feel. We need them to give us purpose by loving us and allowing us to love and care for them in return. We need their approval in order to feel good about ourselves, and we need their protection in order to be safe. Or so we're told. Over and over and over again.

Why do so many men feel entitled to set the frames of reference for human existence?

Let's go back to Marilyn Frye's theory that patriarchy conditions men to believe that they are the 'authors of perception' and that they therefore have the right to 'construct reality'. Patrolling the perimeters of this self-serving reality, men reserve the right to eject or erase women who threaten its integrity. If a woman challenges male authority or attempts to assert a reality that contradicts the male viewpoint, she will be met swiftly with some form of punishment.

In the most extreme of circumstances, this translates to physical violence—or at least the threat of it. History is full of stories of women whose transgressions against patriarchal reality have been met with a retaliation so sadistic it's almost too painful to contemplate. Murder, torture, rape, sexual violence, theft of children, imprisonment, institutionalisation—men have no shortage of ways to keep women in line. In *The Handmaid's Tale*, Margaret Atwood describes how the city walls of Gilead are lined with hanged bodies, a reminder that anyone trying to organise against the regime would be dealt with harshly. Inspired by the oppression of women during the Islamic Revolution in Iran, Atwood might just as well have mimicked the weapons of fear and retaliation used during the persecution of witches; the brutal slaughter of women during the Nanjing Massacre of 1937–1938; the stoning of women found 'guilty' of adultery, as recorded in the Bible (which is really recording actual practice in society at the time), replicated around the world now as 'honour killings'—for what else can it be called when a man murders a woman and/or her children as punishment for leaving him? Patriarchy and its twisted perception of men's power has led him to believe that he owns them all but especially her, and if she 'dishonours' him by asserting differently, he'll remind her who's in charge.

The bodies may not be lining the city walls, but we see them there, nonetheless. Those of us who dare to point them out will be told in no uncertain terms that we're *wrong*. That what we're seeing isn't just invisible, it's not even real. We're clearly deformed in some way; morally, yes, but physically, too—and it's in this physical deformity that our true anguish lies. If we were attractive, men would like us. And if men liked us, they would bless us with their attention. We'd be invited into the reality, and in being invited in we'd see that not only is it beautiful, but it also provides us with everything we could ever need, and that's because it's been built *for us* by people—men—who understand women better than we could ever understand ourselves.

———

[Women] have been lied to by their society forever. That you can be a Girl Boss, and you can do anything a man can do. Which, everyone who's ever seen a woman back up a vehicle knows that's not true, but either way they've been told that they should do career, don't do a family or anything like that. Soon you're Chelsea Handler. Soon it's Valentine's Day, and your womb resembles a dried-up tumbleweed blowing down an old western town, and your Valentine's Day date for the tenth year in a row is a ten-year-old copy of *Magic Mike* and a half-full bottle of Xanax. And you're trying to pretend that you're happy, and you're not happy. And it's actually not her fault; she's been lied to by a country that has lost its way.

—Jesse Kelly, walking sphincter who appears on Fox News

You'll find few women who are less interested in doing what they're told than Chelsea Handler, the bestselling writer and wildly successful stand-up comedian whose hilarious online tributes to being single and child-free have found favour (and viral shares) with women of all ages and nationalities.

In early 2023, Handler was invited to fill in hosting duties for Trevor Noah on *The Daily Show*. During her tenure, she presented a video titled 'A Day in the Life of a Childless Woman'. It was funny not just for the scenes in which Handler hams up the use of her free time, but in how increasingly unhinged the day becomes over the course of the short sketch. It begins with her waking up to a breakfast of edible marijuana. She then goes back to bed to masturbate for a bit before waking up again just after noon. This completely benign and obviously silly joke proved so *offensive* to the pundits at Fox News and Breitbart that they had no choice but to pull out all stops and set her straight.

Ben Shapiro, a tiny little garden gnome who has miraculously gained the power of speech, said it was 'written all over her face how miserable [she] is'. Tucker Carlson, who looks like the mayor of a Lego city and spits more often than he speaks, called her an 'aging, deeply unlikable woman who never had kids'. Boom! Candace Owens, a Black woman who appears to hate both women and Black people, warned that if the young girls on TikTok—'who are really just selfish brats' (girls love when you call them that FYI)—listened to Handler, they were at risk of winding up old and alone. And Jesse Kelly launched into the tirade quoted above.

It's an astonishing response from a group of people who otherwise pretend to champion free speech, and mock tHe WoKe LeFt for being unable to take a joke. (The pearl-clutchers excluded from their commentary the second part of the sketch, in which Handler teleports home from Paris then invents time travel so she can go back and kill Hitler—the joke being that when you don't have children, a woman can get a lot of shit done in the day.)

When conservative men subject progressive women to an onslaught of jeering, misogynistic abuse that focuses on their looks, mental acuity and physical usefulness to men, it's defended as a form of legitimate critique and highbrow humour. If you can't hack it, this must be because you're weak and you can't handle jokes. But when women retaliate in kind or mock their opponents, they're accused of being abusive and unprofessional. (When Handler thanked Shapiro for providing a '100 per cent foolproof contraceptive' in the form of his voice, he responded by accusing her of 'attacking' him and his conservative colleagues. *How dare she!*) If their opponent also happens to be a woman, they're accused of being guilty of the worst kind of misogyny while those otherwise strong women who've never witnessed even an incident of sexism *in their lives* act scandalised at the lack of solidarity.

Buried deep within the terms of service in the patriarchy's 'What Women Need' contract lies the following clause: *Transgressive hags must be held to account and vilified in the public discourse to dissuade other impressionable women* ('selfish young brats', say) *from getting any ideas.*

It's generally an effective approach, because it gives tacit permission to everyone watching to continue the public flaying via social media comments, talkback radio segments, their own response videos and, of course, abuse sent directly to the woman herself. Women dragged through the muck of the Fox News machine and its ilk not only have to contend with people like Jesse Kelly trying to form words, but they also have to deal with the million or so other walking bedsores whose dicks get just that little bit stiff from bombarding women with abuse.

But, then, it isn't called abuse when men do it. It's called 'telling it like it is'. This is another thing only men are allowed to do, because only men have the skills and wherewithal to know what 'it' even is. They determine the reality, remember? We just live in it.

———

What can never be allowed to enter the constructed reality of patriarchal men is a fully formed woman who believes herself to be human in all the same ways they are. If she asserts herself as human, she can't be dismissed as merely a default man. She doesn't just get to live in reality—she also gets to construct it.

Obviously the most frightening thing a patriarchal man can imagine is a woman who constructs reality for herself, living happily alone, providing for her own needs, none of which are reliant on the attentions of men. But as haunting as this image is, it's compounded when the woman in question has the audacity to speak. A woman living alone is bad enough; that she doesn't have the good grace to do so *quietly* and out of public view is an abomination.

Chelsea Handler is just one of many transgressive women who refuse to conform to patriarchy's demands. When the cold fist of patriarchy tries to slam her down, she doesn't just laugh in the face of its owner and tell him to go fuck himself; she'll also make a comedy show out of it and invite millions of other women to come watch and laugh. Margaret Atwood once said men are afraid women will laugh at them while women are afraid men will kill them. As an enthusiastic laugher-atter of men who has received countless death threats as a result, I can attest to the fact that Atwood's premise sometimes occurs on a loop: women like me are often more afraid that men will kill us because we laughed at them.

It took me some years to get to the point where I feel confident laughing at men, and I can understand why so many women avoid it. It isn't just that a man's *good* opinion seems to carry so much currency (however superficial that turns out to be); it's also that his *bad* opinion can be so angry and hostile. Patriarchal culture has been extremely successful in conditioning women to crave its approval, providing its most committed soldiers with a vocabulary of insults, taunts and basic clapbacks designed to strike fear into the hearts of women everywhere. Though they may vary in tone or inventiveness, the thrust is always the same: *Your strident views and obvious physical shortcomings make you unappealing to men, and this failure to please them in all ways is the true source of your unhappiness.*

Patriarchy's finely tuned messaging service operates twenty-four hours a day, seven days a week. It's the white noise of living, the tinnitus you no longer even hear, a steady stream of instructions beamed directly into your brain. I didn't dream of marriage when I was young in quite the same way we're told all little girls do, but this may have had less to do with my own fierce independence and more to do with the fact that I believed myself too unwieldy, too difficult, too fat and even *too tall* to aspire to any of the rewards offered to those girls who played by the rules.

This belief I had about my inherent *wrongness* was confirmed to me over and over again not just by boys and men, but also by girls who, having won men's conditional approval, now lived in fear of losing it. I could never figure out which I felt more let down by: the boys inflicting the damage or the girls telling them how clever their jokes were. But, then, I'm sure other women have wondered the same about me in the past, when I looked away or stayed silent or laughed to show I was *on his side*, my hand held out to receive whatever pathetic crumb patriarchy was offering as its Good Girl treat that day. One thing you learn as you get older that you wish you could tell your younger self: the crumbs will never fill you up, but they will give you a scorching case of heartburn.

Not all of us are lucky enough to learn this lesson. And even for those of us who do, it takes some practice to free ourselves of the conditioning. To express ourselves without fear and in allegiance to our own humanity, we have to risk the possibility of men dehumanising us, which invariably involves calling us hysterical banshees driven mad by sexual frustration. How many women stay meek and silent in the face of sexist behaviour, because we're afraid of inciting men's wrath and being labelled some variation of an ugly, unfuckable cunt? And more to the point, how many men know that this is all they ever need say when conversations with mouthy women become too confronting for them to manage? This age-old rhetorical bait and switch is twofold in its purpose. It succeeds not only in keeping women silent but also in bolstering the currency attached to men's opinions of us. Because it isn't just men's lack of desire that we've been taught to fear—it's the violent intensity with which they express it. Better to appease the beast than risk being mauled to death by his fragile insecurity.

When the Baby Boys of the right wing went after her, Handler refused to follow the rules the way Good Girls are supposed to. Instead of cowering beneath their attempts to shame her, she responded by ridiculing her detractors and inviting her millions of fans to ridicule them alongside her. And boy, did we laugh! All of us sad, old swamp monsters, draped in our cats and the stench of decay, laughing to try to fill the empty hole inside us that grows deeper each year we live without the love of a man! Conservatives hate women like Chelsea Handler, and not just because she can't be told what to do or because she mocks them when they try. They hate her because she exists in larger-than-life, defiant and *funny* opposition to the patriarchal lie that wants women to believe that being single is a fate worse than death— that a single woman is destined to be not just miserable but also impoverished and helpless. Handler isn't just happy without marriage and children—she's also enormously successful and completely self-sufficient as a result of that. Her success has been possible in part because she's chosen to live only for herself. All the energy that would ordinarily be directed towards supporting a man in his pursuits (and which patriarchy certainly relies on in order to keep itself chugging along) while raising his children is instead used by the woman for herself.

When you liberate women from the constraints of domestic service and allow us to forge lives on our terms, it becomes clear that, despite what they would have you believe, it's *men* who benefit from marriage across a variety of metrics. They live longer, they register as being happier and their mental health scores are higher. Married men also tend to be more economically secure, because workplaces see them as a safer bet. On the contrary, in comparison to married women, single women live longer, report higher levels of happiness and have greater economic opportunities.

Sure, Handler's is a unique case. I'm not suggesting that her success means the rest of us can easily share in it. She's incredibly wealthy, privileged, white and able-bodied. She has access to spaces most of us could never dream of. Her income makes it much easier for her not just to live without a man, but to thrive without him.

And therein lies the problem: one conservatives are desperate to keep hidden from ordinary women. In fact, it might just be the thing they're most determined to conceal. If women had the same economic opportunities as men—indeed, if women's right to economic independence was considered as sacrosanct and vital to their self-esteem as it is to men's—then the dream of domestic bliss with the white-picket fence would very quickly reveal itself to be as flimsy as a house of cards. If we believed at the most basic level of our existence that our lives belonged first and foremost to us, we'd soon see that the options presented by the patriarchy as necessary to our fundamental happiness aren't really all that great. Marriage has maintained its vice-like grip on women because the vast majority of us have been denied the same rights to financial liberation and independence as men. Things may have improved since the days when we were legally unable to own things for ourselves, but we are still hampered by the gender pay gap, the cost of raising children and the threat of late stage homelessness that looms over the sixty-five-plus age group. Few things have paupered women more than divorce, and the reality of this invariably leads to women making choices to *stay* in marriages that are manipulative, abusive or just downright miserable because the alternative is considered even worse.

Conservatives need the exploited labour of women to maintain the capitalist patriarchal system that gives them so much privilege. Financially independent women are a looming threat to the security of this system, because they're less likely to make relationship choices based on economic need rather than emotional satisfaction. As a figurehead, Chelsea Handler undermines every lie conservatives have told to try to coerce them into a life of domestic service taking care of men. Because if women with economic means can live happy, fulfilling lives all by themselves, then maybe what we need isn't men at all.

It's money.

10

THE PROTECTION RACKET

'Every man I meet wants to protect me.
I can't figure out what from.'

—Mae West

You don't have to be a feminist to know that money is a great liberating force. You don't even have to be an economist. You just have to be a person in the world, with some understanding of what it means to have autonomy and agency over your decision-making. I guess this is why women have been denied the right to amass any of it for most of human history—because, to paraphrase Zawn Villines, men steal women's potential in order to buy their own power. If you can control the means by which someone is able to provide for themselves, it becomes that much easier to lock them into a contract whose conditions are terrible but from which they can't ever hope to escape.

Controlling women's economic independence and thereby forcing them into a relationship of subservience and inequality has been one of patriarchy's key assaults on women. Men will deny this, of course, because it doesn't suit the narrative of courage and noble sacrifice they love to tell anyone who'll listen about who they are and how the world came to be. You know, the one where dudes fondly describe themselves as the natural leaders, visionaries, rescuers and benevolent defenders of humanity, and as such the deserving recipients of all its songs of praise and glory. From wrestling sabre-toothed tigers to feed the tribe, storming battlefields for the sole purpose of protecting women and children, being Jesus, conquering new lands (which involved absolutely no violence or anything against which the men already there would possibly need to defend 'their' women and children) and basically inventing everything that's every existed, the sweeping saga of Man's Greatness is well known to us all.

When men control the means of production—not just in terms of a society's material gains but also the manufacturing of its mythologies—they also control its rewards. Sign on the dotted line, girls, and men will agree to meet just enough of your most basic needs (shelter, food and a nominal promise of protection against other men) in exchange for an endless supply of domestic labour, obedience, care and sex. This is what patriarchy calls 'providing'. And the expectation that women repay men's marginal economic investment with a lifetime of service? Well, that's just what's required to 'keep up their end of the bargain'.

An entity that is provided for but unable to ever evolve beyond the role of dependent is indistinguishable from livestock or real estate. To say that men provide for women (but only 'their' women) is to say that they'll bother to look after their property as long as it's producing something useful. If a cow stops producing milk, it's slaughtered for meat. If a car breaks down permanently, it's sold for parts. And if a woman refuses to perform her job as expected, she'll be summarily torn apart and discarded. She's a failed investment—and on a farm, even one that just pumps the toxic fumes of patriarchy out into the atmosphere, everybody works.

But women's work is never done, primarily because no amount of women's contributions will ever be considered equal to the incredible sacrifices men have apparently made. *We bloody well provide for you, don't we?* they scream, as if somehow we're to blame for our economic disadvantage. As if *we* were the ones who denied ourselves the right to an education, or to work, or to vote, or to marry who we wanted, or to not marry at all. As if *we*, the women who were not allowed to become lawyers or judges or even readers, were somehow responsible for writing legislation that removed all agency over our own bodies and transferred them into the ownership of fathers and husbands. As if *we* were the ones who decided one day that we'd be better off letting men tell us what to do, forcing them into the untenable position (which they didn't even want!) of now being our *protectors*, soldiers and guards at the gate. (To be clear, this is not the same gate women are meant to barricade shut in order to keep men from trying to get into our pants. That one's on us.)

Patriarchy does indeed work by insisting on a commitment to both provide and protect. But it isn't women who benefit from this exchange—it's men. Patriarchy promises to provide men with power. And in return, they pledge to protect it with their lives.

The feminist narrative is that I'm a controlling man who wants control over women. And the actual truth is I'm a protective man who wants to protect. And being a man in a position is not always a good thing. I feel indebted and have a duty to myself and my honour, meaning if I'm walking down the street with a beautiful woman and three men want to attack her, I have to risk my life now. I can't live my life letting my wife get gang-raped on a fucking street and running away. I can't take it as a man. So I have to now die. I have to die. Or try. I have no choice. So that's my duty. But they'll ignore that part. They'll ignore the part where I risk my life.

So said the notoriously misogynistic social media influencer and accused rapist Andrew Tate on a men's rights podcast recorded at the end of 2022. The episode was recorded shortly after Tate had been banned from the biggest social media platforms, following a growing international backlash against the self-described 'Top G' of the manosphere.

For months, perhaps even years, Tate had been using digital media—video shorts, podcasts, YouTube and even an online course offered through his 'school', Hustlers University—to radicalise men all over the world through an especially potent form of misogynist rhetoric that upholds the idea of innate male power bolstered by female subservience. Some of Tate's fans are as young as twelve; others are already collecting old-age pensions. Most of them are white and evidently lacking in life experience, particularly with women. They feel robbed of the privileges they believe were freely claimed by their grandfathers and are furious at the women they hold responsible for denying them what they believe is theirs by right.

Such a group makes easy pickings for a grifter with a video camera and a plan. Compelled by the markers of patriarchal success that Tate and his bombastic behaviour assure them can be theirs if they just embrace what it means to 'be a man', these men and boys are willing to fall in line behind him and follow him into battle wherever he decides his army is needed. Their mission? To destroy the woke left, the feminists, trans people, the fake news media—whoever and whatever is standing in the way of men claiming their right to lead once more.

But although he might be selling (literally) the promise of a throne for each and every one of his would-be kings, Tate's objective is a little different. Like all modern-day misogynistic gurus who've managed to slip their reptilian bodies through the gaps in reality, Tate believes in nothing so much as he believes in himself.

And his fans believe in him, too. More to the point, they believe that he can provide them with the lifestyle he flaunts. Mansions. Money. Luxury cars. Scantily dressed women who'll fuck them for free and say thank you. According to Tate, feminism has stripped men of their capacity to lead, and *real men* must reclaim their power. Apparently, this can be done through cage-fighting, sucking on cigars (an extremely phallic ritual, it has to be said) and letting women know who's in charge of them.

On this last note, Tate seems especially appealing to his teenage fanbase. Scores of teachers and adolescent girls from all over the world (because Tate is an international juggernaut) have reported frightening interactions with the boys being indoctrinated into his ideology. Female teachers have been told to shut up by boys who refuse to recognise their authority. Girls who consider these boys their peers have found themselves subject to an increasingly dark and threatening kind of misogyny, which is dismissed as 'just jokes' when protested as serious violence. Despite their young age, Tate's teenage fans are already fluent in the language of abuse and intimidation. Who can say how many young men are now shifting from what was an already intolerable scuffle of play-ground gender politics into the more intentional use of genuinely terrifying threats and actual criminal acts of violence? There are already women reporting stories of abuse suffered at the hands of ex-boyfriends radicalised by Tate.

Tate, though, insists that he loves women. He *protects* women. He thinks men and women are *equal*. It doesn't matter that he's also said women who are raped are partly to blame, or that women shouldn't work and have careers because they belong at home, or even that *his* women aren't allowed to leave the house without his permission. It doesn't matter that he brands the women he calls 'his' with tattoos confirming his ownership, or that there are videos of him miming how a man should choke a woman who dares to contradict him. It doesn't even matter that numerous allegations of rape and battery have been made against him, or that four women are currently bringing civil proceedings against him for rape, or that there's digital evidence of him admitting to having repeatedly raped an ex-girlfriend *and liking the fact she didn't want it.*

None of that matters, because in the world of the Tate acolytes, none of it is true. I mean, he *says* he doesn't hate women, so that's what we're expected to believe. Only an idiot feminist with no sense of humour would think he actually meant any of it! No, when Tate gets online and talks about bitches and hoes and tells men exactly what they want to hear about their own divine power, it's all just bluff and swagger, merely part of a character he plays; none of us are meant to take it seriously.

This is the bait and switch at work again. If Tate admits the truth, that he hates women—which he very clearly does, and which he encourages his fans to proudly embrace for themselves—then he can't claim to represent the kind of noble manhood defined by its reverence for the 'nurturing sex'. If he admits that he sees women as little more than chattel for men to exert their own power over, as objects for raping, beating, controlling, profiting from and trading between men—in short, the way men throughout history have violated and abused women—then he has to sacrifice the narrative that men are women's 'natural protectors'. And if he also admits that he sees women as being little more than a group of animals from which 'Top G' men have the right to extort labour, be that domestic, sexual or economic, then he must also give up the pretence that masculine leadership at its core means providing for women.

If you remove the ability of men like Tate to use words like 'protector' and 'provider' to define *who* they are, you make it that much harder for them to shield exactly *what* they are: a weak piece of shit whose masculinity is predicated not on noble sacrifice but on violent exploitation. In short, a Bad Guy.

Tate makes for a perfect study of the most extreme of the self-appointed male 'protectors', and their unwavering belief in their right to women's obedience and service. His ideology and business model represent patriarchy's most perfect metaphor. In order to maintain its appeal to the men who sign on to it, it has to stop just short of giving voice to the violence that it encompasses. Whether the idea of controlling women appeals to men or not is largely irrelevant; most of them will never admit to it out loud. They can't, because that would involve admitting they aren't good people. And most men *need* women to see them as good, because being reassured of their goodness by the women they're exerting power over goes a long way to convincing them that they're only doing what she really wants.

Leaving aside his repulsive views towards women and the terrifying way he's managed to assemble an international move-ment of misogyny under the pretence of 'male empowerment', Tate is, more than anything, an enormous loser. And that calls into question what it is that men—and young men in particular—find so appealing about him. Across the board, it seems to be that he represents an unapologetic insistence that men are owed some kind of service from women, one that feminism has come along and stolen from them. Rather than learn how to adapt to a new social order in which women are finally able to make some headway in terms of providing for ourselves (and thus also circumventing men's other great complaint, that women see them as 'wallets' to fund our grand lifestyles), Tate and his acolytes are furious that they don't get to have their cake and eat it, too. If women can make our own money, we can choose how we spend our time and with whom. If women no longer have to go to men cap in hand, asking them to pretty please put a roof over our heads, support us and our children and 'protect' us from the claims to this resource that men have historically used to bully us into submission, then men ultimately lose the right to be the masters of our lives and bodies.

Men don't 'protect' women to keep the monsters from getting in. It's to keep us from getting out.

———

As I wrote in the previous chapter, women don't need *men* to be secure and happy—what we need is *money*, and the agency that comes from having it. But money, as we know, belongs to men. See also: ambition, science, politics, ideas, culture, dreams, exploration, adventure, engineering, authority and women. To ensure its control over women is maintained, patriarchal society makes it impossible for women to provide for ourselves.

Of course, we've made some headway through the years. Our feminist foremothers were successful in establishing property rights for married women, with America setting the tone in 1839, the United Kingdom following in 1882 and Australian states bringing up the rear in 1884. Eventually, we were even allowed to have our own bank accounts! And credit cards! Isn't that *amazing*? Young women today may not realise that women in Australia weren't even allowed to apply for a bank loan without a male cosignatory until 1974. To put that in perspective, that was the year Leonardo DiCaprio was born. Bank loans for women are literally only as old as two of L.DiC's girlfriends added together.

I'm so glad the relentless onslaught of men's oppression was finally resolved for good, less than fifty years ago, with just a few simple bureaucratic changes. So inspiring, ladies! #wedidit

To understand why the thought of economic independence for women still gets men so riled up, we have to go back once more to the British legal principle of coverture. Under coverture, everything a woman owned was considered the property of her husband, from the clothes on her back to her family name to her children and to unqualified access to her body. We were denied access to education and political suffrage, while working women were denied equal pay (still are!) or the opportunity to work in higher-level employment. All of this makes it even more galling that men today have the audacity to claim our economic disadvantage is the result of us *not trying hard enough* or, my favourite, *choosing lower-paying jobs*. You know, those economically meaningless jobs like teaching, health care, caring for the elderly—basically anything in the nurturing industries (our forte!), which are pointless and unnecessary, and have absolutely nothing to do with the formation of a strong and economically successful society. Because patriarchy has also organised to make care the natural prerogative of women, the idea that it should be remunerated with monetary payment is somehow gauche or greedy. Women shouldn't charge for their 'natural' skills! After all, do men charge women to provide *protection*? No! They give that to us for free, in the same way they give us marriage for free, babies for free and the privilege of not growing old alone for free.

As feminists successfully fought to change legislation that had denied women basic rights to identity and economic mobility, coverture as a legally enforced doctrine began to dissipate. But now that so many of us have relative freedom of choice, the fear of what it means for women to be fully independent has struck men once again, just like it did a few centuries ago when the establishment of the middle class created a whole swathe of women unwilling to marry and give up the modicum of independence they'd carved out for themselves. Men's God-given role as the 'provider' has been threatened, and feminists must be held accountable.

Burn the witch!

One of the things you'll learn early on about being a feminist is that men don't like you. I'm not talking about all men, although of course I shouldn't have to include a disclaimer about that here. We get it. Not all men.

But honestly? It's enough of them. And sometimes, the hatred isn't about violent comments or threats against your life. Sometimes, it's just expressed in the casual dismissal of women's ability to care for themselves.

It's impossible to talk about marriage (and all the reasons why it's still incompatible with women's freedom on the whole) without men popping up to remind you that not only are you WRONG about its negative impact on women but also that women wouldn't have survived without men. Without men, we would have starved to death on plains, frozen on mountainsides, dehydrated into dust in the desert or fallen victim to any of the terrible, intangible dangers of the world that swirl around us (or *in* us, when you consider the demonic portals we're carrying around in our tum-tums).

In short, stop being so grotesquely ungrateful, *you fat bitch*— don't you know that without men you'd be *dead*?

Only good, compliant girls get the protection men bravely provide. Nasty, outspoken, rude mean *cunts* get nothing but back-lash, because they need to be shown their place.

Once you know how it works, it's easy to sidestep it. Men try their hardest to eject women from the reality they've created, but if you remove yourself first, then these attempts to shame and belittle don't work. I don't consider myself part of the reality that men have created for themselves, so it doesn't matter at all to me if they don't like me. I won't hide their true faces from the world just because that's what they demand of all other women. Nor will I hide my own face behind that of a man, because this is the only way I've been told I can be seen.

Some men are good. Some men are bad. Most men enthuse about the universality of the former while being neutral at best about the latter. The violence that I've been subjected to at the hands of men—which, it has to be said, barely even touches the side of the violence so many other women have had to endure—has most often been dismissed as some kind of anomaly. (Men protect women! Men provide for women!) I have been expected to over-look threats of violence against me because 'most men' are good. The 'jokes', comments, memes and rallying cries made by and shared between men with the express intention of dehumanising me are nothing more than harmless words or casual insults that I have to get over, or just accept as being part of the consequences of *my* actions. When I've fought back against men who openly fantasise about *smashing me*, beating me, hitting me with objects, anally raping me so that it *really hurts*, stringing me like a pig and raping me with a baseball bat covered in barbed wire or fucking me with a butcher's knife so that I never reproduce—in short, forcing me to *learn my lesson*—I have been framed as the villain.

Because by making their words public I've embarrassed men. Exposed them. And they aren't really threatening me with violence, I've been told. They're just 'disagreeing' with me.

As I've aged out of impressionable young girl and into fully fledged woman, it has become clearer and clearer to me that *I* am not allowed to protect myself. That I'm not allowed to provide for myself. That I'm not entitled to be judged fairly for what I do and say, only for how I make men feel about those things. So much of my career has been tainted by men's insane reactions to it that even now I can rarely have conversations about my work without being asked, *How do you deal with all the abuse?*

It's useful to lay this all out, not because it shows the individual feelings of men towards me in particular. But because it demonstrates how insincere the pretensions are that these men have to being 'protectors' at all. It shows how eagerly men seek first and foremost to protect *themselves and each other* from the consequences of their own actions, choices and attitudes towards women. Think of every single example in recent years that's involved women speaking out against male violence, misogyny or just plain old sexism—the first impulse has never been to believe the women speaking for themselves, but to rally around exactly the kind of mentality codified in law by all the male experts who've assembled over thousands of years to decide what women are, what women need and what damage women are willing to do in order to destroy the world of men. Men don't provide women with a measure of faith or trust in our ability to testify to our own experiences, and they certainly don't protect us from the critique of other men who seek to discredit us. The idea that men are owed deference and subservience because they've 'protected' women from the big bad world is a nonsense, just as is the idea they've devoted their lives to providing for our needs and wants.

Because really, who gives a fuck what women need and want?

Certainly not men. If they did, a majority of them would be willing to listen when we told them what it is we actually need. Women wouldn't be howled at, berated and abused whenever we spoke about the material conditions of our lives. We wouldn't be called paranoid when we asserted boundaries around men who made us feel uncomfortable. We wouldn't be labelled hysterical man haters when we campaigned against men's violence against women. We wouldn't be sneered at for wanting some kind of financial independence, or mocked for wanting reproductive labour to be recognised as an economic contribution to society. If men really cared about what women need and want, the idea of fighting for our reproductive and abortion health care would be relegated to dystopian fiction—because our rights to control when, where, how and even if we became mothers would be considered sacrosanct. If society cared about women's needs, no woman would ever have to choose between raising a child in poverty or staying in an abusive relationship. Abuse itself would be a rare phenomenon, with the perpetrators of it not only punished accordingly but treated like social pariahs. A society that cared about women wouldn't allow itself to ask questions about whether or not she drove him to it, let alone allow such reprehensible takes to be broadcast on mass platforms. A society that cared about women wouldn't call the perpetrators of such abuse 'good blokes' or talk about what horrendous stress they were under or boo hoo about how sad they were that she decided to leave him. We wouldn't have to deal with endless bullshit about how there are two sides to every story and he's only ever been good to me and women lie, *look at that Amber Heard.*

If society cared about what women need, none of us who fit into that category would ever have to deal with the aftermath of a sexual assault by considering whether or not reporting it would lead to more trauma. Sexual assault itself would be rare, because the idea of what women need would be so finely attuned to the idea of communicating with women and respecting them, that it would become automatically more difficult to dehumanise us. Boys who cried for their mothers when they were scared wouldn't turn into men who got off on scaring women. If society cared about women enough to listen and follow through with what we actually want and need, young men furious at having their entitlement threatened wouldn't be hungry for the teachings of misogynists and male supremacists. If society cared about women, there would be no possible path to success for these online preachers of hate who are making millions from telling boys and men that what women need is to be slapped around, choked, spat on and reminded always that she's a slave to the dick.

Instead, they seem more interested in collectively covering their ears and blocking out any remaining unwanted sound by droning on about history, tradition and how everyone knows what works you dumb bitch.

Maybe it's true that most men don't perpetrate the worst of misogyny's violence against women, not publicly at least. But even if they're not contributing, they still mostly stay silent—because the very same threats of expulsion from reality that work to keep women in line also work to keep men there, too. Men are afraid of other men turning on them, and exposing themselves to the viciousness of the pack.

Ultimately, what I really find telling about the myth of male protection is how it's really used to make sure women don't protect ourselves. Women aren't allowed to fight for ourselves when the target is men who try to harm us. Because we can't be allowed to decide who those men are, only told by other men what reality looks like. Instead, we are forced to accept even the most blatant, enthusiastic and salivating jokes about raping women, beating women, killing women (you know, things that men actually do to women every day) as 'harmless jokes'. We're told that only CRAZY women who HATE MEN would object to these things— and because everyone knows that the worst thing a woman can possibly do is hate a man, we must assure *all* men that we'll devote ourselves to protecting them against the terrifying crime of women's fury.

I don't need or want male protection; I can protect myself. In fact, I will *always* protect myself and other women from the threats men so gleefully employ to try to keep us afraid of them.

246

I will *never* protect men from the consequences of their own actions the way they furiously demand I must.

And I don't need or want men to provide for me. What I want is the right to provide for myself. To not have to negotiate through a line of male authoritarians what it is I'm allowed to strive for in this world, the world that I have also had a part in creating.

The fact that marriage is thrust on women in part because we're told we somehow need men to protect and provide for us is *revolting*. I will not be the mirror that reflects men back to themselves at ten times their size. What I will be is the loudspeaker that amplifies their abuse, and the magnifying glass that makes visible their private rage.

You want to protect?

Protect yourselves from the rage that's coming your way.

You want to provide?

Provide us with a reason to spare you from it.

11

WHEN YOU WISH UPON A STAR

'I'll have what she's having.'

—Woman in diner, *When Harry Met Sally*

When Melbourne entered the first of its long Covid lockdowns, I decided to rewatch all of my favourite childhood movies and post breakdowns of them to my Instagram stories. Thanks to a childhood spent largely in front of the television, I had extensive knowledge of all the greatest hits of the eighties and nineties. Most of them would be considered wildly inappropriate for a child's viewing by today's standards, but this was the eighties and the concept of exercising parental responsibility was often considered more of a suggestion rather than a hard and fast rule. Still, what I lost in emotional stability I gained in creative inspiration, the fertile soil of celluloid storytelling producing a rich crop of scenarios for me to place my Barbie dolls in, most of which seemed to involve stolen boyfriends, thwarted schemes at work and Barbie having a lot of sex.

Working Girl was a particular childhood favourite. It had all of the best plot points: a scrappy young female underdog beating the odds to win at life, a makeover scene (crucial to ensure the underdog's success), glamorous clothes and some key scenes providing instructions for flirting. It was endlessly inspiring to watch Tess McGill (played to raspy throat perfection by Melanie Griffith) rise from lowly secretary to junior executive, but there was one thing that took her triumph over the silver-tongued Katharine (Sigourney Weaver) from good to *great*—that she also got the guy, and he just happened to be her mean old boss's boyfriend.

Of course, Tess doesn't know that Jack Trainer (Harrison Ford) is Katharine's beau when she picks him up at a cocktail party she's snuck into. It would be much harder to sympathise with her if she did, just as it would be harder to cheer for Katharine's downfall if she weren't conniving, bossy, entitled and emasculating. But as I said, this was the eighties, and it would be many decades before screenwriters bothered to give their female characters any kind of nuance or depth.

Tess has always been presented as a protofeminist heroine, the girl from Staten Island who breaks into the big league without losing what it is that makes her special in the first place. Clearly, it had to be on my lockdown #deepdive list. As the first bars of Carly Simon's triumphant anthem 'Let the River Run' began to play, I settled in and prepared to cheer.

But revisiting *Working Girl* as a feminist adult is a different experience altogether; one that leaves you with a distinctly bitter taste in your mouth. It's clear that what made the movie compelling to audiences back in the day wasn't just that Tess made something better of herself—it's that she does it in distinct opposition to the shrewd, imposing and 'bony assed' Katharine, who she also manages to defeat. Jack, meanwhile, is never held to account for the fact he cheated on his girlfriend *and* revelled in her downfall. How could he be, when Katharine was such an emasculating *shrew*? Tess hasn't landed herself an untrustworthy lover with a wandering eye; instead, she's rescued a man from his entrapment under the feminist thumb and restored him to the full glory of his golden manhood, winning the great gift of his devotion in return—something those dragon-skinned women's libbers wouldn't know anything about.

Working Girl might have been set in the fast-paced business district of New York City, but it's a classic Cinderella story. Katharine's the Evil Queen, threatened by the bouncy fertility of the nubile young princess. Make no mistake—she may have a 'head for business and a bod for sin', but Tess is as much a Disney princess as Cinderella, Snow White, Sleeping Beauty and Belle. And just like those sweet, rosy-cheeked young girls, Tess embodies the same patriarchal ideals necessary to make a 'good' and therefore desirable woman. Someone whose kindness, innocence and beauty all come together to make her worthy of the biggest prize of all.

True love.

———

You'd be hard-pressed to find a woman today who hadn't grown up under the influence of fairytale magic and true love's kiss. But unlike our foremothers, the fairytales used to enchant us weren't dark and twisted. Our mermaids didn't end up as foam on the ocean, but were married on ship decks. Beauty's imprisonment in the castle of a beast was made more bearable by the company (and entertainment) of singing, dancing furniture, and Sleeping Beauty didn't have to sleep for one hundred years before Prince Charming awakened her with true love's kiss.

We're so familiar with Disney's retelling of classic fairytales that, to a good proportion of people at least, they *are* the classics. When it was revealed that the live action version of *The Little Mermaid* would feature a young Black actress named Halle Bailey in the role of Ariel, a deluge of racism was unleashed. *Ariel isn't Black!* grown adults screamed on the internet. *Ariel has RED HAIR!*

The original version of *The Little Mermaid* was written by Hans Christian Andersen in 1837, and it was an allegory for the terrible pain of unrequited queer love. Christian Andersen had fallen in love with a friend who was engaged to be married. When he confessed his feelings to the young man in question, Christian Andersen was told that they could never be reciprocated. The allegorical mermaid is Hans Christian Andersen, begging the sea witch to transform him into a person for whom this love could be returned.

The (unnamed) mermaid accepts the deal from the sea witch, but there are other conditions aside from losing her voice. Her new legs would allow her to walk among humans, but each step would feel like it was on a thousand knives. If she couldn't convince the prince to kiss her by the end of the third day and night, she wouldn't just lose her voice forever—she'd lose her life, turning to foam on the ocean's surface and lose the chance to gain the eternal soul that gives humans passage into heaven.

The story most of us are familiar with has Ariel trying to make Eric fall in love with her (silently!) with the help of a talking crab named Sebastian. When she appears to be close to succeeding (because, yes, let's teach little girls that having a voice and something to say isn't necessary for a man to fall in love with you—in fact, it's kind of preferable if you don't), Ursula bewitches Eric and tries to take her place. A battle ensues, Ariel's voice is restored, Eric realises she was the girl who saved him from drowning three days ago (!!!!) and now he knows it's her he loves. Phew! He kills Ursula, marries his child bride and they live happily ever after, far away from her family which is totally fine and nothing a parent would ever be worried about.

In the original version, the mermaid comes to shore only to find her beloved prince has shacked up with a girl from a nearby village, assuming her to have been the one to have rescued him. He's indifferent to the attentions of the mermaid, but accepts her as a companion because of the power the sea witch has given her to dance (remembering of course that this comes with excruciating pain). Her misery is profound, especially with the approaching nuptials between the prince and his chosen bride. Terrified of losing her to foam on the waves, the mermaid's sisters cut off their hair and give it to the sea witch, begging her to release the mermaid from the deal. The sea witch agrees, but on one condition—the sisters will take a dagger to the mermaid and tell her that she must kill the newly married prince and his bride while they sleep. If she does this, she can return to the ocean as a mermaid. If she doesn't, she'll die and turn to foam on the waves. The mermaid takes the dagger to the fickle prince's room, but cannot bring herself to kill the man she loves. Instead, she falls into the ocean and awaits oblivion.

But the mermaid's sacrifice has not gone unnoticed. A higher power grants her the right to a second chance, telling her that if she spends the next three hundred years (the life span of a mermaid) performing good deeds on earth, she will earn her place in heaven.

Knowing its origins as a queer love story makes *The Little Mermaid* all the more melancholic. But it seems to me a perfect depiction of marriage, too. To be blessed with a man's love, women must leave their families, silence their voices, stamp down their needs and change themselves completely to fit into his world. There's a degree of irony in the fact Ariel begins Disney's retelling of the Danish tragedy by fantasising about what it's like up on the shore. With so many new things to discover, people to meet and words to learn, she dreams of life unfolding before her only to have the ambition of that life reduced to marrying a boy she got hot for on the beach and saying goodbye to everything she's ever known.

These were the kinds of stories women of my generation grew up with. We never questioned them. Well, I certainly didn't. On the contrary, I was smitten with the idea that love could come to all of us in time—provided, of course, that we worked hard enough at being *good*. I sucked every last one of these romantic fantasies up, imagining a transformation for myself that mirrored my beloved underdog tales involving mermaids, ambitious secretaries, unpopular teen witches, never-been-kissed Drew Barrymores, hookers with a heart of gold and poor girls from the wrong side of the tracks. The heroines of these stories weren't the beautiful, thin popular girls I felt so envious of. If anything, those girls were more likely to be the villains of the tale and we could enjoy watching them get their comeuppance at the end.

When I was young, I thought these stories were just about falling in love. But really, these are movies about girls being *seen*. In being seen, she gets to be made exceptional. They work by appealing to the childish insecurity so many girls have about being failed girls. Not thin enough, not pretty enough, not interesting enough, not human enough, not awake enough, not loveable enough; not enough of the things a girl should be in order to make a boy love her.

Part of the heroine's journey in the romantic landscape she's been confined to is to make the boy see her. Some element of transformation is always required, whether that's via aesthetic makeover, disguise or body swap. But none of it really matters in the end, because he can see inside her *heart*. This is what makes him see who she really is, and that one little glimpse of her interior self is enough.

The thought that someone could see beyond your physical self and into the *real* you is an intoxicating kind of magic for young girls taught to hate themselves. This is what makes it so powerful.

It's also what makes it so dangerous. Because it makes us believe that being picked is the *same* as being seen; that having a boy or a man come along and pick us (of all the girls on offer!) off the shelf is somehow meaningful.

What so many of us learn far too late is that there's a huge difference between the stories girls are told to aspire to, and the ones boys are taught they deserve. For us, the boy *is* the quest. For them, the girl is just the reward.

What happens when the hero takes his prize back to the castle? Why, they live happily ever after and the story ends. What else is there to say? When a princess completes her transition into marital bliss, we can expect never to hear from her again.

She's part of *his* world now.

———

In Plato's *Symposium*, an imagined conversation between Plato's contemporaries, the playwright, Aristophanes, describes a time in which humans moved rapidly across the earth in giant cartwheels. The speed and size of these whirling circles agitated the gods, who were nervous the humans might one day defeat them. To prevent this, Zeus split the humans down the middle and left them to wander the earth. This yearning for what Plato called the 'soulmate' supposedly comes from trying to find your other half; only once reunited could a person feel truly whole.

Two thousand years after Plato dangled the promise of a soulmate, Cameron Crowe would fell a generation of women already raised on a diet of romantic comedies, modern pop songs and fairytales packaged as feel-good cartoons when he committed three simple words to the zeitgeist: *You complete me.* Seconds later, he issued the knockout blow when Renée Zellweger's single-mother-in-need-of-a-hero replies to Jerry Maguire's declaration of love with her own iconic entry into the catalogue of Great One Liners: *You had me at hello.* The idea that love could be as easy as this (even if it has some narrative hiccups along the way) is a particularly male fantasy. Writing a woman (and a single mother, no less!) as two dimensionally as Dorothy Boyd is also a mistake typically made by men, who seem to collectively believe women are all gazing adoringly at them from the sidelines and just waiting to be noticed.

Crowe's own symposium resonates with that of another iconic duo, roughly from the same era. Seven years before the release of *Jerry Maguire*, Nora Ephron brought together two of pop culture's most enduring lovers: Harry Burns and Sally Albright. Released in 1989, *When Harry Met Sally* remains one of the most popular romantic comedies ever made. A cinematic tribute to New York City, it's beloved for its crackling dialogue, will-they-won't-they storyline and its iconic contributions to the zeitgeist. Sally (played by the adorable Meg Ryan) faking an orgasm over lunch with Harry to prove to him he couldn't possibly know if a woman's done it before has gone down in cinematic history—so much so that in 2022, the United States National Film Registry selected the movie for preservation in the Library of Congress, listing it as 'culturally, historically or aesthetically significant'.

But what makes *When Harry Met Sally* so compelling is how LONG it takes the characters to get together. Rather than falling in love at first sight, their first meeting ends with them hating each other. When they meet again a few years later, Sally doesn't remember Harry. On their third meeting, they become friends. It takes twelve years for them to get it together, which also means the characters mature a lot along the way. Summarising it together in the film's final scene, they say: 'We were friends for a long time. And then we weren't. And then we fell in love. Three months later we got married.'

When Harry Met Sally didn't reinvent the rom-com genre, but it managed to nail a particular kind of nineties neurosis that also happened to be incredibly *Noo Yawk*. Sally might be as cute as a button, but she's notably different from other romantic heroines. She's very particular about what she likes, driving waiters crazy with her extremely specific food orders. She's argumentative, but not in the kind of Katharine Hepburn way where it's considered foreplay. What makes her so appealing to a female audience in particular is the fact she *doesn't* change for Harry. In fact, he says as much in the film's denouement when he races to find her before the clock strikes midnight on New Year's Eve. The pair have had a falling out, because they slept together and Harry—who always said men and women can't be friends because sex gets in the way—went and let the sex get in the way. Soon enough, he realises the enormous mistake he's made and runs to tell her he loves her, and every last one of her annoying idiosyncrasies. Then he delivers this immortal line: 'I came here tonight because when you realise you want to spend the rest of your life with some-body, you want the rest of your life to start as soon as possible.'

When Harry Met Sally is a brilliant movie, there's no doubting that. But it still hooks into this idea that life doesn't begin until we find *the one* (or 'our person' as *Grey's Anatomy* would go on to call it). Only then can we be seen—and in being seen, we can finally see ourselves.

———

There's a political history behind the popularity of romance propaganda, and it's worth looking at. Marriage propaganda has always targeted women, but the success of the women's suffrage movement coupled with the shift towards companionate marriages really forced the practice to become more insidious. With middle-class white women (marriage's target market) able to politically organise themselves, own property and even work, marriage was no longer necessary for a woman's economic survival. In a post suffrage world, where political progress seemed to be happening all the time, marriage reinvented itself as the ultimate indicator that a person was *loved.*

It's no coincidence that this cultural shift occurred as women began claiming more of the legal and social rights that had been denied to them. For most of the first half of the twentieth century, the world was locked into major military conflict. Men went off to fight (and they've never let us forget it!) while women pulled for the war effort back home (wherever that may have been). A world war is the kind of thing that allows people to abandon social mores and conventions (at least for a time), and so the sheer scale of both of these global events meant women of all backgrounds could finally participate in the kind of public, *valued* working life that had always been denied to them, simply because all of the men were off shooting guns at each other.

Frightening, yes. But imagine the excitement at finally being a part of it all!

Remember, a little girl born at the start of World War I in 1914 would have been only thirty-one when the second world war of her lifetime reached its conclusion. She may well have been married by this point, but whether or not her husband survived the war was up to the hand of fate. We know for sure that she wouldn't have spent six years hiding behind curtains and wandering listlessly among drawing rooms and parlours, which really upends all the Victorian bullshit about women's fragile dispositions and delicate nervous systems. More likely than not, she was engaged in the war effort, working either as a mechanic or a munitions expert. She may have been a nurse. She might even have been a spy. Whatever she chose to be or do, one thing was clear: she'd be having a great fucking time.

How do you make women who've won the right to vote AND come through two world wars (both of which provided opportunity to leave the home and contribute meaningfully to the war effort, drastically expanding the social spheres that had previously been available to women) willingly return to the home and the domestic roles they had always been forced into?

You make them believe in the myth of True Love, soulmates and the magic of a life-saving kiss.

Disney's first three princess cartoons came out in 1937, 1950 and 1959, which seems like less of a coincidence and more of a coordinated campaign. That little girls born in the post-suffrage, post-war eras of where the boom was big and opportunity even bigger were suddenly being fed stories of princesses tormented by bitter, twisted old women (feminists!), who were really just jealous of their youth and beauty. Poisoned into submission by these madams of misery, our young heroines are all saved at the end by a handsome prince and his moist lips.

Yuck!

Snow White, Sleeping Beauty and Cinderella were released at a time when the status quo desperately needed its newly liberated women to stay in the home. The men had returned from war, and they couldn't have their sacrifices undermined by a bunch of girls in the lunchroom. The first step was to romanticise marriage. The second, to demonise working women. It was a mighty success. How many of us were raised on a diet of romantic comedies where the careerist woman learns that true happiness comes from being loved and getting married? I can list about ten off the top of my head right now, and those are just the ones starring Sandy Bullock.

Is it any wonder patriarchy has made villains out of the women who finally understand what the fuck is going on? The witch in the woods. The wicked stepmothers maligned by male writers as being consumed with jealousy over the blossoming fertility of their stepdaughters, furious that their own is withering to dust. The women driven to revenge and characterised as 'mad' by the violence men inflicted on them: Medusa, Clytemnestra, Medea, Lilith. Women who challenge male power have always been ridiculed as dangerous and evil. Crazy. Hysterical. Old. Ugly. Bitter. Rude. Unfuckable. Life imitates art, and art has a shitload of women it's fed to the wolves.

It's ironic that all of our most popular and well-worn fairytales feature a gnarled old woman at the centre, fiendishly trying to destroy the happiness of the beautiful young maiden at the story's centre. The world and its male authors have taught us to believe that witches are the ones determined to rob a young woman of her future, when maybe the truth has been concealed in a magic mirror this whole time: that the witch, knowing as she does what awaits the young girl at the end of the happy ever after, intervenes not in an act of destruction . . . but of rescue.

Haven't you ever asked yourself why all the mothers in these stories are dead? It's because dead women can't warn you about what's coming.

It turns out that great danger for young women never lay in the heart of the deep, dark woods but in the bright lights of the castle. *Marriage* is a house made out of gingerbread, drawing young girls in to feast on it with the promise of sugary treats and colourful decorations. Step through the threshold though, and a different future awaits. An oven, warmed and waiting, and ready to slowly cook you until nothing of your once vibrant self remains.

We need to find better stories than the ones that tell us to give up our voices just so we might be loved.

———

In her essay 'Compulsory Heterosexuality and Lesbian Existence', the critical feminist thinker and esteemed poet Adrienne Rich argues that marriage for women has almost always been a decision made easier because of economic concerns. As we know, women have been almost exclusively denied the right to own property or amass wealth of our own. With a variety of different cultural narratives confirming women's responsibility to perform endless reproductive labour (and yet with the absence of effective contraception), women also understood the risks associated with getting pregnant outside of secure economic and domestic arrangements. Even today, the likelihood of women achieving financial independence is diminished considerably by having children—an experience many of us still want and are independently capable of, but that we've been brainwashed into believing must be necessarily linked to romantic partnership. And so marriage has been a practical solution to the obstacles we might otherwise face in establishing some kind of control over our own lives, however superficial and limited that might be. If you keep the women poor, you keep them reliant on whatever makes it easier to get through the day.

But to the economic realities of marriage, Rich adds a more subjective consideration—one designed to significantly reduce women's capacity for freedom, happiness and power in the world, but that also functions to sweeten the deal of aspiring to such a limited state. Beyond economic and practical reasons, she writes, women marry 'because heterosexual romance has been represented as the great female adventure, duty, and fulfillment'.

A woman able to see for the first time is a dangerous beast. I'd known the thrust of what Rich was saying, of course, but never had I seen it articulated in such damning and precise detail. It isn't just that women are tricked by cultural bullshit into serving men, and made to believe that this is where the source of our happiness lives. It's the indignity of knowing how successful this brainwashing has been for so many of us. It's understanding how easy it's been for the system to convince us that nothing we do, create, achieve, say, build or strive for as humans in the world will ever be as meaningful or exciting to us as becoming the kind of woman a man decides to come home to, sometimes. It doesn't matter that the stories we're fed are fake as fuck. We know that love like this doesn't exist, not really. We know that people aren't held in happy perpetuity, frozen in the closing credits of love. Life is complicated and hard, and people are fucked up. But women keep dreaming, because the torrential downpour of love stories that soak us from the moment we're born tell us to *just keep looking for The One*. If we try hard enough, we could find him! Our own Prince Charming, Harry Burns, Jerry Maguire, Noah Calhoun (don't even get me started on *The Notebook*—constantly fighting with someone isn't healthy, and building you a house doesn't make up for that!), McDreamy, McSteamy, McFucker. Whatever the name given to the romantic hero, the bare bones of his character remain the same.

He is not real.

Boys are raised on stories that propel them into the far-off distance. They grow up and out, imagining themselves as pirates, cowboys, pilots, astronauts, inventors—important people doing important things, praised and revered and immortalised in books, movies, songs and folk tales. The phenomenon even has a literary term—*the hero's journey*. In this monomyth, an ordinary hero is called to embark on a quest, taking him outside his comfort zones, both literal and figurative. Over the course of his quest, he confronts enemies, overcomes obstacles and learns something essential about life. Proving himself at last to be a hero, he returns home a transformed man.

Boys have fairytales, too, but they're set in space, underwater or in the Wild West. They get to have *Star Wars, The Lord of the Rings, The Fast and the Furious, Rocky (I–X), Top Gun (I and II), Dirty Harry, Apollo 13, The Martian,* and on and on and on. I could literally list every fucking movie ever made with a male audience in mind, which is approximately 99 per cent of them. Men's fairytales never have marriage at the core; home is only where he returns when his quest is complete. And though he may secure the love and adoration of a woman in the course of this quest, the love itself is never presented as the adventure— merely the reward he gets for having proved his worth *in the eyes of other men.*

This is the noxious shit we all grow up with. Men sailing off into the sunset to conquer the high seas for years on end, fucking mermaids and sirens on their path to glory . . . while women wait dutifully on the cliffs for first sight of their return.

Our great fucking adventure.

Marriage is not the difference between a woman having a happy, meaningful life and her somehow missing out on those things. Women need to liberate ourselves from the need for men to officially pick us. We have to unlearn the fairytales of our youth. Because what lies on the other side of that proposal is very often different from the romantic fantasy we've been drip-fed since birth in order to maintain our investment in our own oppression. The Beast remains a beast, and a prince's charm only goes so far.

———

I'm reminded of a poem my Depression-era grandmother used to recite whenever we left food on our plates.

Waste not, want not
For you may live to say,
'I wish I had the porridge,
that I once threw away!'

I wonder how many women, when presented with the bowl of porridge that constitutes so many men, take into consideration the fact this may be their *only shot to try the slop*. Isn't it better to have some porridge, any porridge, than to have no porridge at all? At least the porridge is there! I mean, at least you could say you've been *offered* porridge. You'd have a first-hand story about porridge, to fit in with the other women who've also had porridge at least once in their life!

Is it that they really, really want to marry THIS guy? Or did decades worth of fairytales, songs and movies just make her want to have a little slice of the story for herself, just in the hopes she might have any kind of story at all? Might as well give it a crack, just to say she didn't waste the opportunity. Maybe the porridge will turn out to be too hot or maybe it will turn out to be too cold.

But maybe, if she's lucky, it might turn out to be just right.

SOMETHING BLUE

'Hell is truth seen too late.'

—Thomas Hobbes, *Leviathan*

12

TROUBLE AND STRIFE, COMEDY WIFE

'John laughs at me of course, but one

expects that in marriage.'

—Charlotte Perkins Gilman, 'The Yellow Wallpaper'

Grooms who flash HELP ME signs while exchanging wedding vows. Men who post videos of themselves hiding in bathrooms as a 'genius move' to avoid dealing with their families. New husbands who smash cake into their bride's face, even though she's specifically asked him not to. If it's highbrow comedy dissecting the human condition you're after, look as far away as you can from the bowels of TikTok, because here you'll find nothing at all to laugh at.

'Marriage humour' (an incredibly loose description, given that it's frequently so unfunny) is probably about as old as marriage itself, with the punchline always being something about how horrendous it is to spend your life locked into a contract with another person. As we know, men are dragged into marriage kicking and screaming and spend the rest of their lives trying not to crumble in defeat. *Marriage!* the metaphorical billboard screams. *It'll drive you to an early grave—but only if you don't drive yourself there first! The only way through it is to laugh!*

Usually at your wife, it seems.

It's unclear if the dire genre of marriage comedy is used by so many people as a coping mechanism for the truly heinous punishment that is marriage, or if its purpose is to function as some kind of humble brag for having 'made it'. The fact that it produces such a glut of tedious jokes, recycled sketches and eager retrosexism is incredibly depressing. If marriage is meant to represent the death of your sex life, your creativity, your youthful optimism and your enthusiasm for living, why are so many of these jokes also laced with pride for having done it?

Previous generations have had to make do with telling their 'take my wife (no, really, take her)' jokes to smaller audiences. Decades worth of Hollywood comedies have also leaned hard into the trope, with an endless parade of slapstick storylines in which incompetent man-babies embark on adventures to distract themselves from the marital hell they've found themselves in. You know, the one in which their objectively much-better-looking wife just rides them day and night (and not in the good way, not in the way she used to before she stopped having sex with him and started wearing thermal pyjamas to bed). She used to be fun, but now she just wears button-up shirts made out of sensible cotton and tells him to get a job. What a nag!

You'd think we'd have outgrown this nonsense, but the rise of online media has made it possible for everyone to have a crack at their spouse. You used to have to be a small-time comedian with a name like Rocket Dickfingers to be given the opportunity to regale the masses with stories about how you tricked your wife into letting you off the hook for dishwashing duties. Now all you need is a smartphone, a TikTok account and the total absence of anything resembling imagination to create the next viral sensation. Chuck in some well-worn hashtags like #marriedlife, #weddedbliss and the staggeringly optimistic #funny, and you're set.

The Cockney rhyming slang for wife is *trouble 'n' strife*, and it's the perfect description for the disdainful humour so many of these men bring to the portrayal of their own marriages. There's a variety of different roles in which the wife is cast: nagging shrew, easily manipulated dummy, emotional crackpot, exhausted mother, ignored personal assistant, unreasonable controller of the sex distribution scheme. For the men behind these videos, the role is more clearly defined: overgrown child who's convinced his wife he's a hapless twit so that she stops asking him to do things he doesn't want to (but will undertake as a gesture of goodwill when he wants to have sex that night). How this fits with men's valorisation of themselves as protectors and providers is anyone's guess, but constructing a reality in which nothing makes sense seems to be a special skill for the dudebros.

A rundown of some of the more popular trouble 'n' strife videos I've seen online:

- Man films himself in shower, his head covered in the lather of shampoo. His caption reads something like: *When you know the kids need to be fed dinner but you decide to have a shower and wash your hair so you 'couldn't hear' your wife yelling at you to come help.*

- Disappointed looking man films himself drying a plate and looking mournfully at the camera. His caption reads: *When you pour your wife a glass of wine and tell her to relax while you clean the kitchen only to have her say she has a headache.*

- A piece of paper rolls slowly out of a fax machine before dropping immediately into a paper shredder. Caption reads: *What your brain does with the instructions your wife just gave you.*

- Man films his wife getting mad or frustrated with him while he pretends not to understand and tries not to laugh. His caption reiterates how crazy women are.

- Man films himself standing cluelessly in front of the fridge (or drawer or cupboard etc.). Caption reads: *When you still can't find what she's describing and she starts walking angrily towards you.*

- Man films himself standing in a field, staring stoically into the distance. Luke Skywalker's theme music from *Star Wars* plays. Caption is some variation of: *Realising you've successfully avoided ever changing a dirty nappy/Congratulating yourself for doing such a bad job of the laundry that she'll never ask you again/Putting literally less effort than it takes to breathe into my marriage and still believing I'm a prize.*

Okay, so that last variation was my own interpretation, but you get the idea.

My disgust for the trouble 'n' strife genre isn't because I consider laughter a criminal offence. And it's not because I 'take myself too seriously'—a quality (usually divorced) men on dating apps often cite as a deal-breaker. I take myself exactly the right amount of seriously, and that means only laughing at men when they deserve it.

Obviously, some marriage humour *is* quite funny. Teasing your spouse isn't in and of itself a detestable act, but one of the basic rules of good comedy is that it shouldn't punch down. Laughing with your wife at her idiosyncrasies is very different from inviting an audience of people (however big or small) to laugh *at* her in a way that's clearly designed to make her feel small and embarrassed. (See: filming your wife while she tries to articulate her frustrations with your behaviour, and then inviting your audience to minimise those frustrations by giggling at how upset she is.)

Similarly, good-faith jokes about things that ultimately read as cute are different from 'jokes' designed to hide harm in plain sight. Consider the above examples of weaponised incompetence, and the not-so-subtle bait and switch that works by concealing genuine exploitation as something that can be passed off as a laugh. There's no clever punchline here. There aren't even any layers. The joke is that he's figured out how to get away with exploiting his wife's time, labour and energy and that this is somehow terrifically clever and funny. What a diabolical genius! Look at him, having his cake and eating it too! Men are so useless—but they also built the world! They invented everything—but they can't use a dishwasher! He can't put his clothes in the hamper—he's too busy being the president!

Whenever I've expressed disgust or even mild derision in response to these kinds of videos, I've been met with a disproportionate level of outrage. The idea that these stale, tired tropes could be received as anything other than harmless one liners is apparently deeply offensive. An attack on all men! Men, who made that phone you're using to type out your half-baked feminist insanity, using technology *men* invented! Show some respect!

Of course, most mobile phones are assembled in factories staffed primarily by women who are less likely than men to own and use one themselves, and the formula that led to the creation of the internet was designed by Ada Lovelace—but again, facts don't matter to the men who construct patriarchal reality for themselves. If they tell you to laugh at something, then you better damn well laugh. Oh, and click the like button while you're at it.

There's a lot about online content creation that I hate. The lack of originality, for a start. I'm going to sound like an old curmudgeon here (guilty as charged!), but creativity seems to be less about originality than it is recreating other people's work. The practice of copying trends has become so ubiquitous that it's hard to know if people even believe in the messages they're sharing or if they just think it will grow their follower counts. Either way, the format has made it more possible than ever for casual misogyny (particularly of the hapless husband variety) to be dropped randomly into your newsfeeds and normalised as a quirky jape.

According to my source in Meta's Australian division, if you want a video to perform well online, the optimum length is fifteen seconds or less. As more online producers become invested in follower growth over actual content, the proliferation of bite-sized videos (YouTube calls them 'shorts') will overwhelm our feeds. Research has shown that excessive use of social media creates a negative dopamine feedback loop. Basically, chomping down on the bite-sized morsels of cognitive junk that floats through our feeds provides little bursts of a mental sugar hit in rapid succession. We comment on posts, receive likes, laugh at other people's jokes and then keep scrolling for more. Sounds nice, right?

But when we flood our brains with too much dopamine without giving them time to release it, we reverse the benefits of the dopamine itself by depleting it all in one great dump. Basically, we feed our brains too much of that sugar and then have to deal with the fallout from a massive crash. To make ourselves feel better, we turn back to our phones, hoping to hit the sweet spot once again.

Professor Anna Lembke calls social media a way to 'drugify human connection'. In an interview with *Teen Vogue*, she said, 'We've evolved over millions of years to want to connect with people because it helps us protect ourselves from predators, use scarce resources, find a mate. One of the ways our brain gets us to make those connections is [to] release dopamine.'

Cool, but what does that have to do with Rocket Dickfingers peddling his comedy schlock on Instagram?

It's all about the algorithm, baby.

Say one of Dickfingers' hilarious 'jokes' pops up on your feed. You think it's harmless enough and it makes you laugh, so you hit 'like' and maybe even start to follow his account. The algorithm takes note of your endorsement and responds by pushing more Dickfingers content into your feed. You like a few more posts, and so the algorithm decides you must like Dickfingers' comedy as a genre. Suddenly, you're seeing other videos and accounts just like his, some of which have tens of thousands of likes, comments and shares. Your feed is flooded with #marriedlife hilarity, and within that feed lies a hierarchy of popularity. Some people even make money from this shit, quitting their day jobs to become professional content creators. Who knows? Maybe one day you could be as big as Dickfingers himself!

You film your first reel—it's a gif of John Cena dancing, superimposed over a toilet bowl, with a carefree pop tune playing over the top. The caption reads: *Kids are crying and wife is falling apart—me taking a twenty-minute dump.*

The reel does okay. A few likes, some comments. It makes you feel good. But then it gets shared by a massive account known for posting memes about dads and husbands. Within days, the repost has been shared more than 427,000 times. The popular dad account's post of your video has well over 5000 comments, and they all think it's the funniest fucking thing they've ever seen in their life. Someone's left a comment just saying 'same!' with a crying face emoji next to it, and there are four hundred replies nested below it from men agreeing that yes, they do indeed also spend concerning amounts of time on the can.

You note that a few women have got their knickers in a twist about it, but they've been set straight by everyone who understands the difference between a JOKE and a humiliating insight into the disregard men so often have for their wives. You like all the ones calling them *ugly cat ladies* and then type out a comment tagging the dad site. *Hey there! Thanks for sharing my video! You can catch more of my insights into the joys of #marriedlife at my account, @TakeMyWife. Hope to see you there!* It's annoying that the dad account has snaked all of your engagement, but it's also kind of inspiring. Now you have something to aim for.

This is a hypothetical scenario, of course. I don't know what prompted the creation of the John Cena toilet video celebrating men who'd rather hide in the bathroom with their own shit than participate in caring for their own children. All I know is that the reel itself exists, and it was indeed shared by a large Dad Meme page filled with comments laughing about how accurate it was. It popped up in my feed not because I follow the page, but because I had recently left a comment on a different post someone had sent me—another one of those here's-how-much-we-hate-our-wives 'jokes' that women are required by law to enjoy. My comment was enough to prompt the algorithm to push the account to me later on as a 'helpful' suggestion for new content to watch: *Because you commented on a recent post from Rocket Dickfingers, we thought you might like this.*

Now, I can just ignore these suggestions. I *should* just ignore these suggestions, because commenting on Dickfingers' genre comedy is a waste of time. No matter how many different ways I've done it, the end result is the same—I'm obviously just a stupid fucking feminist who hates men and can't take a joke. Of course, their rage only increases when I ask them to explain what the joke is meant to be and why *they* find it so funny—but I guess it's hard to say *Well, men hate their wives and kids but sure do love the smell of their own shit* without proving my point.

The problem isn't so much that I have to see shitty (literally) sexism passed off as high art. Shitty sexism dressed up as entertainment has always existed and probably will always exist. The problem is in the resurgence of it as a *profitable* form of comedy, and therefore a ubiquitous one. Dickfingers' comedy might not have the power to turn a genuinely nice man into the kind of person who starts humiliating his partner online for likes, or even a member of the target audience. But the kinds of viewers the algorithm targets—the ones who can be relied on to keep scrolling through whatever wormhole they've been sucked down—might be less critical about what they're being shown. More to the point, women discovering the wilful laziness of their own partners might be less inclined to question what it is they're being subjected to. Because isn't this what marriage is? And if he's broadcasting his treatment of her to millions of strangers, surely it can't be as bad as she thinks? Then there's the *there but for the grace of God go I* responses; women whose husbands objectively do take advantage of them but are perhaps slightly more helpful than Mr Dickfingers are less likely to see their situations as demoralising or exploitative—because, hey, at least he does the dishes *sometimes*. What they don't realise (or are resistant to accepting, for obvious reasons) is that their marriage is in the toilet just the same as those other women's. They might be higher in the bowl, but everything gets flushed down the same way.

This is one of the many dangerous consequences of drugifying human interaction: the algorithm doesn't just interpret what we like—it creates it. And no one is spared from being #influenced.

———

Weaponised incompetence as a cornerstone of #husbandhumour might have found its niche on social media now, but for decades all you had to do was turn on your television and tune into the latest family sitcom. Conservatives might glorify the 'traditional' values of the fictitious June and Ward Cleaver, but the days of men being presented as fully grown adults would be well and truly over by the time Wally and Beaver Cleaver grew up and started to make their way in the world.

Undoubtedly prompted by both the economic downturn of the seventies and the increased presence (and power) of women in the public sphere, this new presentation of family life fixed its humour in the idea of men as deposed kings deprived of their chance to lead even their own households. It's diabolical when you think about it. On the surface, the cultural embrace of men as hopeless buffoons contradicts the idea of women's domestic oppression. *See!* people could argue. *How can men be 'oppressors' when they can't even turn sideways without being ridiculed as useless?* By maintaining the plausible deniability of being hardwired for domestic incompetency, men aggrieved at feminism's theft of their power could focus on delivering consequences to all women trying to rise up out of their station.

Think of the male protagonists of popular sitcoms like *Married . . . with Children*, *Home Improvement*, *Everybody Loves Raymond* and *The King of Queens*. Al Bundy's a defeated, working-class shoe salesman who routinely denigrates his wife, Peg (and is further humiliated by the fact she doesn't seem to care much). Tim 'The Toolman' Taylor is a quintessential dude's dude (to the point that whenever he does something *manly*, he barks). Tim fronts a home renovations show on a local TV network, but he's always messing things up and getting into scrapes. What a goof! The titular character on *Everybody Loves Raymond* is similarly hopeless, lumbering through life cracking jokes and annoying his wife Debra (who never wants to have sex with him, possibly because his parents and brother seem to live in the couple's kitchen). And while I never really watched *The King of Queens*, I do know that it stars Kevin James, whose other credits include *Paul Blart: Mall Cop* and *Zookeeper*, a movie in which, as Amy Schumer reminds us, it requires less suspension of disbelief to accept that James's character can understand the speech of animals than it does to go with a storyline in which Rosario Dawson is desperate to have sex with him.

Hapless husbands are a dime a dozen in the sitcom world and beyond. Think of *The Simpsons* and its cultural elevation to hero status of chief hapless husband, Homer Simpson. The first episode of *The Simpsons* screened when I was only eight years old, with its earliest episodes focusing on the antics of ten-year-old Bart (a sort of modern-day Dennis the Menace). But audiences loved the unrelentingly incompetent Homer, whose working-class credentials only served to further his popularity. This was a man with no discernible social power! He was balding! Let him drink as much Duff beer as he likes while obstinately ruining the life of his cranky wife, Marge! Homer Simpson has become our culture's longest-standing example of the glorified hapless husband, his longevity assured even further by the fact an animated character never has to age. Three decades have passed since the show's debut, but Homer Simpson seems permanently frozen in time as a thirty-something loser with a hot wife he routinely undermines and humiliates, but who sticks around in accordance with one of the unbreakable rules of the sitcom universe: no matter how useless the leading man is, he *means* well—and because of that, his wife knows in her heart that she's lucky to have him.

Almost all sitcom wives are better than their husbands. That isn't the misandry speaking; it's the formula. They're hotter, smarter, more competent, more talented and more demonstrably adult. Why they stay is anyone's guess; in the real world, half of them would have hightailed it out of there by now. (Maybe not Marge Simpson. That poor lady surely has some form of complex PTSD and/or Stockholm syndrome.) But consider Jill Taylor, the fictional wife of Tim 'The Toolman' Taylor (*arf arf arf*). Jill was intelligent, funny, acceptably mom-sexy and leagues ahead of Tim when it came to being a competent adult. She had just the right balance of soft edges and stern authoritarian to help keep their three sons in check (boy moms, am I right?!) and certainly didn't suffer from a lack of confidence. Ditto Debra, whose marriage to Raymond seemed to involve her telling him off weekly, managing the relationship with his overly familiar parents and cleaning up a never-ending mess of spills. Jill and Debra were feisty! They may have been married to overgrown babies, but they didn't suffer fools!

Except . . . they did. All stereotypical sitcom wives are designed to suffer through the foolishness of whatever harebrained scheme their husband comes up with next, and to fix his mistakes when he finally gives up. All sitcom wives have perfected the art of the deep sigh, rolling their eyes while clutching a laundry basket to their hip and shaking their head slightly to convey their disapproval in a way that is obviously frustrated but not overly *feminist*. All sitcom wives eventually have sex with their husbands and enjoy it, and never feel bullied or pressured into doing it for necessary relationship 'maintenance'. By the end of each episode, all sitcom wives have forgiven their husbands for whatever nonsense he put them through that week, just as all sitcom wives will wake up the next morning to cook him breakfast and send him off to work with words of encouragement, never breaking character for even a moment to gaze off into the distance and wonder what the fuck happened to their life.

The depictions of women as overworked but ultimately proud mothers to the overgrown children they share their bed with have been among the most insidious of tools used to negatively influence women into embracing domestic servitude. Yes, he's frustrating and he increases your workload. But what would you do without him? You'd be alone! A fate worse than death! Women don't learn over time to subjugate their needs to a man's; it's drilled into us from the moment we're born, confirmed over and over again by what we see on television, read in books and witness our own mothers tolerating at the hands of fathers we learn to think are good enough. Accepting this subpar, dehumanising version of love is normalised further by the warnings we receive about not being 'too picky'—the subtext of that being of course that beggars can't be choosers. And it works, because most of us *want* love of some kind. We want to feel cared for, and we want to feel seen. That so few men seem interested in loving us the way we *deserve* to be loved is absorbed as par for the course, and dismissed even in ourselves as being 'unrealistic'. As bell hooks wrote in *All About Love*, 'We fear that evaluating our needs and then carefully choosing partners will reveal that there is no one for us to love.'

I mean . . . except our cats, I guess.

Cue audience laughter.

———

This brings us to today's Comedy Wives. You know Comedy Wife. She's the counterpoint to Rocket Dickfingers, the antidote to the nagging nightmare he has to live with. She's chill, she's cool, she knows how to laugh at herself and she just *loves* being married!

It depresses me no end to see the hapless husband trope being replicated across social media daily, except this time with beautiful, competent women making light of the *arf! arf! arf!*ing of the oxygen thieves they're married to. These are men who can somehow manage to stay up all night playing video games but can't get up with the baby. What a catch! But proving once again how deeply women have been indoctrinated into wanting men to like them, a lot of the Comedy Wife genre is fawning, sentimental garbage.

Oh look, he let me sleep in and then I caught him on camera playing with our kids *isn't he just the greatest man to have ever lived?!?!*

Or:

I asked my husband to put away the leftovers, and then found the entire crockpot, cord and all, just shoved into the fridge. I can't even be mad because this is just sooooooo funny! How is he able to manage a small team of contractors, but he can't even figure out Tupperware?! We couldn't live without him, though—he's our shining star #marriedlife

Or:

Appreciation post for the most AMAZING man I know. I've been working really long hours lately, and I haven't been able to keep on top of the house. But I woke up this morning after Steve let me have a sleep-in to find that he'd folded all of the laundry from last week AND wiped down the kitchen bench. Steve, you go above and beyond for our family every day, and we are so grateful for you. Thank you for choosing us <3

The comments will be full of people saying things like 'awww!' and 'you guys are so cute!' with the occasional 'wish my husband would do that for me!' thrown in. Steve won't write anything, but he might consider liking the post to let her know he's seen it. It goes without saying that he'll never reciprocate with a gesture of public appreciation himself. What would he say? What would any of them say? *Thanks for doing absolutely everything for me save for wiping my butt (which I don't do properly, so thanks for still fucking me, I guess!).*

It might seem like I'm being hyperbolic, but these are all marital tropes exhumed to great degree across social media. Like the formulaic world of sitcoms that came before, I've no doubt you've seen anywhere between one and three thousand entries on the topic. But while a lot of women do tend to feign joy at the depressing lot they've wound up with (I call this the Long-Suffering Comedy Wife), there's a second type who's (thankfully) starting to appear more and more: the When You Stare Into The Abyss, The Abyss Also Stares Into You Wife.

I contend that these are in fact the same kind of wife. The only difference is that the first uses comedy as a coping mechanism for the chasm of despair that being married toppled her into, while the second has been in the chasm for so long that she can't summon the energy to keep pretending anymore. These are the women who've grown fucking tired of dealing with the weaponised incompetence of grown men (or 'weaponised incontinence', as one feminist parenting group I follow calls the guys who disappear into the bathroom for hours on end to watch TikTok videos and shit) and they're willing to pull back the curtain and show people what a deadbeat he really is. We need more Abyss Wives and fewer Comedy Wives, with the ultimate goal of course to turn every last one of them into an Ex-Wife.

Look, there's a reason romantic comedies that start with a meet-cute so often end with a proposal or a wedding. If viewers were to continue on past the happily-ever-after and into the mundane reality of the day to day, most of the women watching would correctly assume we'd had an unexpected genre shift and found ourselves in a movie about casual domestic abuse and undiagnosed depression. (This is the clever premise of the show *Kevin Can F**k Himself,* which exposes the misogyny of the domestic sitcom while providing a thematic way out for Annie Murphy's oppressed wife.)

Society tricks women into aspiring to marriage and then shames them into staying. No woman wants to admit her marriage sucks, because it means *she* sucks. She sees everyone else around her thanking their husbands for being superheroes, and she wonders why they all got so lucky while she got stuck with Rocket Dickfingers. What she doesn't know is that most women are *lying*. To their friends, to their families and even to themselves. The reality they've found themselves in post-wedding is a long way from the glossy heights of domestic bliss they thought they were ascending to. The man who at first seemed capable and steady can suddenly reveal himself to be slovenly, disrespectful, casually cruel and utterly uninterested in the interior life of the woman he's pledged to love forever. (In stating this, we must also remember that the bar for what most women will consider a suitable partner is buried deep beneath the earth's crust, so the fact men manage to burrow even further down is quite an impressive feat.)

I know why men take part in the charade of #marriedlife vom-com, but why would women? Well, it's one thing to acknowledge the deeply entrenched inequality that exists in your relationship; deciding what to do about it is another thing entirely. The general approach women take to try to disrupt the domestic inertia men seem happy to embrace often involves a grab bag of different methods, including pleading, encouragement (like you'd give a toddler or a dog who'd learned to take themselves to the toilet), online gratitude parades, occasional bursts of anger, and expulsions of frustration made privately to other mothers and/or wives in the many online groups devoted to exactly this sort of thing.

Rinse. Wash. Repeat. Ha ha ha.

———

Domestic inequality 'comedy' is really boring. We should just admit it. But it's also dangerous, because it serves different purposes for the men and women who embrace it. Women do it because it solicits chuckling solidarity from other women, which helps all of them to breathe through the crushing indignity of their husbands' disregard for them and believe instead that this is just the annoying price of marriage (which is the ultimate goal). But for men, it functions as a nifty little escape clause for the responsibility they have to be good partners. 'Yes,' they're saying. 'I *am* exploiting her time and labour and energy, and I'm doing it deliberately and laughing at my evil genius. But because I'm admitting it publicly, in this forum, it can't really be that serious an infraction. In fact, I know that women will laugh along and say, *This is my husband!* and men will joke about not giving away our trade secrets. Ultimately, I see my wife as the facilitator of my life and someone who has ceased to even be a real person—but by making videos like this, I can hide the real impact of that in plain sight and be reassured that, actually, all men are like me so it's okay.'

How did men become this audacious?

And yes—I *am* talking about all men, across all demographics. I'm talking about men as a class of people, whose beliefs about what they think they deserve and what women should provide to them aren't confined to outliers on the fringes of society. These are culturally inherited ideals that have been passed from generation to generation and enshrined in both judicial legislation and social behaviours. It may not be the case that every single individual man enforces these beliefs, but it *is* the case that men from every different kind of social grouping you can think of have been informed by patriarchy in exactly the same way women from every different region and political class have been impacted by misogyny.

Men today are able to believe that women owe them loyalty, admiration, respect and domestic labour because their fathers and their fathers' fathers and their fathers' fathers' fathers—the fathers of men, the fathers of logic, the fathers of invention, the fathers of creation—made sure to keep passing it down the line to their successors with the same reverence for its importance as they'd reserve for their own names. Because it's not just men of a certain age who express these views, and it's not just men from a particular background or men who have been lacking in feminist education. It's not just men who refuse to eat vegetables and it's not just men who only eat them. It's not just men who hate their mothers and it's not just men who want to marry some version of them. It's tall men, short men, shy men, funny men, successful men, men who work in compassionate fields, men who vote progressive, men who vote conservative, men who were popular growing up, men who were bullied, men who love to cook, men who are active in their local sporting teams, men with sisters they love, men with female friends they treat well, men with long hair, men with short hair, men who like to keep fit, men who hate the gym—all men have inherited the legacy of patriarchy, and as such must accept responsibility for actively purging their system of it, in exactly the same way all white people have inherited the legacy of racism and must actively unlearn it.

These men come from somewhere. And just as they watched their fathers before them, so too are their children watching them now. Sons learn how to dehumanise women by first watching their mother be dehumanised. Daughters learn to expect dehumanisation by seeing it happen to her.

Thanks to science, we know that trauma can be passed down through a genetic line. So if we know that the experience of being subjected to trauma can be passed through a family and form part of the genetic blueprint that makes up that ancestral history, is it so difficult to accept the possibility that similar genetic evidence could appear in the intergenerational line of those who inflicted that trauma? Patriarchy mobilises its men to wield a sustained and deliberate campaign of violence against women. We've been raped, abused, beaten, traded as property, exploited for labour, institutionalised, murdered, fucked into submission, starved of our humanity, denied autonomy, forced into mother-hood, forced out of motherhood, denied an education, denied opportunities, dismissed as feeble, dismissed as pointless, blamed for men's violence, blamed for men's failures, blamed for men's loneliness, blamed for men's suffering, blamed for men's inability to compete with other men, retaliated against, discarded, hounded, told what we are, told who we are, told why we are, told told told told told, our tongues cut out so we cannot speak, our hands cut off so we cannot write and our names erased so we cannot be remembered. None of this history can ever be brought into the light, because men have immortalised themselves as the builders of the world and the fathers of humanity—and they'll do whatever it takes to make sure this is the only story people get to hear.

When men make jokes that persistently undermine women for the benefit of bonding men closer together, it has the impact of codifying that ineptitude as an accepted part of the fabric of society. In making it acceptable, it becomes normal—so much so that women are taught to feel grateful when surprise treats are thrown at them instead of a kick.

If you talk seriously about the widespread problem of this wilful incompetence, you're a 'misandrist' (the worst of all the crimes!). You catch the exact same ball they've been throwing around for laughs and you do nothing more than *describe the ball*, and suddenly you've ruined the game.

Because you hate men!

Men will literally show people exactly who they are, but when you repeat it back to them verbatim they get mad at you.

It's all a bit of fun, though, right? Trust the feminists to get upset! If only they could get a dick up them instead! Hahahahahaha.

They call them jokes, sure. But turn down the laugh track, and what you're left with is this: for women in particular, marriage is an exercise in swallowing daily humiliations, ritualised disrespect and crushing disappointment, all meted out by a person who still expects you to suck his dick when he's feeling horny. No punchline, just a punch.

And the audience cheers.

13

ALL THE LIGHT HE CANNOT SEE

'He who robs us of our dreams robs us of our life.'

—Virginia Woolf, *Orlando*

I was twelve years old when I first heard the term 'man cave'. My mother was reciting passages from a book she was reading that purported to be written by a relationship expert. For a long time after that, she used the image with reference to my father, saying, *Oh, he's just in his cave*, or, *I think he needs to spend some time in his cave*, and sometimes, *Darling, are you in your cave?*

As metaphors go, the idea of a man cave was simple: essentially, the author argued, men coped with the stresses of life by retreating into silence, which meant retreating from all of the nagging demands of their overly chatty partners. In order to process stress effectively, men's need for isolation from family and domestic life had to be both honoured and respected, regardless of how long the withdrawal period lasted. Only when the man had willingly emerged from his cocoon could he be ready to listen to whatever problems his wife might be having—especially if those problems were caused by him.

Women were the opposite. Women processed stress and life in general by *talking* about it, which required someone to talk *to* (or at, depending on how you view the situation). This grotesque need the fairer sex had to 'communicate' led to discord between the sexes, because women didn't know how or when to shut up and men couldn't bring themselves to listen or care.

Could a middle ground be reached, do you think? One where both members of a monogamous relationship learned to nurture the needs of the other, asserting themselves sometimes and making themselves adaptable at other times?

No, silly! It was the *women* who needed to learn what was wrong with them, and adjust their own expectations accordingly in order to make domestic life run as smoothly as possible for the men they were so very, very lucky to have!

This was how to circumvent the risks posed in a post-feminist era, grappling as it was with a rising divorce rate. By anticipating his need for silence, seclusion and space (without which he could not function), a woman could strengthen her husband's affection for her and ensure the longevity of their relationship. Once women cracked the code, living with men would be a lot easier. And really, such a misalignment of communication styles was probably to be expected. We do come from different planets, after all.

———

Men Are from Mars, Women Are from Venus was first published in 1992, but—despite a book tour that included an appearance on *The Oprah Winfrey Show*—its sales were modest initially. It wasn't until its author appeared as a guest on Phil Donahue's wildly successful daytime talk show more than a year after publication that it began to gain traction.

The central thesis of the book was that men and women come from different planets. This was the only explanation for our wildly different communication styles, and understanding this was key to creating healthy, intimate bonds between spouses whose relationships were otherwise hanging by a thread. As premises go, it's entirely non-scientific—but presenting men and women as having an intergalactic-sized reason for why we're just so *different* is no doubt appealing to the kinds of people who think dogs are always boys and cats are always girls. It *feels* true, and feeling like our convictions are correct (despite a lack of evidence to support them) is usually enough to convince most people that they are. Everyone knows that!

The book's author, John Gray, styled himself as a relationship guru and academic, and claimed for himself the academic title of 'PhD'. The qualification, both impressive and reassuring, was spelled out loud and clear not just on the cover of *Mars/Venus* but also the franchise of titles it subsequently spawned, which included a diet and exercise guide. This wasn't just any old guy coming along and trying to get into the self-help market. This was a *book-smart* guy!

But Gray wasn't a trained counsellor, nor was he an academic. What he had was a bachelor and master's degree in the 'Science of

Creative Intelligence', both of which were obtained at a 'university' run by his former employer and mentor, the Maharishi Mahesh Yogi. Gray did *pay* for a PhD, but it was obtained via a correspondence course from the now-defunct Columbia Pacific University, whose closure was forced by court order in 2000 after a years-long legal battle in which the Californian institution—which had been described in a lawsuit as a 'phoney operation' and a 'diploma mill'—was found to have 'failed to meet various requirements for issuing PhD degrees'.

Would John Gray, graduate of a metaphysical university who specialised in transcendental meditation, have been as successful in convincing millions upon millions of people to take his advice seriously if he'd been honest about his credentials? I doubt it. But those three little letters after your name can open a lot of doors, and I guess a lot of charlatans have figured out it's much easier to sell the snake oil to people if you can convince them it might have been made in a lab.

So what was Gray peddling in the book he later boasted took him only twelve weeks to write?

As it turns out, just a lot of pop psychology and unsubstantiated gobbledegook.

Here's some of the 'facts' Gray asserts as immutable in regard to men and women's essential natures. There's the aforementioned 'cave', a place to which men could both physically and metaphorically retreat from the obligation of communicating with their partners until they had gathered the strength to deal with it. There's also the 'wave', which was Gray's way of explaining how women's 'nature' is to experience unexpected changes in mood. Men were told not to try to understand the wave, or force it to be stationary; instead, they were advised to ride it out, letting her *feel* things like the Venusian weirdo she was. Men, logical beasts that they are, were also advised not to offer solutions when women shared their problems. Women didn't want solutions! They just wanted to talk, and men could navigate this by repeating what women said back to them!

It's unclear to me whether Gray has ever spoken to a woman let alone observed the interior motivations of a scientific sample size. This is the same man who described a light-bulb moment in his understanding of women as the moment when his wife, who was one week postpartum and bedridden following a traumatic birth, became upset with him after he responded to her pleas for help by getting angry and attempting to storm out. Such a Martian thing to do!

But my favourite part of the book is Gray's explanation for why men don't 'help' around the house as much as they should, and how women can modify their own behaviour in order to fix this. It isn't that men are lazy sacks of garbage who use what Deborah Cameron (author of the academic text *The Myth of Mars and Venus*) calls 'tactical misunderstanding' and weaponised incompetence to avoid being a contributing member of the household. It's that women *ask* for this 'help' in the wrong way!

See, according to Gray, men love being helpful. But they want to *choose* when they offer that help, and they want this incredible act of service to be acknowledged as having gone above and beyond the call of duty. They don't want some nagging woman-lady from

Venus making them do shit they don't want to do! Where's the reward in that? These Martians are simple creatures. They just want to live their lives peacefully, spending copious amounts of time alone in their caves to power up their energy bar, and every so often—when they *feel* like it—they'll do something huge like take the garbage out or wash a cup without her having to ask. That's how he shows his love! She wants him to show her he loves her, doesn't she?

I'm not exaggerating. This is precisely how Gray explains men's petulant response to being (endlessly) asked to do stuff. But the problem can be resolved easily enough. Instead of saying, 'Can you empty the fucking dishwasher, you soul-sucking piece of shit, I'm sick of fucking asking you?', women should ask (in their sweetest voice, presumably), 'Would you please empty the dishwasher for me?'

The difference between 'can' and 'would' is vital, Gray says. Because when you say 'can you' to a man (who is from Mars, remember!), he unconsciously decides that doing the thing is optional, even if he grudgingly answers yes. Framing the question as 'would you' appeals to his desire to be needed, which makes agreeing to do it seem like benevolent chivalry rather than the obligation of living in a household. And when he completes the task and proudly declares to her that yes, he very generously *provided* for her, he can settle back and enjoy the gratitude and praise she will no doubt want to heap upon him.

Now, girls: say thank you.

———

When I started dating my son's father, he was only recently out of a long-term relationship. I remember asking him one day how he could possibly be ready to move on with someone else when the break-up was so fresh, especially when he hadn't initiated it.

He said, 'When you break up after that long together, you've been breaking up for a long time.'

I took him at his word, but I couldn't relate; I'd never even lived with someone before.

Seven years later, I finally understood what he meant. Our relationship had been in a state of freefall for some time before I made the decision to leave, but the straw that broke the camel's back came on Christmas morning in 2018. My son had turned two a few months earlier, and I was excited for him to open the small array of presents I'd bought. I'd purchased a large cactus in a colourful pot and strung some lights around it in what I hoped made for a festive and reusable setting. I'm generally less thrifty than I'd like to be, but I've always been a bit utilitarian about repurposing things. A Christmas cactus might not be traditional, but it would long outlive the season at least.

As it turned out, the same could not be said of the relationship.

It was the presents that did it. Or, rather, the lack of any present at all. Wanting to replicate the simple joy of my own childhood, I had hung two stockings at the foot of our bed. I had stuffed my son's with a handful of little toys and treats. Into the other, I'd put things I knew his father enjoyed—candy, a jar of smooth peanut butter, a book I thought he'd like to read. I watched as they opened them, the smile tightening across my face as I realised nothing had been organised for me in return.

Maybe he's waiting for when we unwrap the presents under the cactus, I thought to myself.

But no, it turned out he hadn't got me anything at all that year. He waited until I'd handed out the last of the wrapped gifts before telling me. He was very distressed about it, explaining that he hadn't had time to go shopping amid the demands of work.

Seven years later, with the benefit of space and compassion and a lot of water under the bridge, I believe his distress was genuine. He worked until nine most nights and was often gripped by a state of anxious indecision about things such as gift-giving. Since separating, we've worked very hard to return to a state of kindness and love as co-parents, which means I can see once again his many excellent, beautiful qualities. I'm glad that he's the father of my son. I chose well.

But such compassion was beyond me then. The present fiasco was just the latest in a long line of incidents where I felt my needs being minimised while I slowly disappeared into the walls that housed our family—walls, incidentally, that my salary paid to keep us in.

Not even a card?! I exclaimed, the anger rushing through me. I wanted to cry, but—he was already doing that—another thing he got to have that I didn't. Like so many women, I had learned early on to stamp down my own feelings in order to give room to other people's. We have all learned to suck up our anger, breathe through our fury and smile sweetly at our lot. We know how to tuck sad men into bed and hold their hand as they fall asleep.

I had swallowed my disappointment with men so many times in order to save them from having to feel bad, but I couldn't do it that day. And so instead of crying, I let the fury I had been repressing for so long erupt out of me. It wasn't about a meaningless material item. I could buy myself a fucking book. It was about being reminded, once again, how far down the list of priorities I came. I had always been responsible for the running of our lives, and it was a task I was generally well suited for (as much as I might have liked to have a break from it). I had found houses to rent, organised our bills, planned and paid for our holidays . . . hell, I'd even built us a new bed when I was five months pregnant. No one asked me to do these things, it's true. But I also knew that if I didn't, then they wouldn't get done.

This is the role all too many women occupy in the domestic sphere: we are the safety nets held up to catch men felled by their own inertia. They're so accustomed to us being there that they don't even need to look at us anymore to know they'll always have a soft place to land.

In the early years of our relationship, my son's father liked to tell a story about one of our first dates. It was a soft summer's evening, the kind that makes it easy to fall in love. We were walking hand in hand down the street when we saw a person in front of us struggling to get a mini fridge into the back of a car.

'I can help with that!' I called out, racing towards them.

It was an easy task, but I felt the warm glow of approval when I saw my new beau looking at me, grinning.

'You just threw that thing in there like it was no big deal!' he exclaimed as we walked away.

I had always been proud of my can-do attitude. But as our relationship combusted, I realised that what had once seemed impressive to him had become just an ordinary fact of my existence. *She can do it, so she will.*

It wasn't just him. I had spent years throwing proverbial fridges into the backs of cars, trying to signify to men that I was a person in the world. Most hadn't noticed, which made the one who did seem all the more special. But the time came when he was no longer impressed by the sight of me doing something unexpected. Throwing fridges was just a thing that I did, commonplace enough to have faded into the background.

Like me.

The lack of acknowledgement that day brought to the fore the feelings I'd been trying to suppress since our son had been born. The resentment that had begun as a slow leak was now a broken water main, pouring through me and poisoning my insides. I knew that it couldn't be fixed—and, more to the point, I was beyond *wanting* to fix it. I was already responsible for the maintenance of so many things in our life, things I hadn't even asked to be responsible for but ended up managing anyway in order to keep the machine of domesticity running smoothly. I didn't have it in me to take this task on as well.

And so I left. Not that day. Not the next day, or even the next week. Leaving took me a few months, but eventually I did it. Late in the summer, on an evening not unlike the one that saw me throwing a fridge into the back of a stranger's car, I drove to the flat I had found to rent and moved into what would become *my* bedroom, *my* living room, *my* kitchen. I sat on the balcony and gazed out over the train tracks that ran alongside the building, and I felt something unlock inside me. I didn't know what the future held, but I knew I could handle whatever challenges came my way. I had carried more than my share for the past few years, and the decision to just let it all go unburdened me like none other. I had tried being a wife (in all but official title, at least). I would always be a mother. But for the first time in a long time, I felt like I could be me again. I was alone, at last.

And I was finally enough.

———

Perhaps we might have rubbed along for years more if we hadn't had a child. But the inescapable truth is that children permanently alter more than just the body of the person who creates and births them, and that's as it should be. My child had changed me, but he wasn't the one who had worn me down. I loved being his mother, even when I hated being *a* mother. And it wasn't as if the child had done something to the relationship between his parents, creating difficulties where previously there had been none. All the child had done was expose the fault lines between us. Even this is normal enough when a relationship undergoes sudden and substantial change. The problem wasn't the chasm that had grown between us; it was that I seemed to be the only one working to bridge it.

It's a common enough story, but one most women are unprepared for. How can you possibly anticipate the metamorphosis you'll undergo when you become a mother, particularly if you've also experienced the intensity of pregnancy and childbirth? Nothing can prepare you for what happens when theoretical fantasy becomes daily reality.

This is yet another in a long list of ways that women are actively harmed by fictional narratives of romance and happy-ever-afters, especially in a cis-hetero context. I experienced it myself, to the letter. Prior to becoming pregnant (and then prior to giving birth), I spoke about what was coming with the kind of wide-eyed naivety common to expectant first-time parents. We wouldn't change much about who we were, because the baby would adapt to our schedule and lifestyle. Sure, it would be hard—but it couldn't possibly be as hard as other people made it out to be. Besides, we had a reasonably equal relationship (didn't we?) and that was half the battle (wasn't it?).

I soon learned that having a child isn't as simple as adding one extra person to your table setting. It's a fundamental reconfiguring of everything you thought you were an expert on, most of all yourself. I think a lot of women believe that 'having a man's children' (and can we reflect for a moment on how gross that description is—that women are somehow merely the vessel for a man to ensure his genetic legacy, and that being entrusted with the responsibility is a privilege akin to being honoured by the king) will automatically strengthen the love that exists between them, not to mention increase the reverence in which he holds her.

It's a belief formed by the representation of love in popular culture rather than the experience of it in reality, delivered by stories that have mostly (ironically) been written by men and that only serve to uphold a regressive commitment to the notion of a woman's sacrificial love. By being chosen as the mother of *his* children, she's somehow been elevated in status. She has succeeded where previous girlfriends failed, and her victory can never be taken away. To show her gratitude for the incredible honour bestowed on her, she can spend the rest of her life taking care of everyone and everything.

You know, just like his mother did!

The romanticised idea of woman-as-carer has been so successful at least in part because it works alongside the idea of woman-as-exception. The cultural narrative positions society's desirable men as being either diabolically resistant to relationships or relentless bed-hoppers (and the *most* desirable of all of these are at least initially characterised as being both). No woman is good enough to hold his attention for long and certainly none is worthy enough to inspire him to change his ways.

Until he meets *her*. The one who shows him what love is. The woman who makes him want to be a better man.

Having tamed him, the next step is to produce a child to solidify that commitment and love. This act of devotion—the ultimate mark of your connection with someone—can only further expand his love for her, triggering all those latent biological urges to protect that we keep hearing are inherent to men. His love for her will reach transcendent new heights because of the child, and she believes that his transition into the role of father will expand her love in similar ways.

For some people, maybe it does.

But reality has a way of unpicking your dreams. Although everyone's experience of motherhood is different, generally speaking the act of growing a human inside you and then birthing it creates a bond that can be unexpected in its ferocity. Unexpectedly, it is *she* who becomes the protector, this defenceless creature having triggered primal emotions inside her that exist beyond our limited understanding of love and all its rational edges. She may not even love her child—not yet, at least—but outside of circumstances in which she is prevented from being fully present for her child, she will feel the animalistic urge to protect not only her baby but also herself, the one charged with transporting the creature to safety.

Historically, this has meant mothers shielding children from obvious predators and/or environmental threats. As a matter of course, mothers have always been the ones who make sure their children have enough to eat and drink, even at the expense of our own survival. To the best of our abilities, we've used whatever resources are available to make sure our children are kept healthy and clean. Even today, mothers in war zones and environmental disaster regions work overtime to protect their children in a way men have simply never taken responsibility for. I'm talking here about the micro reality of protection, as opposed to the macro fantasy of it. The one that involves mothers scavenging for food to feed children, desperately trying to keep them warm, seeing to their daily needs to ensure they grow up. Mothers are the ones who undertake negotiations with dangerous men to shield their children from the violence those men mete out . . . especially when those men are also the fathers. Women have always protected and provided for their children in ways that men don't and refuse to acknowledge.

Even outside the dangers of societal collapse or immediate risk, women's protection of their children very often leads to the realisation that the man she once believed she'd love forever is actually a useless sack of garbage who'd rather play video games or cycle for hours on end than learn how to change his own baby's wet nappy. For mothers, the sting of this is twofold. There are the obvious resentments that arise from being lumped with managing the bulk of household tasks and the administrative details of all of its residents. More than enough has been written about the mental load that falls to women, and the invisible labour that consumes our time and energy.

More than being unfair, it's soul-destroying to realise the extent to which someone can so casually erase all the things about you that make you special until all that remains are the things that make you useful. There's a reason men on the whole don't want to undertake this labour, and it's not because of the oft-quoted excuse that women are 'just better at it'. It's because it's fucking boring, endlessly demanding and performed entirely without reward. (Well, unless you're a man, I guess, in which case the basic act of folding the laundry is announced to the world as if somewhere within an errant sock he discovered the cure for cancer.)

The toll ongoing domestic disparity places on women is indisputable. A recent Roy Morgan poll in Australia showed that women spend an average of eight hours more per week on unpaid domestic work. This can't be attributed solely to who works in paid employment. The same survey showed that women in full-time paid work still spend four more hours per week than men on domestic tasks. This unpaid labour blows out even more when there are children in the house. Then, women perform a whopping total of 35 hours of unpaid domestic work, compared to men's 19.7. The kicker? Men are more likely to assess their contributions as equal. Little wonder that married women report being exhausted and single women report being happy.

But exhaustion is only half the picture, especially when child rearing comes into play. Spend even a cursory amount of time in online mothers' groups and you'll find women buckling under the weight not just of domestic tedium, but also the terrible realisation that the men they have poured love, care and time into show no desire to reciprocate at the time these women need it most. It's not just that some men are 'absentminded'; it's that they seem to enjoy reminding women just how little they matter. Every online mothers' group I've ever been in—and I've been in a lot—has broadcast the same chorus of despair, especially on days when women could reasonably expect to be *noticed* for what they do. Mother's Day brings out the most complaints, with woman after woman lining up to confess the deep shame they feel at having been left to organise their own celebrations. Sure, it might be a bullshit day designed to reinforce the idea of mothers as self-less angels—but it's the only one we have. And having 'partners' justify their refusal to participate because they don't *care* about it and shouldn't have to because 'you're not *my* mother' is just another of the tiny cuts that work to bleed a woman out over the course of her life. He empties the dishwasher and he expects a parade, but she births a whole human (or a few) and it's too much to get her a card.

Instead, they behave as if nothing much has changed for them, save for gaining a tiny and often fractious roommate. They sleep in on the weekends, go out in the evenings, indulge their own interests and hobbies whenever they choose and for however long they like, and sulk like teenagers when asked to do anything towards the functioning of the house. They get mad when women do things for themselves, or are validated for things outside of the domestic duties considered to be their responsibility. On the rare occasions they agree to 'babysit' their own children, it's still done on their terms—which can often mean with only half an eye on the baby or children, while still doing the things they consider an important use of their time. Like playing those cursed video games, fiddling about with machinery or musical instruments, or setting up secret accounts on Tinder. I've lost count of the number of complaints I've read from women who've carved out a couple of hours of respite for themselves only to come home to hungry babies weighed down by dirty nappies, entertaining themselves while a useless lump lies on the couch playing *Gobshite* or *War of Wankers* or *Garbage Men Unite* or whatever fucking game they think is more important than being a functioning adult.

(Sidenote: a lot of men today love to romanticise 'traditional' women, bemoaning the fact these abrasive banshees are nothing like their grandmothers—but no one could be less like the adults of our grandparents' generation than the overgrown boys who sit in their own stench shooting fake guns on a widescreen TV. Go fight a war, dipshit.)

For the women who view creating a family as the next step in their Great Adventure, what their partners bring to the table—or, rather, what they don't—can be a rude reminder that how we love someone can be very different from how we are loved *by* someone. Countless women have fantasised about what their male partners might be like as fathers, expecting that his transition into this state would only deepen their admiration for him and enrich their love. The trope of the Sexy Dad At The Park (an incredibly low bar, let's be real) is widespread for a reason, and that's because fatherhood is rewarded and revered in a way that motherhood isn't and never has been.

This lack of interest in mothers generally might be tolerable if it were only experienced outside of the home. But the salt in the wound for a lot of women is that, instead of their partners loving them *more* as a result of their transition into motherhood, all too many of them continue to 'love' them in exactly the same kind of superficial way as they did before, with absolutely no curiosity about the multiple, fundamental ways that motherhood has changed them. In these situations, men want women to stay *unchanged* by motherhood—or to keep those changes invisible and unassuming, at least.

Women may well be from Venus. But rather than hailing from Mars, men like this instead consider themselves to be the sun at the centre of their own solar system. Fatherhood isn't seen as an irreversible shift in the structure of their universe; like Venus, the child is merely another planet to be added to the gravitational pull, increasing their power as the burning, gaseous star around which everything revolves.

The unavoidable problem for these men (and their marriages) is that the act of becoming a mother cannot help but pull women out of the sun's gravitational slipstream and blast them apart to form entirely new universes. Once you become the creator of your own universe, returning to a solar system that offers nothing but the chance to orbit the same unmoving, boring sun for the rest of eternity seems like a pretty insulting request. It isn't just that we don't have the energy to worship a man and his petty, frivolous needs anymore—it's that we can't.

But voicing this out loud isn't easy. Giving up on the dream we thought we wanted—or the one we were told we *needed*—takes time. And this is also why so many women are so fucking tired. It's not just because we're overloaded with the physical and mental burden of men's existence, even as we wonder why they're not more interested in ours. It's because we're so conditioned to care for their *egos*—the sons of the world, the suns in our world—that we keep dashing back and forth between the new, unbelievable universe of our creation and the old, suffocating solar system in which he keeps us tethered, each time wondering if he's even noticed we've been gone.

Children don't ruin relationships. What they do is lead mothers into new realities, ones of their own construction. In these new realities, mothers can recognise that *they too* have the capacity to build worlds. That they can be the architects and the creators of dazzling, enormous things. They can be the ones who *see* and the ones who *speak*. Discovering this magic in us is exhilarating and of course we want to share it. Excited, we call to the men whose realities we've spent our entire lives witnessing, decorating and being instructed within. *Follow me! I have the most amazing things to show you!*

Maybe later, they say.

14

THE PRICE OF ENTRY

'Because I have other professions open to me in which the hours are shorter, the work more agreeable, and the pay possibly better.'

—Miss Florence Watts, 'Why am I a spinster?', *Tit-Bits* magazine, 1889

If marriage gives women cultural value, motherhood is supposed to bring us true happiness. Becoming mothers is what we've always been told we were born to do. It's the one thing that can fulfil our purpose on earth, the only thing that can really bring us to life. And because we're also tricked into believing in the myth of male protection and provision, we believe that *what we get* is a reflection of *who we are.*

When children arrive, mothers begin critically assessing the qualities and benefits of male partners more than we might have previously, when all we had to do was worship the sun. And yet, despite being fundamentally unhappy and feeling terribly betrayed by the realisation that men will only see what you *don't* do for them, most women will valiantly push through the inadequacies of male partners while those children are small because:

a) they're overwhelmed, and tiny dribbles of 'help' seem to be better than nothing;
b) they're legitimately scared of being financially destitute while trying to raise a small child; and
c) they're embarrassed.

This last one is key. Significant numbers of women are not only dissatisfied with the reality of marriage, but they're also embarrassed about what their lives have become. They're ashamed to admit to being the cliché of the overlooked housewife, the past-it mother who can't make her husband care about her. To mitigate the sting of this, they participate in toxic humour about hapless husbands and overgrown children, because admitting that they feel small and exploited by men to whose every need they tend is too awful to admit.

What is the point of marriage, when this is the inevitable result—and the cost—for so many women who throw themselves into it wholeheartedly? No one wants to admit that they're treated like garbage. And no woman wants to admit that her husband *is* garbage.

But further demonstrating their lack of engagement is the fact so many of these 'proud husbands and fathers' appear oblivious to this unhappiness, choosing instead to complain about all this boring new shit they have to do and that she can't stop nagging them about, while moaning that if she wanted them to do something then *she should've just asked.*

Laura Danger (who goes by the name @thatdarnchat on Instagram) calls this the Nag Paradox. Basically, when women complain about a lack of equal contribution (we don't call it 'help' because that implies that domestic work belongs to women), men counter with complaints that she didn't tell him what to do. But when women *do* tell men what to do, by begging, pleading, demanding, encouraging or even just asking, those same men will complain that she's nagging him.

The reality men have set up for themselves is deliberately filled with these kinds of paradoxes and contradictions. Men need to be dragged to the altar, but are enraged by the thought of women not wanting to get married at all. Women are the nurturers and are better placed to do most of the caring for the kids, but fathers are equally important, especially when it comes to custody battles. Women baby-trap men and then ruin men's lives by leaving them. He treats her like shit, but she's so lucky to have him. Around and around we go, with women doing everything to meet the needs of men and getting absolutely nothing in return.

Please understand that this isn't a deviation from marriage's original purpose.

It's precisely how marriage as a *system* has been designed, whereby women are expected to provide for the needs of others. Initially this was represented via property transference; women were traded like objects by men who wanted to build their own capital. Here! Have this donkey! She's a hard worker and she'll give you lots of babies to add to your stables!

Women may not always be explicitly traded for marriage now (although it certainly still happens worldwide), but the purpose of this exchange is still economic. The writer Elizabeth Gilbert has pointed to women being used as the 'building blocks of society'; in essence, we're the ones who assure a shit ton of the work involved in creating strong societies is done in small blocks, for free. As Gilbert says, a state that cares about its citizens would provide free health care, free education, free child care, stable housing, nutritious food and so on. But the capitalist state doesn't want to *pay* for these things, even though it needs to ensure an endless supply of productive citizens to maintain its function. This work is therefore outsourced to women. Having been brainwashed for centuries to believe that our biological role is to nurture—which conveniently includes caring for *men* as if they were children—we are that much easier to coerce into marriage. Once locked into it, we can be relied on to assume the care of anywhere between two and five people on average. Women will keep these people safe, fed, educated, clothed and healthy to the best of their ability, which means these people can be productive for the state. Women are literally building the world, but because the work has, like women, been made invisible, it's not considered to have any value whatsoever, least of all economic. (And if you want to get into world building, think again about how the labour of Black and brown people has been stolen for centuries and used to prop up white economies. Women of colour, in particular, have been exploited as wet nurses, nannies and domestic servants for white women, whose status as wives and mothers rose in direct corre- lation with how much of this labour they could source. When white women today joke about 'needing a wife', we would do well to remember that what this usually means is wanting a servant. One demographic's gauche fantasy is another's lived history.)

In the 1970s, a collective of feminists co-founded by American scholar and teacher Silvia Federici called for a national wage for housework. Although their demands were ignored (of course), they spoke to the very real exploitation of women not just within their own marriages but for the benefit of the larger state for the reasons Gilbert would go on to reiterate. The refusal to pay women for the domestic labour we provide (which in Australia alone has an annual value of A$434 billion, almost half our total gross domestic product) isn't just to discredit that labour; it's also to keep us trapped in it, by virtue of having nowhere else to go. As the Nobel Prize–nominated economist Marilyn Waring notes, 'Men won't easily give up a system in which half the world's population works for next to nothing.'

Modern marriage has in part been sold to women as a means of securing economic stability. We can't get around the fact our societal cost of living has increased dramatically. As we learned in 'Honey, you're home', the conservative nostalgia for the booming 1950s ignores the unsustainability of this time period. Despite patriarchy's millennia-long obsession with women reproducing, it's also clear that pregnancy and childbirth alone are not enough. How those babies are made and by whom is key—we can't just have *random* women out there doing it by themselves, *stealing* not just men's progeny but also their entitlement to a lifetime supply of woman's labour and flooding society with undesirables. John Gray was able to sell what was essentially unfounded rhetoric as legitimate relationship advice, because the largely white middle-class demographic who formed the bulk of his audience had already been primed by decades' worth of similar pseudoscience, which itself was borne out of class and white supremacist anxieties over what President Theodore Roosevelt had almost a century earlier called the risk of 'race suicide'. Basically, the advances in political and economic opportunities for women were most keenly felt by (and all too often sought in service of) white women of financial means. If too many middle-class white women pursued new avenues of education and independence, where would the nations' (white) babies come from? And who would be left for the white men to marry? With divorce on the rise and marriage rates on the decline, marriage needed a rebrand.

To counter the number of white women who might abandon the domestic sphere entirely for the public one (further threatening the security of those men who dominate the latter), the culture reframed the idea of a 'successful' marriage as being integral to a woman's social status, and divorce (the right to which has been a cornerstone of women's liberation) a sign of her failure. Marriage became work, in both the literal and figurative sense—and like most things in the domestic sphere, it was work that fell to women. By reinforcing the ideological and moral status of a 'successful' marriage (or at least the appearance of one), whiteness is maintained as a gold standard of 'family values', with white women, in particular, heralded for the same things marginalised groups are punished for: having lots of babies, choosing to be stay at home mothers rather than working in paid employment, and living in siloed enclaves.

Not all women want to be mothers, although it's fair to say it's a desire for many of us. But as we've been shown repeatedly throughout history (and are still being reminded today), women are not allowed to control the means of this reproduction. Patriarchy claims that right and wields it over us, which means it tells us when, how, if and with whom we're allowed to do the one thing it also insists we *must* do in order to realise our true potential on earth.

This is another one of those convenient paradoxes that keeps women permanently two-stepping in the artificial reality we're forced to live in. I've written it here as a haiku.

Listen, you women
Become a mother, or else
No, slut, not like that.

The right way to become a mother is by marrying a man, having his child and giving that child his name. The correct way to *stay* being a mother is to never complain about the circumstances of the motherhood, and to enthusiastically and lovingly devote your life to caring for the family you were blessed to be given. If you leave, you're selfish. If you leave, you're hurting your children. If you leave, you didn't deserve any of it after all.

And who's going to take care of you now?

The wrongest of all the wrong ways to become a mother is either to deliberately do it alone or to do it in a way that threatens structural power. Science has made it possible for us to circumvent having sex with men in order to get pregnant, but we're only a whisper away from the brutal legacy of forced adoptions. As recently as the seventies, unwed mothers were having their babies ripped from their arms and given to 'nice Christian families' to punish them for becoming pregnant outside of marriage. White Australia has still not properly reckoned with or made reparations for its dehumanisation of First Nations people, and the barbaric, racist abduction of Aboriginal children that was carried out as a matter of government policy. Women must be mothers, but only if they're the right kind of women, the *white* kind of women. All the others—the poor, the disabled, the sex workers, the singles, the working women, the sluts, whores and *witches*—well, they just get to be the wombs.

It is baffling how deep this conditioning still runs, that we are still forced to deal with the contradiction that positions mother-hood as both essential to our wellbeing but also something only the righteous (and whiteous) among us are *allowed* to have. Even financially secure, middle-class women (whose reproductive obligations we are being constantly reminded of) face backlash and horrifying abuse for choosing to become mothers on their own. Selfish! Children need a mother and a father! This is the problem with feminists today!

Again, a contradiction: women are biologically built to nurture, which is why they're best suited to do the child rearing and stay at home raising the babies. But when it suits patriarchy, fathers are also essential and important and denying your child the right to have one is *cruel*.

If I have the physical capacity to carry a pregnancy and birth that child into the world, then it means I have the capacity to become a mother. If it's true (as patriarchy asserts with its wolf-like smirk) that my biology pushes me towards motherhood, and that *not* achieving it will leave me unfulfilled, having failed to reach my full potential, then why is my right to do that dependent on something as unpredictable as *finding a guy*?

Am I only allowed to climb a mountain if I find a man to accompany me to the summit?

Looked at like this, it seems clear that what men have needed from women all along is not for us to accept our 'natural' role as mothers; it's to allow ourselves to be trapped by motherhood, so we can continue to nurture *them* in their quest for power while being prevented from ever discovering the breadth of our own. If we can raise children without men—and it's clear not only that we can but also that we *have done* and continue to do so, even in the face of enormous structural oppression—then motherhood itself becomes divested of men entirely. If the state recognised maternal labour as vital to its economic and social success and cared for mothers accordingly, all women and children would be supported to thrive. Mothering itself would be tangibly respected but also recognised as a choice—one that a decent number of women (and other people capable of becoming pregnant) would still make, knowing that it wouldn't entrench them in lifelong poverty. A new reality would emerge, one constructed with the needs of women and children in mind. In that reality, men would have to work harder not only to take care of themselves but also to be worthy of whatever attention we may still be inclined to give them. Partnership then becomes a matter of choice rather than necessity. Freed from the anchor of domestic labour performed in service to men, we would see the full extent of women's capacity to lead, build, create and love.

But because we don't live in that reality, women who want to become mothers (or think they do) are still constrained by the economic reality of how expensive it is—but only for them, the ones tasked with all the labour of it. In America, single women without children boast a median family wealth that is nine times that of single mothers—US$65,000 per annum versus $7000. By contrast, single men without children have a median family wealth of $57,000, while single dads register *slightly higher* at $59,000. The punitive cost of child-bearing is borne solely by women, with children also being the primary reason women suffer as a result of the gender wage gap.

And again, the system is designed this way. It needs women to have babies, but to ensure the productivity of its male workers it needs to tether those women to men. One-third of all single mothers in the US and Australia live in poverty; in the UK, it's half. If men are the only ones making the money (or the bulk of it), women often have no choice but to stay. When men leave, it's women who not only risk being thrust into poverty but who will also be stigmatised for being the 'wrong' kind of mother. For being a 'drain on the system', a 'welfare queen' (a particularly racist term primarily used to demonise single Black mothers), someone with a string of children from different dads—which is apparently far more serious than fathering multiple children with multiple different women and abandoning them from the beginning.

Under these conditions, of course it seems sensible to women to combine two incomes and create a buffer for when and if the mother takes time out of paid employment to do the much harder work of raising children. And so couples move in together, thinking that this is the start of a chapter of new growth. But the rude and unexpected reality is that a woman's economic prospects decrease even as her unpaid labour increases, and these trajectories differ even more starkly if she decides to have that baby. Now she's not only earning little to no money, but she's also missing out on superannuation and on-the-job training that leads to the possibility of promotion. Meanwhile, men's economic prospects go *up* when they start to cohabit (and again when they become fathers) while their domestic workload goes down (and that's with or without children, and regardless of whether or not they're earning less than their wife or girlfriend).

But don't forget! Motherhood is the most important job in the world! I guess that's why the state doesn't pay for it. Putting a price on it would make it transactional, and that's unseemly.

Let's be real. There's nothing more fucking transactional than the system of baby-trapping women into caring for men whose justification for this inbuilt misogyny is always to say, *We pay the bills and put a roof over your heads, so you should do the housework.*

Leaving aside the fact that 'housework' in their mind very often includes 'sex on tap', let's just consider the facts for a moment. In America, three-quarters of all mothers are in some kind of paid employment. Despite this, they're also pulling what second wave feminists called 'the second shift' at home, doing the bulk of the domestic work plus raising the children. Men are paying a reduced part of the bills for a house they would have been living in anyway . . . except somehow the fact they (might) pay slightly more means they get to have literally EVERYTHING done for them? They dropped their junk into someone, did nothing to help grow that baby or raise it, and now believe they deserve a full-time domestic staff *for life* in exchange for this? How can she ever get ahead when he's always holding her back?

I liken this system to Terry Pratchett's 'boots theory' of socio-economic inequality. Say there are two people, a man and a woman. They're both looking to buy a pair of boots. But the woman's circumstances (marriage) have made her poor, and the only boots she can afford to buy are the kind that will wear out quickly. In a year's time, she'll need to buy a new pair of boots. She'll have to buy a new pair every year, if she wants to have any boots at all.

The man, on the other hand, is rich. Because he's married! He can afford to invest a whopping great sum in a beautifully made pair of boots with real leather that will never crack and soles that will never wear out. The man can strut in his boots forever, over which time the leather will just grow more and more comfortable. Sure, they cost a lot—but he'll never have to replace them, so in the end he's saved money.

Pratchett's theory is designed to highlight how socioeconomic inequality not only favours the rich but prevents the poor from ever moving forward. Over the course of her lifetime, the woman who is poor will spend significantly more money on boots than the man who is rich—but although she's spending more money, she'll never be able to have the luxuries that are accessible to him.

When we use the argument that marriage is 'economically beneficial' for women, what we really mean is 'the system is economically punitive for women, and marriage is a means of securing superficial relief despite the long-term cost'.

Denied the ability to reach our full potential on our own, women walk into the trap of marriage on the promise of being given shoes to wear. What we don't realise is that the ones we get are cheap, uncomfortable and require constant replacement. We can never get ahead as long as we're buying the cheap, shitty pair of boots year after year. But we still need to wear boots, right? So we stay, continuing to invest in the shitty plastic crap year after year, reasoning that it's better than the alternative, which is to go barefoot.

For men, marriage represents wealth and privilege. Gaining a wife is like buying a pair of the best handmade leather boots. The initial investment might seem huge (the old ball and chain, giving up the single life, being 'trapped', marriage is the end!!!) but damn are those boots comfortable! They can wear them year after year, never having to replace them or spend any more money than they already have. The boots only get better with age, as the leather stretches and breaks and moulds to fit them exactly. When their wife complains about how unfair it is that he gets to walk around in luxurious comfort while her feet are blistered, he'll say, 'They look like the same boots to me. I can't help it if your feet are more sensitive.' Or, 'You should have worked harder to afford a better pair.' Then he'll get her to polish his boots for him, because 'she's better at it'. If she stops or doesn't want to, or he finds someone different or younger to bless with that privilege, he'll walk on out of there in his fancy boots, leaving her with nothing to show for the years she spent keeping them nice for him. Because she did nothing to *earn* those boots. He bought them all by himself. That was *his* work. She just sat around in her shitty pair of boots, complaining about how tight they were. So she gets nothing. She deserves *nothing.*

This is at the root of why it's so important for men to maintain their position as 'providers'. Because it's the only way they can continue to drain labour out of women and call it a reasonable exchange—a generous one, even. Women have long been denied access to anything that would allow us to have agency over our own lives. We've been kicked out of our own specialist professions, refused education, equal pay, respect and reproductive autonomy, prevented from doing or having anything at all that would give us basic *choice* in the world. We have been handcuffed to men and forced to manage their every basic need, while they claim access to our work, our time and even our *bodies.*

And we're supposed to be fucking grateful when they *put a roof over our heads*? That they've fabricated some bullshit mythology around 'providing' for us, when in actual fact they just figured out how to steal our opportunities and consequently our money? We're meant to hold out our hands gratefully as they throw a sliver of our own resources back at us and call us *lucky,* unbuckling their belts to accept the sex they're owed in exchange?

When I think about how women have been taught to view marriage as essential to our wellbeing, I am overwhelmed with fury. Because it's not just about the limitations this places on us as people, conditioning us from an early age not to look beyond our horizons but to aspire instead to stay firmly shackled within them; it's because for so many women, marriage is the *mechanism* through which violence is perpetrated against us.

And we're the ones who pay.

15

MOTHERFUCKER

'If women, as I hope, wake themselves from the lengthy slumber by which they are oppressed, then these ungrateful and overbearing men would learn humility.'

—Lucrezia Marinella, *The Nobility and Excellence of Women, And the Defects and Vices of Men*, 1600

Like many expectant mothers, I approached the birth of my child with a mixture of excitement, trepidation and total disregard for the experiences of those who'd come before me. I knew there would be hard moments, but I felt equipped to handle them. I understood that my body would change—the baby had to come out, after all—but I had unwavering faith in my genetics. That is to say, I assumed my broad hips had to have a greater purpose than just making it hard for me to buy jeans. And while I expected to lose a bit of sleep, I wasn't too worried about that part of the job. I'd pulled all-nighters to get essays done, stayed out until the wee hours partying and then gone to work on little to no sleep. How much harder could it be with a baby?

In what should have been the most predictable twist in the world, it turned out to be a lot harder than I ever thought possible. It wasn't just the traumatic birth (turns out the size of my hips *was* just about making jeans shopping an exercise in self-loathing). Having gone sixteen days past my due date, I'd finally consented to an induction. It had dashed my dreams of a water birth, but I was nothing if not adaptable. I could manage. When hours of excruciating labour had passed and I'd dilated less than a few centimetres, I begged them to give me the epidural I'd been determined to avoid. I didn't think I was too good or pure for drugs, nor did I care for the bragging rights of having done it 'naturally' (which is little more than misogyny); I just didn't want to lose the feeling in my legs, because I thought that would add to the already heightened anxiety of childbirth. But when you think you're dying, your perspective changes somewhat. The epidural was called for, and I was finally able to rest before the big push.

This final obstacle wasn't without its turmoil. I was told that because I'd been in labour for so long, I'd have less time to try to get the baby out vaginally before they'd have to make the call to cut him out of my belly. I dug deep, calling on the deepest reserves of my being to will this human life out of me and help him to take his first breath. I got to my knees and gripped the bedhead, a guttural sound rumbling out of my mouth. I could feel him moving through me, but there was so much further to go and I was running out of steam.

'I can't do this,' I wept to my friend, a student midwife whom I'd asked to be with me.

'You *are* doing this,' she replied calmly, rubbing my back.

I gritted my teeth and continued to push, somehow tapping into what felt at the time like the collective strength of every single person who'd been called on to do this completely impossible, completely ordinary thing.

Just when it felt like I might be close to releasing him, his shoulder got stuck behind my pubic bone. I was directed to come down off all fours and turn on to my back, but his head was half protruding from my vagina. Miraculously, despite being completely drained of mental energy and almost at the end of my physical capacity, I managed to carefully execute the manoeuvre without sitting down and crushing him. As I lay on my back, a pair of midwives grabbed my knees and pushed them out and up to my shoulders while a third reached in to twist both the baby and his shoulder free. He burst out of me and my flesh tore in a ragged line along my perineum.

'Here's your baby!' one of the midwives called, holding the blood-soaked child over my head and then whisking him away to the resuscitation table. He'd been born covered in meconium, which meant he'd pooped while in utero. If a newborn inhales faeces there's a risk of pneumonia or even death. I didn't know this then, which was probably a blessing. Instead I just lay there, exhausted and spent.

I didn't notice as the room filled with concerned-looking doctors and my son's father was pushed away from the bed. They were there not just in case it turned out the baby's precious new lungs had been flooded with shit, but also because I was haemorrhaging. I didn't know this either. All I knew was that I was tired, so tired, the tiredest I had ever been in my whole life.

I could sense that my son's father was concerned about something, but I didn't want him to worry. 'It's okay,' I said to him dreamily, as a midwife started to palpate my belly aggressively, trying to stem the blood flowing out of me. 'This is normal.'

When it comes to childbirth, the word 'normal' is so often used in place of the word 'common'. For women and girls of reproductive age (and I use the word 'girls' deliberately, because patriarchy's view of females as walking incubators extends even to children), the transition into motherhood is treated as a mundane inevitability. Regardless of the fact not all women can have children or even want them, not to mention the fact that not all people who can bear children are women, in the eyes of patriarchy, the role of women is set in stone. As we saw in 'A womb of one's own', women's baby ovens must be put to good use lest our domestic hands become idle, our brains become too active and our presence in the world becomes too . . . well, *present*.

In farming, the term 'animal husbandry' is used to refer to 'the branch of agriculture concerned with raising domestic animals'. Through the course of this book, we've seen how powerful institutions have weaponised women's reproductive capacity against us. Whether by law, violence, economics or social brainwashing, we have at least six thousand years of recorded history demonstrating patriarchy's obsession with filling wombs. And what has this necessarily involved, in order to prove legitimacy of the child?

Husbandry.

Yes, it's a play on the word. But what better way to illustrate the act of turning women into domestic animals and raising them to produce an endless supply of resources for their masters to consume?

The pressure women face to reproduce has never gone away. Isolating our ambitions to reproduction prevents them from being projected outwards, into the world of men. The *Malleus Maleficarum* identified ambition as one of three major indicators of witchcraft in a woman, along with lust and infidelity. To desire a life outside of domestic service is *not normal*, nor is it safe. Women who reject motherhood are inherently twisted or broken in some way, and must be convinced to change their minds lest they invite upon themselves the misery of a sad and lonely old age. *Normal* women want babies, ergo women who don't are *not normal*. End of.

Here's what they don't tell you about giving birth: *women still die.*

Like, a lot.

Globally, the maternal mortality rate (MMR) is 810 deaths per day. That amounts to 295,650 women dying per year. Although there can be underlying causes, three-quarters of maternal deaths during childbirth are caused by severe bleeding, infections, high blood pressure, pregnancy complications and/or complications from unsafe abortions. It's true that the majority of these maternal deaths—94 per cent—occur in places where women have little or no access to medical resources, but what this really tells us is that childbirth *is fucking dangerous and always has been*, and poverty is a literal killer. Roughly 70 per cent of maternal mortalities happen in sub-Saharan African regions, where poverty is high, health care is scarce and child exploitation via forced marriage is common.

Common. Not normal.

In some areas, around one-fifth of mothers who give birth do so before their sixteenth birthdays. When children are impregnated and forced to give birth, it increases the risk of complications, which in turn increases the risk of death. Girls who are forced into motherhood too soon are significantly more likely to miss out on receiving an education—the same education European scientists in the nineteenth century argued would damage a woman's fertility. When a woman is educated, she tends to have fewer babies, which not only keeps her alive and healthier for longer, but also equips her to keep her existing children alive and healthier.

But that's in Outland! That doesn't happen here!

Firstly, gross. Secondly, ethnocentric thinking won't save you. The risks of pregnancy and birth are faced by women all over the world, perpetuated by the institutional insistence on our obligation to breed. For example, while the United States may love to refer to itself as 'the greatest country in the world', its MMR is not only much higher per capita than other OECD countries, it's been rising steadily for two decades. This is hardly surprising given that there is no universal health care. But it's Black women who bear the brunt of this statistic; they are three times more likely to die during pregnancy than white women, because the deeply entrenched racism that still underpins western medicine dehumanises Black bodies and discredits Black women's testimony of pain and reports of things being wrong. And while Australia has a much lower MMR, Aboriginal women are still three times more at risk of death during pregnancy and childbirth than non-Indigenous women.

Serena Williams, the greatest tennis player of all time, an athlete whose body is in peak physical condition, has spoken about almost dying following the birth of her daughter. When Williams tried to tell health professionals that she believed she was suffering from a pulmonary embolism, not only did they not believe her, one nurse called her 'crazy'. In May 2023, Tori Bowie, a Black athlete and Olympic gold medallist, died after developing eclampsia during the eighth month of her pregnancy. Two of Bowie's three other teammates also experienced serious complications during their pregnancies. Black women in the United States are 60 per cent more likely to develop pre-eclampsia than white women, but less likely to have their symptoms recognised. The racism doesn't stop there. Black children are also less likely to be given adequate medical care, and more likely to die as a result of hospital malfeasance.

Despite the lack of adequate care provided to pregnant women and people, in 2022 the US Supreme Court voted 5–4 in favour of overturning *Roe v. Wade*, the landmark 1973 legal ruling that enshrined the constitutional right of pregnant women in the United States to seek an abortion. Of these nine Supreme Court justices, six were men and three were women—and of the three women, none was still young enough to become pregnant. Nine people deciding the rights of millions of women and girls in a country that will not provide adequate social welfare and where 30 per cent of all single mothers are living in poverty. Five people who voted yes to making theirs a nation in which ten-year-old rape survivors are now forced to carry pregnancies in bodies that are too small to safely do so before being forced to give birth. When I was ten years old, I was still playing with Barbie dolls. But a 'god-fearing' nation whose conservative lawmakers are obsessed with spreading transphobic hate under the guise of 'protecting children' will not only stand by and allow little girls to be torn apart psychologically and physically because *an adult man raped them*, but will actively oppose any measures to stop this from happening.

Suffer the little children indeed.

Pregnancy is dangerous. Childbirth is dangerous. Both can be navigated safely, but they're not easy and they certainly aren't meaningless. We shouldn't consider it *normal* for women to emerge from the experience of creating life having half-wrecked their own. We shouldn't accept as commonplace the fact that one in three people who give birth will deal with ongoing incontinence. Men have forced women into this labour for their own benefit, not for ours. To satisfy their own egos and maintain their fortunes, they created a contract that would tether women to them permanently. Marriage wasn't created to liberate women or even to benevolently provide for us; it was created to enslave us and to confer ownership rights to men wanting to amass a collection of heirs. Those women who did bear children out of wedlock were ostracised, and their children punished for 'illegitimacy', because caring for the fate of children in the noble world of the patriarchs has always come with provisos. Perhaps the most egregious lie of all is the one in which patriarchy pretends to *love* the women it ensnares. It claims to revere mothers, while denying us dignity, adequate health care and opportunities. It pretends to value this 'essential work', calling motherhood 'the most important job in the world' but it won't pay us for it, because economically empowered women are a threat to patriarchy and, besides, how can you put a price on something so *pure*? It claims that men protect women, and protect especially the women who are carrying 'their' children, even as evidence to the contrary washes through like a tsunami. Men are not our valiant protectors; they are our most dangerous predators. They collectively represent the biggest risk to our health and safety. And during pregnancy and postpartum, we confront the most terrifying reality of all: when we are doing what it is we are told we must do, either growing life or caring for new life, the likelihood of domestic abuse, including sexual abuse, perpetrated by our partners, our husbands, our 'protectors', *increases*. Becoming mothers places our lives most at risk not because our child could kill us accidentally—but because their father could kill us on purpose.

If nothing else in this book has convinced you of the great lie told to us by marriage and its PR team, I implore you not to minimise the impact of what you're about to read. We've seen the myriad ways men have worked together to punish women in the public and legal spheres. But it would be a mistake to think the enthusiasm of misogyny and the violence it engenders has been left in the past. You cannot know what an otherwise 'nice' man is capable of until you're weakened by the physical impact of child-bearing and trapped by the need to care for a newborn child—but a frighteningly high number of women find out.

The monsters aren't outside the castle walls. They're often found in the man who sleeps next to you at night. The same man who can look at everything you've done—the feat of physical endurance you've just pulled off, the weeping body that remains, the work you're doing to keep a tiny child alive—and declare that you've been off the clock for long enough and it's probably about time you gave his dick a good seeing-to.

After all, it's not just your head he's putting a roof over now. It's that squalling baby's, too.

———

One of the most confronting things new mothers are faced with is the realisation that some men—so many of them, in fact—still expect to have their sexual demands met.

I say 'demands', although of course men and mainstream sexism frames them as 'needs'. He *needs* to have sex in order to feel loved. He *needs* to have physical affection in order to feel close to her, the mother of his child or children. He *needs* to be indulged on a regular basis otherwise he'll stray. He *needs* to have access to his wife's body, because that's the unwritten contract of marriage—and why did he marry her if all he was getting in exchange was this bloody drama, and no puss-on-tap?

These are the same beliefs that informed the legal scholar Sir Matthew Hale's view on conjugal rights, outlined in his immensely influential *Historia Placitorum Coronæ*. As we've already seen, laws denying the possibility of marital rape (at least in the western world) persisted until the 1970s at the earliest, and weren't abolished in Britain until 1991. You can get rid of a law, but it takes a lot longer to unpick the social attitudes that supported that law—and a significant number of men *and* women still believe that marriage (or committed domestic partnerships) automatically gives men the rights to sexual 'maintenance'.

We looked at the tedious rise in #marriedhumour in 'Trouble and strife, comedy wife', but perhaps more disturbing than the regurgitation of retrosexist jokes are the skits in which couples film themselves navigating the approach of the day marking the end of the recommended healing period for bodies postpartum. If you've had a baby, you'll know that this is around six weeks, and penetrative sex is generally advised against prior to that. I guess the joke is meant to be that six weeks without fucking is enough to turn a man into a raging bull who'll chase his (still-healing) partner through the house while roaring, because that's exactly what so many couples commit to video every day in the attempt to go viral online.

Ha ha.

These flaccid, unfunny attempts to assert sex as something men *need* and women gatekeep are nothing new. But they're made especially worse in this case by the fact postpartum sexual assault is a lived reality for millions of new mothers every year.

A few years ago, I started collecting stories about coercion and sex on my Instagram page. The conversation started because I was talking about abortion as a life-saving medical procedure. I didn't mean 'life-saving' in the way we usually frame this topic, which is as a kind of morally ambiguous ditch that pregnant women and people allow themselves to fall into, and from which they can only be justifiably rescued if they prove genuine need. I was more interested in presenting abortion as a legitimate counter-procedure to the inherent dangers of pregnancy and childbirth. I had experienced a traumatic pregnancy and birth myself, and I resented the implication that because I hadn't died, and my baby was 'fine', I should shut up and get on with things. The fact that I spent the first eight months of my child's life wearing urinary incontinence pads was apparently no big deal. That so many women endure significantly worse birth injuries (and some of them irreversible) and yet are met with silence should be viewed as an outrage. We know it's easier (and cheaper) for a man to be prescribed Viagra than it is for a woman to receive care for a prolapse or pelvic floor dysfunction. Imagine if a man's dick exploded every time he became a father, or his sexual capacity diminished considerably or disappeared entirely. Imagine if his ability to reach orgasm was forever changed because crucial nerves needed for sexual pleasure had been permanently damaged. We'd never hear the bloody end of it.

I knew that scores of women were suffering through such things in silence. The culture we live in doesn't consider women's bodies to be worthy of protection or respect, and certainly holds no regard for our right to sexual freedom and pleasure. But as more and more women replied to these stories, a theme began to emerge—the emotional and sometimes physical violence inflicted by male partners who still saw these women's freshly postpartum bodies as *theirs* and had no qualms about doing what they thought was necessary in order to get their dicks inside them.

Often, this involved a lot of whining. Women exhausted by the intensity of breastfeeding an infant for hours a day found themselves further burdened by the childish tantrums of grown men who wanted to know when they were going to 'get a turn'. Others talked of receiving text messages from husbands taking luxurious eight-hour breaks at their paid employment wanting to know if they 'could at least get a hand job' that evening because it had been *weeks*. Still more talked of being given the silent treatment, backs turned on them in bed after they'd said no to him pawing them.

These were the least distressing stories, which is saying something.

On the other end of the scale were the horrifying stories of coercive sex (and sometimes explicitly defined rape). Bodies that were still bleeding mere days after giving birth being penetrated by men who would almost certainly swear they were kind and loving husbands, absolutely thrilled with the arrival of their children and definitely keen to have more. Some of the incidents recounted disturbed me deeply, not just because of what they involved but because I suspected they weren't all that uncommon. The woman who had 'let' her husband fuck her in the hospital bathroom the day after their baby was born, because 'he was used to having it every day'. The woman whose (now-ex) husband had insisted on fucking her while she was in labour, because—and steel yourself for this one—*he said he was turned on by seeing her in pain.* I remember the woman in my baby centre cohort who once asked for advice on how to deal with a 'horny hubby'. We were all of us almost full term by then, but she was still getting on her hands and knees to scrub the bath. She was met with hostility and belligerence, too, after responding to her husband's insistently groping hands (which, unlike hers, were not at all chapped from cleaning products) by saying gently, 'Do you mind if we don't tonight? I'm really tired.' He turned his back on her and huffed that she hadn't let him do it for months (which, depressing sidenote, she said wasn't even true because she'd given in the week before) and then he refused to speak to her again.

'How do you all deal with hubbies wanting sex when you're tired from being so pregnant?' she implored.

Arsenic, I thought to myself.

As I've been writing this book, I've encountered more and more of these horrifying revelations about the objectively torturous treatment of women committed by men beneath the supposedly respectable veneer of domestic partnership, related to me by women on the other side of this kind of abuse or still very much caught in the thick of it.

I don't know if these men realise how disengaged they are from their wives and partners as actual people, or if they even care. But the fact remains that a not-insignificant number of them treat women like multifunctional appliances. This one does the cooking, this one handles the cleaning, and this one lies back and acts like a porn star while I get my dick sucked.

And if his dick doesn't get sucked? I can guarantee you the whiny ones will be on the apps quicker than you can say 'could this man please die already'. He'll lie about the situation, pretending to be single ('I can't share photos because of work') or claiming he's in a 'sexless marriage'. One woman who contacted me reported that her then-husband had warned her that if she didn't do something to alleviate his sexual frustration, he'd have 'no choice but to go elsewhere'.

It had been four weeks since her caesarean.

Despite expecting regular servicing from their sex appliances, these men do fuck all to 'help' parent or care for their own children or the houses they live in. They don't see that as being their job. Why would they? They're out at work every day *putting a roof over their heads,* which is also why they don't think they should have to wake up in the middle of the night to do any feeding, nappy changes or even to fetch her a cup of tea. I have read story after story posted in online mothers' groups about men who claim separate rooms for themselves so they can pop their earplugs in at night and make sure they have eight hours of undisturbed sleep. In one instance, the husband kept the bedroom while the mother and her baby slept on the couch. 'He has to work!' comes the apologetic explanation, as if he's responsible for defusing landmines and not just tweeting garbage all day when his boss isn't looking.

But none of these comes close to the story I was told by a woman whose (ex-)-husband exemplifies the depth of hatred men can feel towards women even while believing themselves to be 'good'. At the end of her first pregnancy, the woman suffered the devastating loss of her baby in utero. Having almost reached full term, labour was induced and she had to go through the traumatic experience of giving birth. While waiting for the contractions to begin, and in the midst of their mutual grief, her then-husband suggested that it might make him feel better if she gave him a blow job. Because he was sad. Stunned by the request, the woman replied that she couldn't bring herself to do that . . . but she could give him a hand job instead.

And he let her.

There are so many stories like this. Too many stories of women being objectified, assaulted, grabbed, coerced into sex and raped because taking care of 'his needs' is part of the deal. We may have outlawed marital rape, but that doesn't mean it's not still happening across the country, in our neighbourhoods, on our streets and often in our own houses. As we're constantly reminded, becoming a mother is the most important thing a woman can do, and as a man her husband is biologically wired to protect her and the baby—but only if he gets to empty his balls in her like a Twinkie or on her like a toaster strudel at least three times a week.

You know, people spit the accusation *man hater* at me like there aren't five billion fucking good reasons why I and any other woman with a brain have no choice but to hate them. But it's not really accurate to say that I'm a man hater. Saying I hate men gives them too much power. What I think I really am is a man *seer*. I see men the way we're not supposed to see them, in the endless ways they contradict the myths of their morality and greatness and the ways in which they enforce their hatred of women over and over again.

I see men for who they are, and I know too many of the secrets they want to keep hidden. It's not why *I* hate *them*. It's why *they* hate *me*.

———

Let me be extremely clear about this: everything I have just described is domestic abuse. Ordinary men do these things. You know them. They are your colleagues. Your mates. Your brothers. Your teammates. The blokes you watch the footy with. The men playing the footy. The men you listen to on the radio, watch on the TV, read in the paper. None of them think they're bad men. They all think they're good men. But they also believe that it's their right to be serviced, because patriarchy has told them women exist to serve men. In the constructed reality, we don't get a say over what we want because we can't even see what's good for us and what we *need*.

What women *get* is so often not what we deserve or need, but it is exactly what the system wants for us. New mothers discovering the extent of their so-called partner's disdain for them rarely have the financial means to walk out when they have a newborn baby to care for. Even in the rare circumstances where they are financially independent, their emotional wellbeing is still tenuous after such a life-changing event. It's hard enough just to make it through the day keeping the both of you alive; the prospect of having to navigate a break-up with someone who might become violent, toxic and/or punitive is unthinkable.

And so they stay, being further abused by men who realise on some level that she *can't* leave—and if she can't leave, then they can do pretty much anything they want (which is often nothing at all when it comes to domestic labour). They can and will punish her for her public joy and accolades, reminding her in the privacy of the home she's built that she's *not that special.* If the relationship does end up breaking down, it'll usually be for one of two reasons:

1. She'll have come to a point where she feels capable of wearing the emotional and financial fallout of leaving, and has realised that even the hardship of being a single mother is preferable to staying with someone who's draining her life force.
2. He leaves her for a new (often younger) girlfriend who doesn't whine about shit, has sex with him whenever he likes *and* who finds his status as a single dad impressive enough to willingly sign on to start taking care of his kids.

Men are not held to account for anything, not even the role they play in disintegrating their own relationships and families. They act as if going without sex is the same thing as abuse. As if it's psychological torment to be denied a fucking orgasm. As if she's manipulating and exploiting him, coercively controlling him by keeping the doors to the pussy—*his* pussy—closed. But despite all this *torment* they claim to be experiencing (and certainly use as justification for their endless infidelity), they won't actually leave. Because marriage is designed FOR THEM, as it has been since the beginning. Giving it up would mean giving up their free maid, free nanny, free secretary, free cook and free therapist. It would mean giving up everything that makes their life easy and nice. Everything that makes them feel *powerful* and god-like. And damn it, he deserves to feel those things!

Yes, I'm dealing in stereotypes and generalisations here. And yes, I know there are many men who are actively engaged with their families and committed to being equal partners. But there are scores more who consider the minuscule contribution of their sperm and their physical presence to be all that's required of them in exchange for a lifetime of domestic and sexual labour, undertaken without complaint. Worse, there are men who believe that they're the ones sacrificing happiness and freedom in this scenario, not the women they've trapped into being their caregivers—and because of this, their sacrifice, entitled to her subservient devotion for the rest of time.

I think what gets me most is the outrageous expectation these men have of *attention*. As if by being roughly in the vicinity of a woman and a child, they've done something monumental at great expense to themselves. As if the women stuck at home with these fuckbags don't feel chronically neglected! As if they wouldn't *love* to go out and have no-strings-attached sex with someone or have a fling and feel special again. To feel like a *person*! As if they don't deserve that one million times more than the fucking losers they married. Women deserve the fucking world, but instead we get married and learn soon enough what that really means.

A picket fence is just a pretty cage with a fresh coat of paint.

———

Marriage needs to be destroyed because it's the linchpin in the maintenance of the patriarchal family unit. And the patriarchal family unit needs to be destroyed because it is overwhelmingly hurting women. I don't think men, for the most part, have proven that they deserve women's care and love. Men have built their legacy in the world by stealing everything they can from us—our labour, our resources, our bodies and our very lives—and nothing has changed in the prison of marriage except the furniture. Our expectations of basic decency and respect have been obliterated by the legacy of oppression, so all it takes for a woman to feel 'lucky' is a man who isn't the *worst* of men. He doesn't need to properly parent his own children, just be nice to them sometimes. He doesn't need to respect or care for her body, just not completely dehumanise her. He doesn't even need to know a single thing about her, just to be able to say that he likes how she takes care of him. He doesn't even need to love her. She just needs to be there at the exact moment he's ready to take a wife, and take a load off.

This is an unacceptable metric for excellence and good fortune in love. Frankly, men should be thanking us daily for even continuing to speak to them.

And yet most of us do. Because despite it all—despite everything they've done and continue to do, every dismissive comment made about our worth, every insistence that we are *nothing*—we continue to put faith in them. We continue to love them.

We continue to build them.

Andrea Dworkin once said of men: 'Have you ever wondered why [women] are not just in armed combat against you? It's not because there's a shortage of kitchen knives in this country. It is because we believe in your humanity, against all the evidence.'

We believe in their humanity. But after all this time, they still refuse to believe in ours.

Motherfuckers.

Epilogue

THE PRINCESS SAVES HERSELF

'The time when mountains move has come

People may not believe my words

But mountains have only slept for a while

In the ancient days

All mountains moved,

Dancing with fire,

Though you may not believe it.

But oh, believe this.

All women, who have slept,

Wake now and move.'

—Yosano Akiko, 'The Day the Mountains Move', *Seito* magazine, 1911

Here at the close, I have just one more thing to say: it is never too late to start again.

When you take even the most cursory glance at patriarchal history and the violence men have wreaked against women, it's difficult to understand how we arrived here, in the heteronormative hellscape of marital aspiration. Logic would dictate that women should reject the male class entirely, refusing to hand over even a whisper more of the labour and time that's been shamelessly stolen from us.

But this isn't the case.

Now, we not only willingly surrender ourselves to patriarchy's domestic demands, but we also participate in the charade that says this is what we need to be happy. We've arrived at a point in time where the prospect of being a single woman living alone isn't considered a progressive step forward for a culture that once denied women the right to own property for ourselves, but the terrifying consequence that awaits she who aspires to be seen as human. We have come so far, only to find ourselves right back where they want us: pleading for mercy and hoping like hell they'll spare us the fullness of their wrath.

To learn how to find our way out of the woods of our own exploitation, we need to understand the various methods that have been used to entrench the denial of our personhood, and we need to be across how this has manifested throughout history. This is what I've tried to do in these pages. To paint a clear picture of what has been done to women in order to keep us from articulating reality for ourselves, as fully realised humans living in the world. I hope I've succeeded. Because this is what it comes down to: who gets to be people, and who gets to be women.

Patriarchy's denial of our humanity has proved such a successful act of violence that women, desperate to negotiate some scrap of respect, are still called to the endless labour of reassuring men that we aren't really women at all. We can be ciphers, mirrors, cheerleaders, maids, therapists, sex objects, mothers and champions—but what we can never be is women with agency, because to believe in our own agency is to believe we are *people*. And only men can be people.

If women are afforded superficial social rights only in so far as we prove ourselves to be useful and willing domestic animals, then patriarchy has conditioned us to believe personhood can only be bestowed by our agricultural masters. Personhood isn't something we claim for ourselves; it can only be identified by men, and men can and will only transfer some of its privileges to us if we perform as dutiful and subservient pets.

We know that men fear women, and have done so since time immemorial. We know that men's fear of women is a killer, both figuratively and literally. But how to make us fear *ourselves*? How to make us fear our own freedom, to the degree that even seeing it embodied in other women is experienced as a terrifying virus we might catch? How to make us keep doing the work of the witch-hunters, centuries after the last of their flames burned out?

You use every tool at your disposal (sharpened as they have been by patriarchy's blade) to make us fear the alternative—a life spent cast out of the benevolent glow of the male gaze, cold and alone. Women who actively resist marriage or express even mild disregard for it can never be allowed to take their place in society as anything other than the laughable example of a Woman Gone Wrong. To aspire to independence as a woman is to admit to having dreams and ambitions beyond the domestic sphere, to imagine for ourselves a world of adventure and autonomy that has always been reserved for men. The more independent a woman makes herself, the less she resembles a woman at all. Twisted, bitter and gnarled from the poison that runs through her veins, she becomes a parody of herself.

A woman stripped of her femininity has no purpose at all to men, which nullifies her entire reason for being. Too late, she'll discover that what she really craved all along was to become a wife and mother—but given her transformation into withered old crone she'll have no choice but to spend the rest of her life in abject misery, a formerly ripe plum turned sour.

It doesn't have to be like this.

We don't have to let them set the terms of the game, gaslighting us into believing that life only has meaning if a man invites us to experience it. We are full and whole human beings in our own right, and no one else gets to determine that. Let them rage from the pulpit, let them spit their fury over the internet, let them melt in anger at the thought of losing control over the thing they have never been able to tame. Cats or no cats, I would rather wake up every day knowing that I live in service to no one but myself. No one will ever pin me down again, nor will I be forced into the straitjacket of marriage. Let them call me a witch, a demon, a miserable old hag, a crone, a rammy slut, a spinster, an old maid, a pitiful cat lady. These are just words they use to avoid calling me what I actually am, which is the thing that terrifies them most of all.

Free.

As I've said, I'm not here to offer solutions to people looking to save their marriages. You cannot save an institution whose purpose is to entrench oppressive ideals, and nor should you want to. Every woman believes they'll be the exception to patriarchy's grand plan, and only a handful of them get lucky.

The odds are rarely in your favour.

Locking yourself into a contract that's both legally and financially difficult to leave is insane. Would you accept a job on that basis? Would you refuse to negotiate the fine print on a house sale because caring about the details is somehow 'unromantic'? Of course not. Marriage is the only life-altering legal contract women are willing to sign with their eyes closed, often on the strength of nothing more than the person is *there*. And why? Because we're told that having someone is better than having no one. To have no one is to *be* no one—because how could we possibly be enough, just by ourselves? We're women! Who would want to spend time with us if they didn't have to?

My darlings. Fierce, incredible women in the world, breathing and living and loving with every fibre of your being. I am *begging you* to want more for yourselves than the garbage they tell us to be grateful for. Women are thrown slops from a dirty bucket and told we're being fed champagne and caviar, and the great fucking tragedy is how many of us believe it.

Dig in, girls! Get your slops! But be quick . . . because there's only so much to go around, and you don't want to miss out.

Marriage has sustained itself largely by convincing women we're nothing without it, and codifying all the rituals that accompany it as being some integral part of a woman's life. Humans love a good ritual. The Ancient Romans knew it, as did the women who learned to throw their bouquets into the madding crowd. Queen Victoria's ceremonial garb spawned over a century's worth of sartorial ritual, and capitalism eagerly exploited the cultural stories it could get its hands on to create a shit ton more.

Here's a crazy thought. What if we made *ourselves* the ritual?

What if we marked our tangible achievements—the graduations, the promotions, the books written, awards received, children had, lives just fucking lived freely and enjoyed as we choose, etc.— with the same fanfare accompanying this one superficial and ultimately meaningless milestone? I want a world where women feel free to host parties both ostentatiously and quietly intimate, for no reason other than that they feel compelled to celebrate themselves. I want to give speeches broadcasting the brilliance of my friends, shouting from the rooftops about how fucking great they are for finally completing that PhD or walking across the country or being an incredible single mum or having amazing style or painting a fucking picture or just continuing to live as large as they can in a world that tells us that if we want to be loved, we have to make ourselves small.

I want a world where women are celebrated for who we are, not for who we're sleeping next to at night. Where weddings, if they must happen at all, are just *another* thing a woman might do in her life but not the most exciting thing and certainly not the *only* thing. Whether or not a woman is married is literally the least interesting thing about her, yet it gets more positive attention than anything else—because if we can keep marrying women off despite all this freedom we're supposed to have now, then we can ensure men continue to benefit from all that work being done for them.

I want a world where women remember what it was like to be girls, before life came along and knocked the wind out of their sails. Girls who laughed and danced and played and allowed themselves to dream that one day, they might get to be the main event. She's still in you, that girl. She's still waiting for you to put the spotlight on her. You hold her future in your hands. She's trusting you to take care of her.

You can be the one who saves her life.

The world is full of incredible women doing incredible things every day. For some that might mean driving scientific progress, changing the world politically, advocating for the world's most disenfranchised or figuring out solutions to climate change. Others exhibit their greatness by raising the next generation of humans, caring for the people around them and making it through the day. But it tells us everything we need to know about how the world values women's contributions that the only thing we're *really* allowed to publicly congratulate ourselves for is being saved from the shelf of forgotten nobodies, dusty and alone, and becoming someone's *wife*.

Fuck that. Fuck all that bullshit which wants us to believe this is the start of our life and not the end of our freedom. Fuck the cultural narrative that tells women this is what we've dreamed of ever since we were little girls, marching down make-believe aisles with pillowcases pinned to our hair. Fuck the money that's wasted, the debt people get themselves into, the photographs taken after the ceremony featuring couples fist-pumping the air as if to say, *We did it!* Fuck the jokes made at the bride's expense, from the videos of grooms standing at altars flashing signs asking to be rescued to the cake smashes she specifically said she didn't want. Fuck the speed with which women race to change their names on social media, fuck how 'proud wife' has become a job title, fuck the suspicion levelled at newly separated women as if they would ever want your shit-for-brains husband, fuck the men who think that buying a ring is their lifelong insurance policy against ever having to do anything for themselves ever again and fuck them most of all for stealing a woman's years and sucking her spirit dry.

So you want a party? Throw a party. You want the excuse to wear a pretty dress or a cool suit? Fucking do it, sister. You want to hire someone to take photographs of you with the kind of vintage wash that looks perfect on an Instagram carousel? Go for it! There is so much waiting for you to discover! There is still so much time left for you to *shine*.

Because here's a little secret about that sad, scary shelf: the view is fucking incredible from up here. Nothing is more powerful than a woman who regains control over her own perspective. When you are able to see, you learn, finally, that you are real.

Fuck marriage. You can be the great love you're looking for, if you raise your standards. You can honour who you are every day. You can obey the call you feel inside, the one that tells you there's something else out there just waiting for you to find it. Live courageously, be wild and untethered. As Mary Oliver says, 'There are moments that cry out to be fulfilled . . . Your heart is beating, isn't it? You're not in chains, are you? There is nothing more pathetic than caution when headlong might save a life, even, possibly, your own.' You only get one chance so dive in, headfirst, and make the most of it because there's no prize at the end for who suffered the most. You can have a better dream for yourself. You *deserve* a better dream, for you and every single version of yourself that you've ever been or will ever be. YOU and you alone are the longest relationship you'll ever have, till death do you part. Let no man tear that asunder.

Princess for a day? No, thank you.

Queen, commander and general in charge of my life for the rest of all time?

I fucking do.

Now you see. Now you know.

Now you go tell.

NOTES

EPIGRAPHS

'In education, in marriage, in religion, in everything': Lucy Stone,
'Disappointment is the lot of women', speech delivered at the National
Women's Rights Convention in Cincinnati on 17 October 1855.

'Every one of my female friends is too good for her boyfriend': Lane Moore,
Twitter, September 2020.

SOMETHING OLD

'She hears her own thick voice deep inside her ears': Charlotte Wood, *The
Natural Way of Things*, Allen & Unwin, Sydney, 2015.

CHAPTER 1: IN THE BEGINNING

'I have always thought that there might be a lot of cash in starting a religion':
George Orwell, *Collected Essays, Journalism, and Letters of George Orwell*,
Harcourt, Brace & Co., New York, 1971.

'one of the reasons cited for opposing marriage among the clergy': A.W. Richard
Snipe, *Sex, Priests and Power: The anatomy of a crisis*. Brunner/Mazel, Inc.,
New York, 1995.

'entangled men in the slimy glue of their sexuality': Stephanie Coontz, *Marriage,
A History: How love conquered marriage*, Penguin Group, New York, 2005,
p. 121.

'bitches, sows, screech-owls, night-owls, she-wolves [and] blood-suckers':
Anne Llewellyn Barstow, 'Married priests and the reforming papacy: The
eleventh-century debates', *Texts and Studies in Religion*, 12, Edwin Mellon
Press, New York, 1982.

'cannot under any circumstances be without blame': Coontz, p. 86.

'The sanctity of human life is a foundational principle': Mitt Romney, June 2022.

CHAPTER 2: CAT LADY

'If man could be crossed with the cat it would improve man': *Mark Twain's
Notebook*, Harper & Brothers Publishers, New York, 1935.

'discourage girls and women from venturing out of bounds': Kate Manne,
Entitled: How male privilege hurts women, Crown, USA, 2020.

'How many of the women rallying against overturning Roe': Matt Gaetz, Twitter,
May 2022.

'We are effectively run in this country—via the Democrats, via our corporate
oligarchs': J.D. Vance, *Tucker Carlson Tonight*, Fox News, July 2021.

'Parents have a stake in the game': Will Cain, *Fox & Friends*, July 2021.

'The rise of lonely, single men': Greg Matos, 'What's behind the rise of lonely,
single men', *Psychology Today*, 9 August 2022.

'the Devil descends as a black cat before his devotees': Walter Map, *De nugis
curialium*, 1180.

'The witch-hunt reversed the power relation': Silvia Federici, *Caliban and the
Witch: Women, the body and primitive accumulation*, Autonomedia, New
York, 2004.

'some of the most sadistic tortures ever invented': Frederici.

'would be whipped in front of the stake': Frederici.

'inviolable mystery': Federici.

'an accusation easily to be made and hard to be proved': Matthew Hale, *Historia
Placitorum Coronæ* (*The history of the pleas of the Crown*), printed by
E. and R. Nutt, and R. Gosling (assigns of Edward Sayer, Esq.) for F. Gyles,
T. Woodward, and C. Davis, London, 1736.

'the wisdom of all nations had provided laws against such persons': Hale.

CHAPTER 3: SPINSTER CITY

'I put in my list all the busy, useful independent spinsters I know': Louisa May
Alcott, *Her Life, Letters, and Journals*, Little, Brown and Company, Boston,
1898.

'finally die, fat and alone': Helen Fielding, *Bridget Jones's Diary*, Pan Macmillan,
London, 2016.

'And my wyf . . . Spak to the spinsters for to spinne hit softe': William Langland, 'Piers Plowman', United Kingdom, circa 1370.

'Just learnt that "spinster" was originally the word for a woman': Gemma Milne, Twitter, January 2020.

'As never married women moved to fill a greater physical space': Judith Spicksley, 'Women alone', *History Workshop Journal*, 63, 2007, pp. 312–319.

'a warning to all politically active women': Jennifer Robinson and Keina Yoshida, *How Many More Women?* Allen & Unwin, Sydney, 2022.

'just over half of all adult women at the time were either unmarried or widowed': Amy Froide, 'Hidden women: Rediscovering the singlewomen of early modern England', *Local population studies*, 2002, pp. 26–41.

CHAPTER 4: A WOMB OF ONE'S OWN

'Do you really believe . . . that everything historians tell us about men': Moderata Fonte, *The Worth of Women*, 1600.

'What is a woman, Prime Minister?': Piers Morgan, *Piers Morgan Uncensored*, 3 May 2023.

'Somewhere, Emmeline Pankhurst just vomited': Piers Morgan, Twitter, December 2017.

'man-hating, bomb-threatening brigade': Piers Morgan, Twitter, January 2017.

'hungered for intercourse and pregnancy': Elinor Cleghorn, *Unwell Women: Misdiagnosis and myth in a man-made world*, Weidenfeld & Nicolson, London, 2021, p. 26.

'unleashing their original sin': Cleghorn, p. 51.

'rebellious lower class': Barbara Ehrenreich and Deirdre English, *Witches, Midwives, and Nurses: A history of women healers*, The Feminist Press, New York, 1973.

'uncooperative or neurotic': Ehrenreich and English, p. 8.

'"crisis" of menstruation caused women to "suffer under a languor and depression"': James McGrigor Allan, 'On the real differences in the minds of men and women', *The Anthropological Review*, 7, 1869, pp. 196–219.

'if a woman showed even an inkling of a man's aptitude for thought': Charles Darwin, in Angela Saini, *Inferior: The true power of women and the science that shows it*, HarperCollins Publishers, London, 2018.

'the most discussed animal in the universe': Virginia Woolf, *A Room of One's Own*, Hogarth Press, London, 1929.

SOMETHING NEW

'Jane, I take your place now, and you must go lower': Jane Austen, *Pride and Prejudice*, T. Egerton, Whitehall, 1813.

CHAPTER 5: PUT A RING ON IT

'I've been dating since I was fifteen! I'm exhausted': *Sex and the City* (TV series), 2000.

'love and personal fulfilment': Ellen Lamont, *The Mating Game: How gender still shapes how we date*, University of California Press, Oakland, 2020.

'Boys seldom make passes at girls who wear glasses.': Dorothy Parker, 'News Item', *Enough Rope*, Horace Liveright, New York, 1926.

'It would have been better had she died.': Jane Austen, *Pride and Prejudice*, T. Egerton, Whitehall, United Kingdom, 1813.

'on the eve of World War II only about ten per cent of engagement rings had diamonds': Richard Shotton, *The Choice Factory: 25 behavioural biases that influence what we buy*, Harriman House, Hampshire, United Kingdom, 2018.

'the abolition of "breach of promise" acts first established in Indiana in 1935': Margaret F. Brinig, 'Rings and Promises', *Journal of Law, Economics, & Organization*, 6, 1990, p. 203.

'stay up late with her dogs and write copy': J. Courtney Sullivan, *The Engagements*, Vintage, London, 2014.

CHAPTER 6: THE HAPPIEST DAY OF HER LIFE

'I have in me the germs of intense life': Mary MacLane, *I Await the Devil's Coming* (first published as *The Story of Mary MacLane*), Herbert S. Stone & Co., Chicago, 1902.

'Pelting a bride and bridegroom with old shoes': James Crombie, 'Shoe-throwing at weddings', *Folklore*, 6:3, 1895, pp. 258–281.

'I Thee Dread': Jia Tolentino, *Trick Mirror: Reflections on self-delusion*, Fourth Estate, London, 2019.

'a frenzy of nodding, curtseying, beaming and handshaking': Julia Baird, 'Queen Victoria's wedding night: "I never, never spent such an evening"', *Sydney Morning Herald*, October 2016.

'People have always loved a love story': Stephanie Coontz, *Marriage, A History: How love conquered marriage*, Penguin Group, New York, 2005.

'As of 2021, the average individual cost of a wedding in America was $28,000': Jaclyn DeJohn, 'Wedding Waitlist: How long it takes to save for the big day—2023 study', *Smart Asset*, 2023.

CHAPTER 7: HONEY, YOU'RE HOME

'I would strongly advise every woman contemplating sexual union:' Voltairine de Cleyre, excerpt from a speech given in Scotland, 1897.

'all of the ways the status quo and patriarchy': Susan Faludi, *Backlash: The undeclared war against American women*, Crown Publishing Group, New York, 1991.

'During the day the women and children remain in the residential area':
E.O. Wilson, quoted in Stephanie Coontz, *Marriage, A History: How love conquered marriage*, Penguin Group, New York, 2005, p. 26.

'It's the job of some women to buttress patriarchy': Celeste Headlee, *Men* podcast.

'the idea that women have an inherent material instinct': William McDougall, *An Introduction to Social Psychology*, Psychology Press, London, 1908.

'no other life form on the planet is segregated by sex in this way': Carol Gilligan, *In a Different Voice: Psychological theory and women's development*, Harvard University Press, Boston, 1982.

'typically walked about twelve miles a day': Coontz, p. 37.

'South Dakota was the easiest (if also the most expensive) place for a rich, white woman to escape the bonds of a marriage': April White, *The Divorce Colony: How women revolutionized marriage and found freedom on the American frontier*, Hachette Books, New York, 2022.

'Feminism encourages women to leave their husbands': Pat Robertson, included in a fund-raising letter sent out under Robertson's name to supporters of the Christian Coalition in 1992.

'the inertia suddenly thrust upon women': Barbara Ehrenreich and Deirdre English, *For Her Own Good: Two centuries of the experts' advice to women*, Pluto Press, London, 1988.

'exposing the dissatisfaction of women': Betty Friedan, *The Feminine Mystique*. W.W. Norton & Co., New York, 1963.

SOMETHING BORROWED

'Hope is the thing with feathers': Emily Dickinson, 'Hope is the Thing with Feathers', *The Complete Poems of Emily Dickinson*, edited by Thomas H. Johnson, Cambridge, Mass., 1951.

CHAPTER 8: YOUR FATHER'S NAME

'A wife should no more take her husband's name than he should hers': Motto of the Lucy Stone League, founded in 1921.

'the very being, or legal existence of the woman, is suspended during the marriage': Sir William Blackstone, *Commentaries on the Laws of England, vol I.*, 1765.

'impersonating another person on his driver's licence': Katie McDonough, 'Man who adopted his wife's last name is accused of fraud', *Salon*, January 2013.

CHAPTER 9: CHELSEA MOURNING

'In the beginning, Woman was truly the Sun': Hiratsuka Raichō, *The Seito Manifesto*, Tokyo, September 1911.

'authors of perception': Marilyn Frye, *The Politics of Reality: Essays in feminist theory*, Crossing Press, Berkeley, CA, 1983.

'[Women] have been lied to by their society forever': Jesse Kelly, Fox News, February 2023.

'written all over her face how miserable she is': Ben Shapiro, *Variety*, February 2023.

'aging, deeply unlikable woman who never had kids': Tucker Carlson, *Variety*, February 2023.

'who are really just selfish brats': *Candace Owens* podcast, February 2023.

'100 per cent foolproof contraceptive': Chelsea Handler, *Variety*, February 2023.

'men are afraid women will laugh at them while women are afraid men will kill them': Margaret Atwood, 'Writing the Male Character', Hagey Lecture, University of Waterloo, February 1982.

CHAPTER 10: THE PROTECTION RACKET

'Every man I meet wants to protect me': Mae West, 1940.

'The feminist narrative is that I'm a controlling man': Melissa Fleur Afshar, 'Woman blames Andrew Tate for turning her boyfriend into a rapist', *Newsweek*, April 2023.

CHAPTER 11: WHEN YOU WISH UPON A STAR

'I'll have what she's having': Woman in diner, *When Harry Met Sally* (film), 1989.

'head for business and a bod for sin': *Working Girl* (film), 1988.

'You complete me': *Jerry Maguire* (film), 1996.

'marriage for women has almost always been a decision made easier because of economic concerns': Adrienne Rich, 'Compulsory heterosexuality and lesbian existence', *Signs*, 5(4), 1980, pp. 631–660.

'because heterosexual romance': Rich.

SOMETHING BLUE

'Hell is truth seen too late': Thomas Hobbes, *Leviathan*, 1651.

'culturally, historically or aesthetically significant': United States National Film Registry, *Library of Congress Sound Recording and Film Preservation Programs Reauthorization Act 2016*, section 179.

CHAPTER 12: TROUBLE AND STRIFE, COMEDY WIFE

'John laughs at me of course': Charlotte Perkins Gilman, 'The Yellow Wallpaper' (1892), Virago Press, London, 1981.

'most mobile phones are assembled in factories': Saritha Rai, 'Armies of women earning $4 a day could be behind your next iPhone', *The Economic Times*, 31 August 2019.

'the formula that led to the creation of the internet': 'Ada Lovelace', *Encyclopedia Britannica*.

'Research has shown that excessive use of social media': Jeffrey Davis, 'Breaking out of the doomscrolling cycle', *Psychology Today*, 9 June 2022.

'drugify human connection': Brittney McNamara, 'The science behind social media's hold on our mental health', *Teen Vogue*, 10 November 2021.

'We fear that evaluating our needs and then carefully choosing partners': bell hooks, *All About Love*, HarperCollins Publisher, New York, 2017.

CHAPTER 13: ALL THE LIGHT HE CANNOT SEE

'He who robs us of our dreams': Virginia Woolf, *Orlando*, Hogarth Press, London, 1928.

'men and women come from different planets': John Gray, *Men Are from Mars, Women Are from Venus*, HarperCollins, New York, 1992.

'"phoney operation" and a "diploma mill"': Tanya Schevitz, 'Marin judge orders university in Novato to cease operations/State has wanted it closed for years', *SF Gate*, December 1999.

'tactical misunderstanding': Deborah Cameron, *The Myth of Mars and Venus*, Oxford University Press, Oxford, 2008.

'women spend an average of eight hours more per week on unpaid domestic work': Roy Morgan, 'Taking the pulse of the nation', May 2023.

CHAPTER 14: THE PRICE OF ENTRY

'Because I have other professions open to me in which the hours are shorter': Miss Florence Watts, 'Why am I a spinster?', *Tit-Bits* magazine, 1889.

'building blocks of society': Elizabeth Gilbert. *Bewildered* podcast, August 2022.

'Men won't easily give up a system': Marilyn Waring, 7th Annual Maybanke Fund Lecture, 2019.

'In America, single women without children': Ana Hernández Kent, 'Single mothers face difficulties with slim financial cushions', Federal Reserve Bank of St Louis, 2022.

'"boots theory" of socioeconomic inequality': Terry Pratchett, *Men at Arms*, Victor, Gollancz, London, 1993.

CHAPTER 15: MOTHERFUCKER

'If women, as I hope, wake themselves from the lengthy slumber': Lucrezia Marinella, *The Nobility and Excellence of Women, And the Defects and Vices of Men*, 1600.

'the branch of agriculture concerned with raising domestic animals': 'Animal husbandry', *Encyclopedia Britannica*.

'Black women in the United States are 60 per cent more likely to develop pre-eclampsia': Margaret Osborne, 'What is eclampsia? Olympian Tori Bowie may have died from the rare pregnancy condition', *Smithsonian Magazine*, 16 June 2023.

'Have you ever wondered why [women] are not just in armed combat against you?': Mary Spongberg, 'Andrea Dworkin, 1946–2005', *Australian Feminist Studies*, 21:49, 2006, pp. 3–5.

EPILOGUE: THE PRINCESS SAVES HERSELF

'The time when mountains move has come': Yosano Akiko, 'The Day the Mountains Move', *Seito* magazine, Tokyo, September 1911.

'Hell is truth seen too late': Thomas Hobbes, *Private Thoughts on Religion: And other subjects connected with it*, Rudd and Stockholm, London, 1814.

READING LIST

Sharon Blackie, *Hagitude: Reimagining the second half of life*, September Publishing, London, 2022.

Kristin Celello, *Making Marriage Work: A history of marriage and divorce in twentieth-century United States*, University of North Carolina Press, Chapel Hill, NC, 2012.

Mona Chollet, *In Defence of Witches: Why women are still on trial*, Pan Macmillan, London, 2023.

Gail Collins, *America's Women: 400 years of dolls, drudges, helpmates, and heroines*, HarperCollins Publishers, New York, 2007.

Stephanie Coontz, *A Strange Stirring: The feminine mystique and American women at the dawn of the 1960s*, Little Brown, New York, 2012.

Stephanie Coontz, *Marriage, A History: How love conquered marriage*, Penguin Group, New York, 2006.

Stephanie Coontz, *The Way We Never Were: American families and the nostalgia trap*, Little Brown, New York, 2016.

Stephanie Coontz, *The Way We Really Are: Coming to terms with America's changing families*, Basic Books, New York, 1997.

Caroline Criado-Perez, *Invisible Women: Exposing data bias in a world designed for men*, Random House, London, 2020.

Christine Delphy, *Close To Home: A materialist analysis of women's oppression*, Bloomsbury, London, 2016.

Wendy Doniger, *The Ring of Truth: And other myths of sex and jewellery*, Oxford University Press, New York, 2017.

Andrea Dworkin, *Last Days at Hot Slit: The radical feminism of Andrea Dworkin*, MIT Press, Cambridge, Mass., 2019.

Barbara Ehrenreich and Deirdre English, *For Her Own Good: Two centuries of the experts' advice to women* (2nd edition), Anchor Books, 2005.

Barbara Ehrenreich and Deirdre English, *Witches, Midwives, and Nurses: A history of women healers* (2nd edition), The Feminist Press, New York, 2010.

Silvia Federici, *Witches, Witch-Hunting, and Women*, PM Press, Oakland, CA, 2018.

Cordelia Fine, *Testosterone Rex: Unmaking the myths of our gendered minds*, Icon Books, London, 2018.

Norman Finkelstein, *The Way Things Never Were: The truth about the good old days*, iUniverse, 2005.

Helen Fisher, *Anatomy of Love: A natural history of mating, marriage and why we stray*, W.W. Norton & Company, London, 1992.

Marilyn Frye, *The Politics of Reality: Essays in feminist theory*, Crossing Press, Berkeley, CA, 1983.

Anna Funder, *Wifedom: Mrs. Orwell's invisible life*, Penguin Australia, Sydney, 2023.

Angela Garbes, *Essential Labor: Mothering as social change*, Harper Wave, New York, 2022.

Elizabeth Gilbert, *Committed: A love story*, Bloomsbury, London, 2011.

Carol Gilligan, *In a Human Voice*, John Wiley & Sons, London, 2023.

Carol Gilligan and Naomi Snider, *Why Does Patriarchy Persist?* John Wiley & Sons, London, 2018.

Eliane Glaser, *Motherhood: Feminism's unfinished business*, HarperCollins Publishers, London, 2022.

Germaine Greer, *The Female Eunuch*, MacGibbon & Kee, London, 1970.

Leo Hollis, *Inheritance—The Lost History of Mary Davies: A story of property, marriage and madness*, Bloomsbury, London, 2022.

bell hooks, *All About Love*, HarperCollins Publishers, New York, 2017.

Ronald Hutton, *The Witch: A history of fear, from ancient times to the present*, Yale University Press, New Haven, Conn., 2018.

Alice Kessler-Harris, *Out to Work: A history of wage-earning women in the United States*, Oxford University Press, New York, 2003.

Audre Lorde, *When I Dare To Be Powerful* (preface by Renni Eddo-Lodge, introduction by Sara Ahmed), Silver Press, London, 2021.

Audre Lorde, *Your Silence Will Not Protect You: Essays and poems* (preface by Renni Eddo-Lodge, introduction by Sara Ahmed), Silver Press, London, 2021.

Wednesday Martin, *Untrue: Why nearly everything we believe about women and lust and infidelity is untrue*, Scribe Publications, Melbourne, 2018.

Harry L. Munsinger J.D. Ph.D., *The History of Marriage and Divorce: Everything you need to know*, Archway Publishing, Bloomington, 2019.

Janina Ramirez, *Femina: A new history of the middle ages, through the women written out of it*, Random House, London, 2023.

Adrienne Rich, *Of Woman Born: Motherhood as experience and institution* (introduction by Eula Biss), W.W. Norton & Company, New York, 2021.

Adrienne Rich and Sandra M. Gilbert, *Essential Essays: Culture, politics and the art of poetry*, W.W. Norton & Company, New York, 2018.

Gina Rippon, *The Gendered Brain: The new neuroscience that shatters the myth of the female brain*, Random House, London, 2020.

Angela Saini, *Inferior: The true power of women and the science that shows it*, HarperCollins Publishers, London, 2018.

Angela Saini, *The Patriarchs: How men came to rule*, HarperCollins Publishers, London, 2023.

Linda Scott, *The Cost of Sexism: How the economy is built for men and why we must reshape it*, Faber & Faber, London, 2022.

Mary Ann Sieghart, *The Authority Gap: Why women are still taken less seriously than men, and what we can do about it*, Random House, London, 2022.

Shani Silver, *A Single Revolution*, Shani Silver Inc., New Orleans, LA, 2021.

Christina Simmons, *Making Marriage Modern: Women's sexuality from the progressive era to World War II*, Oxford University Press, New York, 2012.

Maggie Smith, *You Could Make This Place Beautiful*, Atria/One Signal Publishers, New York, 2023.

Valerie Solanas, *Scum Manifesto* (introduction by Michelle Tea), AK Press, Chico, CA, 2014.

Tracey Spicer, *Man-Made: How the bias of the past is being built into the future*, Simon & Schuster, Sydney, 2023.

Nicholas L. Syrett, *American Child Bride: A history of minors and marriage in the United States*, University of North Carolina Press, Chapel Hill, NC, 2018.

Rebecca Traister, *All the Single Ladies: Unmarried women and the rise of an independent nation*, Simon & Schuster/Marysue Rucci Books, New York, 2016.

April White, *The Divorce Colony: How women revolutionized marriage and found freedom on the American frontier*, Hachette Books, New York, 2022.

Marilyn Yalom, *History of the Wife*, Perennial, New York, 2013.

Arlene Young, *From Spinster to Career Woman: Middle class women and work in Victorian England*, McGill-Queen's University Press, Montreal, 2019.

ACKNOWLEDGEMENTS

I am in the extraordinarily privileged position of having had a few books published by now, and what I've learned about the experience is this: it never gets easier. Writers by necessity are intensely self-involved people, determined to prove our genius to all and sundry while buckling under the weight of what we know, in our heart of hearts, to be all the ways we've come up short. In light of that, the acknowledgements section is perhaps the most important part of any book—because it illuminates to the reader the enormous cast of people who come together to bring a piece of work to life. If this book has moved you in the way I hope it will, please take a moment to acknowledge with me everyone who has made it possible, because I am forever in their debt.

First and foremost, I must give thanks to the formidable Jane Palfreyman. Eight years ago, I walked into the offices of Allen & Unwin and my life changed forever. Jane has believed so fervently and so faithfully in my work, and this is truly the greatest gift a writer can receive. I am endlessly in awe of her strength, her generosity and her desire to make the world a better place. The thing that makes Jane exceptional is that she has a magnificent intellect, but she leads always with her heart. It's a rare gift. We all deserve a champion like Jane, because she loves you in the best way—by *seeing* you. Jane, I'll repeat what I said last time, and hope for the opportunity only to say it at least one more time: whither thou goest, I will go. I am devoted to your service, now and always.

To my incredible editor, Ali Lavau. Every argument you see presented in this book has been shaped by Ali. Were it not for her, you'd be reading a waffling rant that splintered off into tangents dealing with little known nineteenth-century scientists and bloviated Greek philosophers. Ali, having edited all four of my books by now, I can say this with total sincerity: you are the sequinned jumpsuit that makes me look far more sparkly than I am and fools everyone into thinking I might be clever after all. Thank you for being stern enough to cut what isn't needed, and kind enough to pretend I have a choice in the matter. As with Jane, I will attach myself to you like a slug and never let you go.

To Christa Munns, who has managed—incomprehensibly, it seems to me—to treat my haphazard approach to deadlines with a patience I do not deserve. It's a rare person who accepts a late manuscript AND a good bulk of that having been submitted without track changes turned on. But you did it, and you managed it with a grace I couldn't summon in the same position. You're the third fairy in the mix, making sure it all works out in the end. As with Jane, as with Ali, if you ever depart then expect to find me peering in your windows demanding you come back (at least just for me).

I am eternally in the service of my agent, Jacinta di Mase. Jacinta has the exceptional ability to make every single one of her authors feel like they might be her only child. Sometimes when she brings us all together, I'm rudely reminded that there are other people whose work she cares deeply about. From a casual coffee in a cafe eight years ago to walking into the Allen & Unwin offices side by side and squealing in an airport bar only hours later, we have grown an incredible friendship. I defer to her wisdom always; for though she may be small, she is but mighty. Jacinta, it has always been my goal to make you proud. I hope I can continue to do so for decades more.

To everyone who works so intensely behind the scenes of the book world, thank you! Special mention must go to Jane Gilmore, who was on hand as my stalwart researcher and fact checker. Your forensic mind is invaluable for a book like this! Immense gratitude also to Lauren Beckmann, who agreed to read the completed manuscript and give me honest feedback about what worked and what didn't. Lauren is a voracious reader and clever policy boffin, and I trust her opinion greatly. To be reassured of her positive thoughts was such a relief—because never forget, writers are desperately fragile creatures with enormous egos and crippling fear of failure!

To my publicist, Isabelle O'Brien, who works so hard to make sure my work is out there front and centre. To the broader publicity team at Allen & Unwin, who really put in the hard yards to sell my books. To the booksellers, whose passion for reading is second to none—authors owe you so much! To the librarians, too, who work in one of the most magical places to have ever existed—a warm retreat, where all people can read for free. To the reviewers, whose thoughtful reflections on new works help to encourage new readers—yours is a tough job, but a necessary one.

ACKNOWLEDGEMENTS

I am an incredibly loyal person, but it's easy to be when your team is made up of such brilliant, fierce women. I have been profoundly lucky to work with so many of them in my life, and to call them friends. Writing this book in particular has driven home to me the enormous capacity women have to get on with things. To build, to survive, to prevail and, against deliberate opposition, to win. We have lost so much due to the erasure of women throughout history—but I find some small comfort in remembering that each of us only ever lives and exists in the time that we are given, and that love thrives even in the face of the most significant opposition. Men may have conspired throughout history to eject women from their reality, but that doesn't mean those women weren't *real*. Throughout it all, they had each other to draw strength from. Patriarchy succeeds in part by drawing men together and tearing women from one another—if you're uncertain where to start on your feminist journey, let it be with rebellion against the conditioning that tells women to mistrust one another. I wouldn't be who I am without the love of good women! Never forget that 'gossip' once meant 'friend'—so resist all impulses to feel as if friendship with women is superficial and nasty.

In light of that, I must acknowledge the wonderful women whose love and support has been my guiding light since long before I could officially call myself a 'writer'. To the women I came up with at university, each of us learning about feminism in our own way but evolving together through discussion, debate and goodwill. Melissa Vine, Anais Chevalier, Penny Chalke, Anna Svedberg—how lucky we are!

Included in that list but necessarily in need of a separate shoutout is my dear Bonnie Cruickshank. Through the long, hard slog of writing, Bonnie has cooked, nurtured, listened and cared for both me and my boy. Bonnie, you'll never be a Trad Wife but it was fun pretending for a bit. I hope I can one day repay the gesture. Together, we're also enthusiastic members of the Sophisticated Ladies quartet of Brunswick—and so thanks too to Emily O'Hannessian and Hannah Douglas (the latter of whom will always be the best thing to come out of a break-up). Here's to more martinis, fancy little snacks and speculating on matters of state importance (read: Scandoval). While we're mentioning group chats, shoutout also to Alice Robinson and Mandy Lee—if there's a more apt name for a chat group comprised of three single mothers than 'Scream Into The Void', I've yet to hear it. You both inspire me daily with your fierce intelligence, love for your children and razor-sharp wit.

Unless you're the kind of writer who fares well in an office, you rely on the kindness of strangers, acquaintances and businesses to provide you with space. I happen to be the kind of terrible cliché who works best on a laptop in a cafe, and I am deeply indebted to the kindness of Michael Bertoncello at Bertoncello Cafe & Bar in Brunswick. The neighbourhood community he has fostered is so generous and welcoming to artists, writers and creators and we are so lucky to have him.

I'm also very grateful for the two weeks I was able to spend at Varuna Writers' House, during both the earlyish stages of this book and the final mad rush to finish. If you are ever inclined to become a patron of the arts, please consider contributing to retreats like those offered at Varuna—nothing is more valuable to a writer (particularly a single mother!) than time and space to write uninterrupted, with meals and solidarity supplied in abundance. With this last point in mind, I also want to acknowledge the care and love given to my son by his godmother, Melissa Fyfe (who also manages Bertie's when it turns into a gin joint! Family affairs and tightknit community is kind of my thing). Thank you for the times you stepped in last minute to look after him. Thank you also to Poppy Paraw, his long-term babysitter and friend—you have been invaluable and we love you very much!

As much as writers might wish to be able to dive into books unencumbered, most of us have to continue working elsewhere to pay bills: thank you to everyone who has been so patient and amenable to me over the last year, working with my schedule to change things last minute. I am especially in love with my brilliant producers at Nova, Edwina Stott and Elle Beattie—I'm so proud of the work we create together, and so appreciative of your flexibility over the last year! I can't wait to do more with you both—and to see what you both do with your own magical talents.

Okay, nearing the end now!

Much of the early research and writing of this book was done from the backseat of a car while I was touring *Love Sermon*. I set myself a goal of writing five hundred words per day, and bashed them out while the car snaked up mountain ranges, navigated flood waters and drove on coastal roads. Afterwards, I would read what I'd written to my bandmates, who would generously offer feedback and mini cucumbers. To Libby O'Donovan and Marty Brown—those touring days will always be some of the most special days of my life. I could write pages just on the three of us, and one day maybe I will. But for now, what I'll say is this—every day with you both is a high-five day. I will love you both for every single moment of our time, which I hope is forever.

To my sister, Charlotte Ford—in many ways, this book is an homage to you. You are the woman who came out the other side, fortified rather than broken. You are the princess who saved herself, and I love you so much.

To my soul sister, Karen Pickering—what can I say here that I haven't tried to say to you in a thousand different ways to capture the strength of feeling I have for you and all that you are? I believe in magic, and I believe you're made of it. Our memories will hold on to us, and I'll be picking up bottles with you on New Year's Day and every day. Harry is so very lucky to have you, and we are all so very lucky to have him.

Speaking of luck, I have been given spades of it with you Papa J. We've weathered a lot but come out the other side stronger and wiser. We are raising the most beautiful boy. I'll repeat here what I said in this book—I chose his father well. You have been an unending source of emotional support and care, particularly through this process. Thank you for always doing what needs to be done, and for championing to our son the qualities and power of his mother. We are all water from the same source, still.

Finally, this book is for all the women who came before and fought so that we could stand here and speak. This book couldn't have been written without you, which is why it's been written for you. I am sitting in a forest whose seeds you planted long ago. This book will hopefully act as another seed for thought, for action, for change. I may not live to see what it grows into, but it's enough to know that some future version of the girls we're all fighting for will know how wild and courageous their lives can be.

I'll finish with these words. Write them down, print them out, stick them up somewhere. Anything to remember that you are not a passenger in life, and you can be your own great love.

If you hear your dreams calling to you from beyond the horizon, swim as fast as you can towards them. Someone has to make it! Why not you?

PRAISE FOR
HOW WE LOVE

'An act of exquisite beauty, generosity and vulnerability from a woman who can also throw a fridge into the back of a car, all by herself. Big-hearted, fierce, tender, and so full of hope, just when we need it.'

Clare Bowditch, author of *Your Own Kind of Girl*

'Sensitive, soulful and utterly captivating. *How We Love* manages to be both beautiful and brutal, at the same time. Clem gives us words for the loves we've never been able to speak about before.'

Jamila Rizvi, author and editor of *The Motherhood*

'Everything in *How We Love* pierced me as I read—the humour, the honesty, the blistering detail. I laughed, and my heart ached . . . *How We Love* balances the specific and the universal so beautifully. It illuminates Clementine's experience, and sheds a light on us all.'

Alice Robinson, author of *The Glad Shout*

'A wise, tender and generous book about the agonies and ecstasies of being a human who dares to love. At once intimate and universal, *How We Love* is an ode to opening our hearts, again and again—despite knowing that pain awaits. Ford reminds us that, even when they hurt, our feelings are the very meat of life.'

Yves Rees, author of *All About Yves: Notes from a Transition*

'How can stories from someone else's life make you feel so seen, so known, so bloody tender towards your younger self? That's the power of great memoir and *How We Love* is glorious. Sparkling prose, heart-in-mouth honesty and Clementine's trademark wit, warmth and sincerity. I laughed, I cried, I cringed, I forgave myself a hundred times. You'll fall in love with Clementine just a little bit more.'

Karen Pickering, writer and host of *Cherchez La Femme*